COMPELLING PEOPLE

THE HIDDEN QUALITIES THAT MAKE US INFLUENTIAL

John Neffinger and Matthew Kohut

A PLUME BOOK

PLUME
Published by the Penguin Group
Penguin Group (USA) LLC
375 Hudson Street
New York, New York 10014

USA | Canada | UK | Ireland | Australia | New Zealand | India | South Africa | China
penguin.com
A Penguin Random House Company

First published in the United States of America by Hudson Street Press, a member of Penguin
Group (USA) Inc., 2013
First Plume Printing 2014

 REGISTERED TRADEMARK—MARCA REGISTRADA

THE LIBRARY OF CONGRESS HAS CATALOGED THE HUDSON STREET PRESS EDITION AS FOLLOWS:
Neffinger, John.
    Compelling people : the hidden qualities that make us influential / John Neffinger and Matthew
Kohut.
    pages cm
    Includes bibliographical references and index.
    ISBN 978-1-59463-101-6 (hc.)
    ISBN 978-0-14-218102-7 (pbk.)
    1. Influence (Psychology) 2. Charisma. 3. Personality. I. Kohut, Matthew. II. Title.
    BF774.N44 2013
    158.2—dc23   2013009024

Printed in the United States of America
10 9 8 7 6 5 4

Set in Warnock Pro Light

A PLUME BOOK

COMPELLING PEOPLE

JOHN NEFFINGER and MATTHEW KOHUT are founding partners in KNP Communications, which specializes in preparing speakers for high-stakes audiences. Their clients include corporate executives, elected officials, and media personalities, and they regularly lecture at universities and serve as commentators on air and in print. Both John and Matt live with their families in Washington, D.C.

Praise for *Compelling People*

"Not only does this book tell you why people react to you as they do, it also provides specific suggestions for managing your image. This book is a must-read for all leaders who want to maximize their influence on others."

—Art Markman, professor, University of Texas, and author of
Smart Thinking and *Habits of Leadership*

"This is not just another pop-psych book: it's the *first* book to capture and share the insights from all the recent groundbreaking research on how we judge and persuade each other. And it translates that into simple, practical terms anyone can use to build more effective relationships at the office or at home. I'm glad they wrote it so I didn't have to."

—Amy Cuddy, associate professor, Harvard Business School

"Human psychology is never more fascinating than in this book. It is both serious and engaging. Kohut and Neffinger will help you to lead—and succeed—in everything from public speaking to love. This is a wonderful read."

—Joseph S. Nye Jr., professor, Harvard University, and author of
The Powers to Lead

"Neffinger and Kohut will blow your mind with their unified theory of everything that matters. *Compelling People* goes deep with an idea that will have you reexamining your instincts and opinions about everyone from coworkers and dates to politicians and celebrities."

—Amy Argetsinger, columnist, *Washington Post* "Reliable Source"

"Thanks to John Neffinger and Matt Kohut, I now have a much greater understanding of how to better influence and connect with all the people I encounter every day. *Compelling People* is a fascinating, beguiling read with the potential to change your life."

—Lynne Olson, author of *Those Angry Days* and *Citizens of London*

"Neffinger and Kohut brilliantly illuminate how successful people negotiate possibilities and pitfalls to find success and avoid failure."

—Liz Coleman, president, Bennington College

"*Compelling People* offers a wealth of practical approaches for understanding and improving how each of us presents ourselves to the world."

—Cheryl Strauss Einhorn, adjunct professor, Columbia Business School

Contents

How to Use This Book

This subject is endlessly fascinating to us, and we hope you feel the same way. This book draws on both our work with clients and a rapidly growing body of social science research. Seemingly every day brings a new study with some fresh insight that further strengthens our thinking, and as we write this on Guy Fawkes Day 2012, we realize that this is by no means the final word on this topic. With that in mind, this book is intended to work in concert with the accompanying website, compellingpeople.com, where we share perspectives on current events and related issues, discuss the latest research and directions for future research, and provide useful tools to bring some of these concepts to life.

We have written the text in a way that we hope is engaging and fun to read. After laying out the basic idea in the first section, we look at what happens when you size someone up—and more important, when you get sized up yourself. We then explore how the basic idea plays out in a variety of real-life settings. The book is written to be read straight through, and everything is meant to relate to people you know and situations you find yourself in. But you can also use this like a handbook and jump around to the sections that are most relevant to your purposes. If you do jump around, know that the "Making It Happen" section and the epilogue offer useful tools and perspectives to help you operationalize the ideas covered throughout. Also, if you are not in a hurry, take a look at the endnotes: You will find research citations, resources, thoughts, and stories.

Preface

Late one Friday afternoon a few years ago, our friend Susan had a chance encounter that changed her career. At forty-five years old, Susan had worked her way up in her company and was feeling good about her job. She had just come from the last meeting of a long week, and was looking forward to losing herself in a good book on the train ride home.

A well-dressed man in his mid-fifties walked up and asked if the seat next to her was taken. When she said no, he sat down and offered a polite hello. She glanced at her new seatmate and noticed he was wearing a name tag sticker on his jacket. She had already opened her book, and debated whether to mention it. But he seemed nice enough, so she decided to make the effort.

"You're a doctor?" she asked.

"Yes, how did you know?"

She pointed to the name tag: Dr. Edward Jordan.

He chuckled and peeled it off. "Thanks for letting me know." Then he kept talking, explaining he had just come from a conference because he was trying to start a business and needed to make new contacts.

Susan nodded silently, trying to strike a balance between being polite and not encouraging him.

But he went on: He was a pediatrician, and he had just launched a company to let patients confer with doctors over the Internet. As he described this venture, Susan recalled taking her daughter to the doctor a month earlier. She would not have wanted to try that over e-mail.

She asked him how he planned to get people to change the way they interacted with their doctors.

He smiled, and turned the question back to her. "You're absolutely right," he said. "That's the big hurdle. How would you handle it?"

Susan was surprised that he asked. In her experience, doctors usually thought they had all the answers. So she told him about her recent experience, and they talked about the kinds of care a doctor could and could not provide over the Internet, and how parents would feel about that. Susan suggested a few ways that Edward might speak to parents' concerns. He nodded, impressed, and asked more questions. She told him about a successful effort she had recently been involved in to market a new product.

By the time the train reached her stop, Susan was on her way to accepting a newly created position as the head of sales for Edward's company.

We all hear stories like this from time to time, and chalk them up to serendipity. To a certain extent, dumb luck put these two people on the same train, and they had skills and needs that fit well together. But there was more to it. In those first moments, what was it about Edward that persuaded Susan to talk with him further instead of diving into her book? After pitching his business to industry insiders all week, what was it about Susan that persuaded Edward to pitch it again to a stranger on a train? And what was it that eventually persuaded each of them to consider taking a gamble on working together?

As they spoke, each of them made a character judgment about the other. Character judgments like these happen quickly, but they are a big deal, shaping every aspect of our lives. It starts on the playground, where most kids form bands of compatriots while a few unlucky souls are almost universally shunned, and a few favored others move seamlessly across cliques. When adolescence dawns, similar judgments dictate whom we can and cannot date, and ultimately who marries whom. They dictate our professional fates as well, determining which candidate gets the job, who gets promoted, and who gets shown the door when times are tough.

This book explains how character judgments work. When people size you up, what are they looking for? It also explains how to make character judgments work for you—what you can do to affect the way others see you.

The Short Answer

It turns out that when we decide how we feel about someone, we are making not one judgment, but two. The criteria that count are what we call "strength" and "warmth." Strength is a person's capacity to make things happen with abilities and force of will. When people project strength, they command our respect. Warmth is the sense that a person shares our feelings, interests, and view of the world. When people project warmth, we like and support them.

So we warm to warm people but dislike cold ones. We take seemingly strong people seriously but often disregard those who seem weak and inconsequential. People who project both strength and warmth impress us as knowing what they are doing and having our best interests at heart, so we trust them and find them persuasive. They seem willing (warm) and able (strong) to look out for our interests, so we look to them for leadership and feel comfortable knowing they are in charge. Strength and warmth are the principal criteria on which all our social judgments hinge.

Once you grasp this insight, it opens up a whole new window on the human experience. You can understand why a person is appealing by looking closely at how they project strength and warmth. Or, if a person is not so appealing, you can see what makes them seem cold or weak. The waitress's sweet talk projects warmth, while her level gaze suggests she does not put up with nonsense. The boss's awkward posture projects insecurity and undercuts his employees' respect for him. The customer service rep projects warmth by sympathizing with the caller, saying that the snafu must have been aggravating—but then expresses confusion about the problem, projecting weakness and losing the caller's confidence. Like a cost-benefit analysis or a pros-and-cons list, the strength + warmth lens reveals something fundamental about our experience.

What About You?

Knowing that strength and warmth matter is one thing, but when it comes to ourselves, acting on that insight turns out to be tricky. Any time we are in the presence of others, we are communicating, sending social signals, even when the message is just "This is who I am." We project strength and warmth using many different signals, including ones we never think about. Most of us generally have only a dim understanding of the signals we are sending. In fact, a stranger who spends just a few minutes in your presence usually walks away with a much clearer sense of the impression you make on people than you have yourself.

But understanding the signals you send is not the biggest challenge. The trickiest thing about strength and warmth is that it is very hard to project both at once. This is because strength and warmth are in direct tension with each other. Most of the things we do to project strength of character—wearing a serious facial expression, flexing our biceps, or flexing our vocabulary—tend to make us seem less warm. Likewise, most signals of warmth—smiling often, speaking softly, doing people favors—can leave us seeming more submissive than strong.

This presents each of us with a dilemma. We get to decide what kind of social signals to send to the world. Do we choose to project warmth, so people like us? Do we instead show strength, so we command respect? Or do we try our best to project strength and warmth, knowing that one undermines the other and we might end up failing at both?

The ability to master this tension, to project both strength and warmth at once, is rare—so rare, in fact, that we celebrate, elevate, and envy those people who manage it. We even have special names for this ability. The ancient Greeks called it "the divine gift," from which we get the word "charisma." Today it goes by different names in different circles: It is called "leadership potential" in the modern workplace, "cool" in social settings, and even just "it" in the entertainment business, as in "She's got it!"

A New Approach

A decade ago, the two of us were both working at Harvard, writing speeches and editing articles for faculty members. We got to talking about why it was that some people lit up a room while others fell flat. The conversation grew to include a friend of ours, Seth Pendleton, a trained actor who had been coaching public speakers for years. Eventually we started working with Seth helping executives and public figures prepare for speeches and high-stakes pitch meetings.

As we worked with clients, we found our advice kept returning to the same themes, even with people facing very different challenges. For one thing, it was striking how we could transform the impressions many people made just by getting them to stand up straight and smile, though that was by no means always easy. We also noticed that our clients' public speaking challenges often fell into one of two categories: They would either come across as too stiff and emotionally distant, or they would seem too hesitant, unsure of their material or apologizing for themselves.

To become better coaches, we studied the most compelling people to see how they pulled it off. From Oprah Winfrey to Ronald Reagan, from Dolly Parton to the Dalai Lama, we saw successful people using the same strategies over and over. Armed with these insights, we were able to develop and refine a coaching approach that helps the rest of us learn what the greats already know.

This book is the culmination of our research and experience helping clients connect with audiences in boardrooms, on K Street, at cocktail parties and Sunday picnics. We have now used this approach over a half dozen years with hundreds of clients, including Fortune 500 executives, members of Congress, TV personalities, leaders of government agencies and national nonprofit organizations, Nobel Prize winners, and NASA flight directors. Our work also benefits greatly from our collaboration with our colleague and friend Professor Amy Cuddy, of Harvard Business School, thanks to whom we regularly guest lecture and work with MBA students there.

Many times we have been asked for recommendations for something to read about the work we do, and have not had much to offer. At long last, then, here is our answer: the story of strength, warmth, and character.

A Look Ahead

We begin with the big idea: What exactly do we mean by strength? What about warmth? We take a closer look under the hood to reveal the dynamics that make it tricky to project both at once.

Next we consider the factors we have the least control over: gender, ethnicity, age, body type, and looks. We examine the role of stereotyping in character judgments and what our basic demographic factors say about us to other people.

With a clear picture of the hand life has dealt you, we then explore the best ways to play that hand. This begins by examining the nonverbal cues that broadcast our inner emotional states in real time. We also use the lens of strength and warmth to take a fresh look at the seemingly superficial but always engaging topic of fashion and personal style.

We then focus on how language projects strength and warmth, from words and names to complex stories. The heart of this section presents a simple and powerful approach to verbal persuasion—"connect, then lead"—which we explain with the metaphor of a circle. You can use this approach with all forms of nonfiction writing, from business proposals to personal e-mails.

Having considered all of your strength and warmth signals in isolation, we turn next to how this all comes together at the office and in our personal lives, including in arenas like social media and public speaking. We also consider how strength and warmth shape our politics and our culture.

Along the way, we share some of our favorite techniques that we use with clients, including showing you how to be your own coach.

Every time we work with someone new, we are reminded just how powerful this framework is. The fact is, once you recognize the dynamics of strength and warmth, you see people in a new way: yourself, your loved ones, your colleagues, random strangers, everybody. And if you understand how to project your own strength and warmth, you will change the way people see you too.

COMPELLING PEOPLE

The Big Idea

Strength

Strength gets things done. As a personal quality, strength is a measure of how much a person can impose their will on our world. People who project it command our attention, in part because we need to know if they are going to use their strength in ways that help us or in ways that harm us. Grudgingly or gladly, we respect people who project strength.

There is no shortage of examples of strong people in the public eye. Corporate downsizers "Chainsaw Al" Dunlap and General Electric's "Neutron Jack" Welch earned their reputations for strength pursuing efficiency above all and showing many workers the door in the process. Former British prime minister Margaret Thatcher cultivated her reputation as the Iron Lady. Supreme Court justice Antonin Scalia projects strength with his scornful wit and sneer.

When people seem weak, we are not as concerned with what they want, because they cannot make it happen anyway. We do not pay much attention to them unless we want something specific, and they generally have less to offer. Our personal ethical code may well dictate that we treasure them as our fellow human beings, but they lack the ability to affect our world. In that sense, they do not matter as much.

Leadership and strength are inextricably bound together. We look to strong people as leaders because they can protect us from threats to our group. Strength is essential to effective leadership, whether the organization is a submarine crew or a school clique.

Strength consists of two basic elements: the ability to affect the world, and the gumption to take action.

Ability

Ability includes anything that lets you affect the world. This encompasses qualities like your physical strength, learned technical skills, deft social skills, and hard-won wisdom. Social scientists refer to all of this together as "competence."

People who accomplish a task that requires a high degree of practice, learning, or judgment command our attention and respect, whether they are brain surgeons or banjo players. These feats do not have to be showy: A top-notch accountant possesses formidable number-crunching acumen, which confers a certain standing among her colleagues.

Within an organization, you may be given the ability to command people to do things, or to hold them accountable if they refuse. Supervisory authority is a primary source of strength in organizational settings. (It is often bestowed on people who have proven themselves especially competent, but not always.)

In civilized company, some of the most critical abilities are social. A diplomat, for example, earns respect and authority by demonstrating mastery of social graces, using both verbal dexterity and a host of nonverbal cues. On the other hand, people who are less skilled at reading social cues or not adept at expressing themselves command less respect.

Social skills are not all about being charming. Getting one's way in social situations—or at least not getting trampled—often involves being assertive. A kid who responds to a mocking comment on the playground with a quick retort is not only less likely to get picked on next time but also more likely to be listened to when it is time to decide which game to play at recess. Delivering that retort swiftly involves the skill to come up with it on the fly, and it also involves something else: the will to stand up to the bully and risk the consequences.

Will

If having ability means you have the tools to make things happen, will is the strength of character it takes to act. Will manifests itself as a commitment to move forward, even (or especially) in the face of obstacles and resistance. We talk about this quality all the time, calling it determination, grit, motivation, ambition, perseverance, or resilience. Gandhi may have put it best: "Strength does not come from physical capacity. It comes from an indomitable will." While we say both ability and will grant us strength, we salute Gandhi's sentiment nonetheless.

Will is not just something you are born with, but it develops early, and some kids have more than others. In a classic study known as the Stanford marshmallow experiment, small children were confronted with a trial by temptation: Each child was placed alone in a room that was empty except for a marshmallow sitting on a plate in front of them. They were told they could eat the marshmallow—but that if they waited fifteen minutes they would get two marshmallows instead of one. Many squirmed, and many succumbed, but others persevered and doubled their marshmallow haul. Years later, researchers found that the kids who had resisted eating the single marshmallow tended to perform better in school and cope better with frustration as adolescents. In other words, they mustered the willpower to handle discomfort and delay gratification in many realms of life.

It turns out that what we call willpower works through a combination of skills and desires. Like a muscle, willpower can be developed and exercised—and get fatigued. Recent research has shown that willpower gets depleted at the end of a hard day, making temptation harder to resist when we are tired. But it can be developed too: The more we ask of ourselves in this regard, the more we can deliver. Our friend Bonnie learned this firsthand when she joined a running club after not exercising regularly in decades. On day one she could run only two blocks, and she was ready to say she had made a mistake and give up. Over a period of months, though, she stuck with it, deciding every day to renew her commitment, and gradually increased both her physical stamina and her ability to persevere through the discomfort of stretching her limits.

Exercising willpower is largely a matter of deciding how badly you want what you are after, and focusing on the emotional consequences of the choice in front of you. This is where personality, values, and character come into play: People persevere longer not only when they want the reward more, but when they take pride in their determination, or feel shame for quitting. Developing willpower is partly a matter of strengthening those emotional associations, both by enjoying small successes and by learning to tell ourselves better stories.

But people tackling challenges like Bonnie do not just grit their teeth harder, they also use other techniques to persevere. Rather than facing down every pain or irresistible temptation, they avoid them. This is the skill dimension of willpower. When pushing through the middle minutes of a hard run, Bonnie learned not to focus on the growing pain. Instead, she thinks about her next vacation or sings along with a song in her head. This passes the time without depleting her reserve of willpower, which she might still need later.

When dealing with inanimate objects, will is pretty simple: You exert effort, and you either achieve the desired effect or you do not. In the social realm, things get more complicated, because people exert their will on others, who in turn exert their will right back. As social creatures, we are surrounded by people seeking to impose their will upon us in ways large and small, from family members wanting favors to work colleagues wanting special treatment to hucksters wanting our money.

People who are not comfortable asserting themselves with others limit their effectiveness in the many social contexts we all inhabit. Even professionals who have spent years mastering a difficult specialty may still lack what it takes to make a point in even a small roomful of colleagues. These people rarely move into positions of leadership, because despite their competence, their submissive social style leaves them unable to lead. They typically reach a plateau as experts who are called on to do difficult work for their bosses.

One client of ours was a senior adviser in the finance department of a multinational company. He was a mountain of a man, well over six feet tall, with broad shoulders and a square jaw. In meetings, though, he shrank before colleagues and could not hold his own in a contentious conversation even when he was sure of his position. With some coaching, he began to approach these encounters with a new attitude and became more comfortable asserting himself, but it took a conscious effort and practice to reach that point.

On the other end of the spectrum are the dominant characters: the bullies and the know-it-alls. These people think their way is the only right way, and they steamroll everyone else, not by praising people who do things their way, but by making life unpleasant when anyone dares to dissent. This extreme willfulness can get results in the short term, but it also comes at a steep social price.

The Biology of Strength

Assertiveness and dominance are tied directly to the presence of certain hormones in the bloodstream. The star of this story is testosterone, which is most commonly thought of as the male sex hormone. It is actually present in both men and women, though in higher levels in men. Elevated levels of testosterone correspond with behaviors associated with dominance and risk taking. Adrenaline can also play a role, surging through our veins when we see a small child toddling toward a busy road and we dash over to intercede. In lesser emergencies, it still gives us a boost of energy and helps us react quickly with either fight or flight. The other hormone that plays a key role here is cortisol, which reacts to stress in less helpful ways. When you get the jitters before a big performance, that is cortisol at work. Cortisol makes people feel anxious and worried, and that undercuts strength.

Skeptics

Most of us recognize and respect people who project traditional strength signals. We are impressed by people who show talent, whether it is navigating around a race course or navigating around a room. Most people perceive dominant people as more credible than submissive people. The very act of asserting yourself boosts your standing as someone who matters. This should not be too surprising: If you won't stand up for yourself, why should anyone else take you seriously?

But not everyone sees strength the same way. Some people are suspicious of traditional strength signals. They distrust the salesperson who booms confidence, for instance, preferring one who expresses more moderate opinions and acknowledges uncertainties. These people suspect the bluster may be masking weakness, that since this person is getting by on style, it is a good bet there is no substance behind it. These feelings can be motivated by jealousy of others' social skills. But even then, they are sometimes right that the emperor has no clothes.

We can learn to project strength and elicit reactions of respect and even fear from the people around us. But strength alone can only take us so far. To move beyond respect to admiration, we also need to be liked. And to do that, we need to project warmth.

Warmth

We all commonly use the term "warmth" to refer to a sense of belonging and feeling cared for. The connection between that sentiment and a physical feeling of elevated temperature is universal. Researchers have found that just about every known human language uses warmth to mean "affection," one of just a handful of "primary metaphors" shared widely across cultures around the world. This seems to stem directly from the primal bonding experience we all have as infants of being held by our parents and experiencing the warmth of their bodies. This association runs so deep that just holding a warm drink will make you act more warmly toward others. On the other hand, being excluded from a group can make you feel physically cold.

For our purposes, warmth is what people feel when they recognize they share interests and concerns. It is the sense of being on the same team. If strength is about whether someone can carry out their intentions, warmth is about whether you will be happy with the result. When people project warmth, we like them.

Warmth encompasses several related concepts: empathy, familiarity, and love.

Empathy

Displaying empathy means putting oneself in the shoes of others. This is not always a pleasant experience: If someone is filled with outrage, sadness, disappointment, or disgust, and you recognize that you share that feeling with them, that is empathy too. Empathy offers us comfort, the feeling that we are not alone. As the actor Bill Murray once said, "Every moment that you share someone else's pain, feel what they feel, makes you more human."

Emotional empathy can be contagious. For instance, it is hard not to yawn when you see someone else do it. (This even works across species: Matt will often fake a yawn at his dog to get her to settle down for bed— and she yawns right back.) This viral quality holds for other seemingly spontaneous behaviors as well, from laughing to crying to cheering. More subtly, when two people are deep in conversation, they will often unconsciously start to mimic each other's posture, gestures, and vocal patterns.

Empathy is not just about feelings. There is also a cognitive dimension to it: The shared feeling is tied to a shared perception. This is captured in the expression "I get it," meaning "I understand why you feel a certain way." It takes mental effort to imagine how someone with a different background, experiences, and values sees and feels about the world, and the greater the difference in background, the more effort that takes.

Journalist Barbara Ehrenreich took drastic measures to bridge a cognitive empathy gap in her book *Nickel and Dimed*. A best-selling writer with a Ph.D. in biology, Ehrenreich took a series of jobs serving food, scrubbing toilets, and stocking shelves. Only then did she fully appreciate just how hard people in those jobs had it. It is not always necessary (or possible) to walk a mile in another's shoes, but her example illustrates how people right next to each other can experience things very differently.

An undercover officer or a spy behind enemy lines also experiences cognitive empathy, but has to be able to draw the line there. Think of a cop pretending to be part of a drug dealer's crew. As he gets to know the people involved, he comes to understand their worldview and concerns, even as he does not feel the same way in his own heart. In that situation, empathy is such a powerful force that undercover operatives are often pulled out of the field so they do not "go native" and adopt the suspects' point of view.

Familiarity

Familiar things are a reliable source of comfort. Of course, not everything familiar gives us warm feelings, and familiarity does sometimes breed contempt. But we fear the unknown, and the more often we encounter something without anything bad happening, the more comfortable we get around it. Imagine, for instance, going to a friend's house and being greeted at the door by a large dog like a rottweiler. Even if you are comfortable with dogs, you will probably be more wary the first time you meet the dog than after you have spent time with her and learned she is a lovable, oversize lapdog. When someone or something is unfamiliar, we are on guard—poised to react with strength (or fear)—until we determine that there is no threat.

When we meet people who are similar to us, we gravitate toward them because they feel so familiar to us. "Birds of a feather flock together" is such a well-established phenomenon that psychologists have a technical name for it: the similarity-attraction effect. For example, studies have found that mothers tend to favor daughters who most closely resemble them physically. Similarity essentially works like a social magnet.

Love

When we feel a whole lot of warmth for someone, we say we love them. This gets complicated because we use the word "love" to describe many different feelings, some of which involve more than warmth. In fact, researchers have identified three different biological systems that get labeled "love," each of which generates a different set of hormones that produces different kinds of feelings: one for romantic love, one for sexual attraction, and a third for general feelings of attachment. Romance and sexual attraction are close cousins of warmth: When someone is either romantically or sexually attractive to us, just looking at them makes us feel good—maybe even literally warm, if there is a flush under the skin. But it is this third feeling—basic affection and attachment—that best fits our idea of warmth.

The Biology of Warmth

The main molecules associated with warmth are estrogen and oxytocin. For a long time both were best known as female reproductive hormones, but they are present in both men and women, and recent research has made their role in warmth much clearer. Estrogen is associated with being "touchy-feely," socially perceptive, and emotionally expressive. Oxytocin is responsible for the good feeling of connectedness and belonging that we associate with warmth. Elevated oxytocin levels are linked with feelings of warmth and behavior that shows cooperation and trust toward people we perceive as being on our team.

In short, warmth is all about sharing feelings, good or bad, happy or sad.

Strength vs. Warmth

Half a millennium ago, in a medieval world of sword battles, palace intrigue, and priceless treasures, an aging diplomat found himself sidelined after choosing the losing side in the latest power struggle. In his long life in politics, he had witnessed the rise and fall of dynasties and popes, and had both held positions of great power and found himself imprisoned and tortured when his chosen faction's fortunes fell. Searching for a way back into the good graces of the latest prince, he hit on an idea: He would write down all the hard-won lessons he had learned navigating these intrigues and betrayals, and make a gift of this knowledge to the new prince to impress him and win his favor. As it happened, the prince was not impressed. But though it did not restore his political career, Niccolò Machiavelli's book secured his reputation as one of history's wisest strategists, as well as his place in our language—the term "Machiavellian" is synonymous with unsentimental cunning.

The most famous of all Machiavelli's lessons is his meditation on the relative merits of fear and love: ". . . whether it be better to be loved than feared or feared than loved? . . . One should wish to be both, but . . . it is difficult to unite them in one person."

This captures the basic dynamics of strength and warmth perfectly: Great strength can inspire fear, and great warmth can inspire love. These are the fundamental forces that shape human relations. In any situation that requires leadership, these are the tools available to motivate people to follow—and it is very hard to wield both at once. This is the leader's dilemma.

Machiavelli did not know it, but the tension between strength and warmth actually has a direct biological basis. Testosterone, the key hormonal agent of strength, turns out to be a potent inhibitor of oxytocin, its counterpart for warmth. It is hard to balance these qualities in life in part because they do battle with one another in our blood.

The Choice

So if you cannot project both strength and warmth, which one should you choose?

Back in the world of medieval Florence, Machiavelli recommended choosing fear over love, strength over warmth, a competitive strategy over a cooperative one. This is a perfectly appropriate choice in dog-eat-dog situations, when cooperation is not likely to be reciprocated and there are no social forces to sanction excessive strength.

Modern society is somewhat more civilized, and research suggests that when people size each other up, warmth is their most important criterion. Janine Willis and Alex Todorov of Princeton University have found that people make warmth judgments within a tenth of a second of seeing a new person's face. This makes intuitive sense: When people meet someone new, they want to figure out this person's intentions.

At the same time, strength matters too. Imagine meeting a pro football linebacker. His size would get your attention, and you would recognize right away that he could cause you harm. Similarly, you might discount the physical abilities of the proverbial ninety-eight-pound weakling. The instinct that drives judgments of both intentions and capabilities is the same: survival.

There is one especially critical difference in the way we judge each quality. Warmth operates under something we call the tomato rule: Just as one freezing night can ruin a garden full of tomatoes, one cold incident—in which you show clearly that you do not share another person's interests or care about how they feel—can make it very difficult to reestablish warmth between you later. If you come across as cold once, the impression sticks. Strength works in the inverse way: Demonstrating your strength affirmatively just once goes a long way toward establishing yourself as strong. That impression sticks. There are limits to this, of course. If you start a new job performing at a high level but then slack off, you will eventually undo your initial impression of competence. But it will probably take a while.

Halos and Hydraulics

Strength and warmth are complementary, not mutually exclusive opposites, and there is a lot of interplay between them.

For starters, there is the halo effect: We tend to attribute positive qualities to people with other positive qualities. If we like our doctor, for example, we might tell friends that she's brilliant, even if we have no basis at all to make judgments about anyone's medical know-how.

Even if she made a mistake and negligently caused us great bodily harm, we might refuse to believe it was her fault. Several studies have found that more likable doctors—ones who take a little extra time with each patient and speak in warm, empathetic tones—rarely get sued, even when their performance might warrant it. Meanwhile, doctors who discount the importance of bedside manner are much more likely to end up in court, regardless of their performance. Once we like someone, the halo effect kicks in, and we find it easy to think the best of them and hard to think anything else.

But there is another dynamic at play here, and it is in conflict with the halo effect.

There is also a hydraulic effect between strength and warmth: When one goes up, the other usually goes down. Raise your voice in order to be heard in a meeting, and you sound angry. Show too much kindly deference toward your colleagues, and you seem like a pushover. In fact, nearly everything you do to increase your strength diminishes your warmth, and vice versa.

While the halo effect seems driven mostly by wishful thinking, the hydraulic effect has some logic to it. As Machiavelli saw, leading with strength and leading with warmth are different strategies for getting along in the world. People who are proficient in one strategy may have less need to develop the other. And it is tricky to do both, particularly if you have spent a lifetime favoring one set of muscles over the other.

A similar hydraulic dynamic kicks in when we compare two people side by side: One person is perceived as stronger and tends to seem less warm, while the other person seems warmer but less strong. This contrast effect comes up in situations like hiring, when a company is deciding between its final two candidates: One gets labeled the strong candidate, the other the warm one. (This is good to recognize whether you are one of the two candidates for the job or the person doing the hiring.)

The tension between the halo and hydraulic effects is evident in the contrast between a couple of old sports clichés. One saying holds that "everybody loves a winner." This is why sports fans adore the star who wins year in and year out. The other old saw is that "everyone loves an underdog." When two competitors are pitted against one another and one seems clearly stronger, many people feel a surge of warmth for the weaker one. This demonstrates that a person's perceived strength and warmth is not absolute or fixed. It is judged in context.

Two Worldviews

Consider these two rags-to-riches stories with very different morals.

A young Jewish woman who lived through the upheaval of the Russian Revolution found her way to the United States in the 1920s and set her sights on becoming a screenwriter. Having witnessed the forced transformation of Russian society under Lenin and Stalin, she developed a worldview that prized the individual above all. The novels that made her famous featured iron-willed men who valued personal freedom. In this distinctly twentieth-century vision of American rugged individualism, the only currency that mattered was strength.

A couple of decades later, four working-class lads from Liverpool took the world by storm. They were pop stars who led the growth of rock 'n' roll from two-minute boy-meets-girl ditties to more expansive musical forms and lyrics that spoke to the issues of the day. At the height of their fame, as protests swelled in opposition to the U.S. war in Vietnam, they sang an anthem that came to epitomize a generational antipathy toward violence: "All You Need Is Love." The title said it all: The world could run just fine on warmth alone.

Ayn Rand and the Beatles symbolize two poles in a deep divide. One champions all strength and no warmth, the other all warmth and no strength. This is a bit of a caricature, but the gulf between the two is real.

The Strong Do What They Can

For the Ayn Rand crowd, warmth is a proxy for the ultimate flaw, weakness. This reflects a fundamentally bleak view of how the world works: "The strong do what they can, and the weak suffer what they must." In this view, strength is the only morality, because it is the only way to survive, and do-gooders who want to help the weak are just too cowardly to face that harsh reality. People who take this view to heart cultivate strength as a virtue, seeing it as the only way to defend what they value from the darkness of anarchy or tyranny.

Strength can make people powerful, influential, and important. After all, strength is about getting things done. But there are things it cannot do. Strength alone can coerce, but it cannot lead. Strength for its own sake is a corrosive force. People who renounce warmth and go over to the dark side are much less likely to end up sharing their lives with people who care about them. Ironically, the stronger people are—the more easily they can bend the world to their will—the harder it is for them to be sure their friends are being friendly for the right reasons. Like spies, they trust nobody, and nobody trusts them either. At best, they inspire fear, or sometimes envy.

Let There Be Warmth

On the other hand, the "all you need is love" hootenanny is filled with the nicest people you know. With this crowd, being important is nice, but being nice is what's important. These people see the best in everyone, but they are deeply suspicious of many forms of strength. In their eyes, strength goes hand in hand with cruelty, brutality, greed, selfishness, aggression, and a lack of caring. Their alternative vision is a world built on cooperation rather than competition, one of mutual understanding and dialogue that leads to consensus and peace. The virtues they hold in high esteem are compassion, patience, and tolerance.

In fact, these folks are nice to a fault. Their judgment can be impaired by the "rose-colored glasses" syndrome, in which they are so busy seeing the best in everyone that they miss clear warning signs about people who may do them harm. Think doormat—the person in the office who continually gets passed over for promotion, the girlfriend who sticks with her jerk boyfriend even though all her friends say she should dump him, the parent who lets his kid call the shots. Old-time baseball manager Leo Durocher coined a phrase to describe what happens to them: "Nice guys finish last." The feeling they inspire is pity.

Each Inside the Other

When you project a whole lot of either strength or warmth, an interesting thing sometimes happens: You can start to project the other trait as well.

Think of Ayn Rand. Her ideas championing the gospel of strength attracted legions of devotees who organized local Ayn Rand clubs and student groups to share their common interest in individualism and not caring what anyone else thinks. She showed no interest in what other people thought either, and yet she drew people to her cause. People loved her books, recognized her strength, and wanted to be on her team. She projected so much strength that people were drawn to it, and they came to see themselves as sharing interests with her. This is how great strength can also generate warmth.

The Beatles were so lovable that their effect on fans merited its own word: "Beatlemania." They attracted millions of fans, to the point where John Lennon made a comment about the Beatles being "bigger than Jesus," which provoked a bit of a firestorm. Their success enabled them to use the loyalty of their supporters to get what they wanted, from making better business deals to advancing social causes. They projected so much warmth that they became a force to be reckoned with. Their warmth gave them the ability to move people, not to mention records and tickets. This is how great warmth can also create strength.

You do not have to invent a new philosophy or reinvent pop music to see how this might work in your own life. You may have colleagues who want to be like you because you are known for being great at what you do—so your strength fosters warmth. Similarly, if you find yourself in a situation full of tough characters, whether in a boardroom or in a bar, projecting strength not only wins you respect; it is also the first step to showing them you are their kind of person. In that sense, it also creates some warmth.

On the flip side, if you are beloved by the people you work with, most of them will side with you if you get crosswise with someone—so your warmth also gives you strength. And if you are doing any job in which you have to be liked to be effective, your ability to project warmth is a key strength you bring to the role.

Overcoming the Divide

One of the wisest strategists of the twentieth century also grappled with the relationship between strength and warmth. In 1967, Dr. Martin Luther King Jr. gave one of his last great speeches to the Southern Christian Leadership Conference in Atlanta. King first spoke of the importance of asserting a sense of dignity and worth, and then addressed the process of gaining political and economic power. He acknowledged that many in his audience were skeptical of power. But, King said, "One of the great problems of history is that the concepts of love and power have usually been contrasted as opposites. . . . What is needed is a realization that power without love is reckless and abusive, and that love without power is sentimental and anemic."

What King recognized on the world stage, each one of us also experiences in person every day. We turn next to this challenge of embodying both at once. It is a little like the old parlor game of rubbing your stomach and patting your head at the same time—definitely doable, not so easy.

Strength + Warmth

Imagine arriving at a party. You show up a few minutes ahead of the friends who invited you. You ring the bell and wait, and moments later the door is opened by a pretty young woman with a blue cardigan sweater. "Oh, hi," she says, looking at you with a note of trepidation in her wide eyes, her head bent slightly as if she were trying to blend into the gymnasium wall at a school dance. You say hello in return, and she looks at the floor and shuffles her feet before looking up at you again with an embarrassed smile. "Um, please come in?" she offers hopefully. You nod, thank her, and come inside.

As you survey the room, a man in a well-tailored suit looks up from the circle of people he is with and strides toward you with a slightly suspicious look on his face, as if calculating whether you are friend or foe. "And you are?" he says, taking your hand into his bone-crushing grip. But before you can say your own name, his gaze shifts over your shoulder toward the door, and a polite smile appears on his face. He hails the guests arriving behind you and drifts away in search of another hand to crush.

You find your way to the drinks and help yourself, and as you turn to look around the room again, you come to the realization that you have company—there is a guy standing just a couple of feet from you. He is short, almost jockey-sized, with a dark T-shirt tucked into his pants, and he does not look friendly. He has his phone in one hand and is scowling as he scrolls around the screen, while he is biting at the cuticles on his other hand—a favorite pastime, judging by the scabs on his fingers. He looks up at you, still scowling, and says "What?" But before you can respond, he has turned back to his phone. You nod vaguely in the direction of his scowl and move quietly away.

Across the room, you notice a middle-aged woman, medium height and build, standing in a semicircle of people. She seems quite pleasant, with a small smile and something of a twinkle in her eye. She has a simple haircut and wears a colorful scarf loosely wrapped around her neck. She listens intently when someone else is speaking: She nods, asks questions, and reaches out to offer an easy pat on their forearm. As the conversation unfolds, with every exchange the center of gravity returns to her. You drift closer to see what is so interesting.

If your friends arrived at that moment and asked how it was going, what would you say about the people at the party? Who did you like? Who did you respect? Who turned you off? Who did you want to get to know better?

Think about these people at the party through the lens of strength and warmth. Start with the young woman who greeted you at the door. Let's call her Emily. She was skittish and awkward, a deer in the headlights, pretty much the opposite of strong and confident. On the warmth front, though, she was both genuine and friendly.

How about your host, Kurt, who accosted you just long enough to make your hand hurt? From his sharp dress to his all-business demeanor to the way he mangled your hand just because he could, this guy was all about strength. Warmth, not so much. Even when he recognized the guest arriving behind you, his smile was nothing more than an appropriate social signal. There was no joy behind it.

Dennis, the scowling guy at the bar, was a piece of work. Did he project strength? Not unless you consider a bad attitude strong. His anxious habit of chewing on his fingers did not inspire confidence either. How about warmth? He came to a party full of people, only to stand alone checking his phone. Even standing next to someone at the bar with plenty to chitchat about, he did not manage to project much strength or warmth.

Now consider the woman in the semicircle, Cheryl, who attracted the sustained attention of several guests. She carried herself with poise and confidence and paired that with a warm, genuine smile. The combination of the two put the people around her at ease. Even though you didn't even meet her, you liked her already too.

If we were to map our partygoers according to whether they are high or low in strength and warmth, it would be easy to see who belongs where. Figure 1 (below) shows the different levels of strength and warmth that each person projected. The more strength they project, the more we respect them, and the further up the vertical axis they go. The more warmth they project, the more we like them, and the further along the horizontal axis they go. Emily projected warmth but hardly any strength. Our host, Kurt, was the opposite—all strength, zero warmth. Dennis, by the bar, struck out on both counts, while Cheryl managed to project a good deal of both.

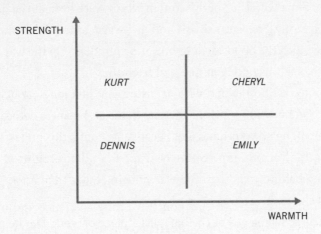

Fig. 1.

It is usually pretty easy to figure out where people fit on this chart. Where would you put Oprah? Even fictional people: How about Darth Vader? Most project some degree of each, but the ratio varies.

The easiest way to think about how much strength and warmth someone projects is to consider the emotions we feel in response. Machiavelli saw that high strength can elicit fear, while lots of warmth can elicit love. The picture is slightly more complex when we look at different combinations of strength and warmth. Our friend Amy Cuddy at Harvard did some seminal work in this area with her colleagues Susan Fiske and Peter Glick. While their research initially focused on understanding how stereotypes work, they went on to identify these two factors as universal dimensions that shape our judgments of others. Figure 2 plots our emotional responses to people who project different levels of strength and warmth.

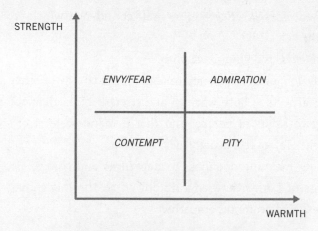

Fig. 2. (Adapted from Cuddy, Fiske, and Glick)

Looking at our partygoers in this context, Emily is so nice and meek that we want to give her a hug. Our hearts go out to her—the beginnings of pity. Our menacing host, Kurt, inspires wariness, if not quite fear. His heavy-duty handshake and in-your-face demeanor show us that he is not afraid to assert himself and not sure he likes your kind. If we even bother to care about the surly Mr. Dennis, the emotion we feel is contempt. Cheryl seems to be winning admirers based on the reactions of those around her, and we suspect we would feel the same way if we got to know her.

As the party scene illustrates, the strength and warmth framework goes a long way toward making sense of what otherwise is just a muddle: what makes some people charming, others jerks, and still others pushovers. Notice also that these judgments do not depend on what we usually think of as personality types. Psychologists generally see personality as consisting of five main traits, the Big Five, and these do track strength and warmth to a degree:

- *Conscientiousness*, which concerns self-discipline and thoroughness, is a form of strength.
- The absence of *neuroticism* allows self-confidence, which projects strength.
- *Agreeableness* is a kind of warmth.
- *Extraversion*, or the tendency to feed off the energy of other people, has aspects of both warmth and strength. It is all about connecting with lots of people, and that demands a level of social confidence introverts usually lack.
- *Openness*, meaning openness to new ideas and things, also has elements of both: Knowledge is power, so the jingle goes, and openness also promotes empathy.

But these personality factors do not explain whom we like or respect. We find some extroverts wonderful and others aggravating. We like some introverts and cannot be bothered with others. And while many neurotic people stress us out, Woody Allen and Jerry Seinfeld have found fame and fortune entertaining us.

When we make value judgments about people, we look past these personality factors to strength and warmth, because a person's strength and warmth are ultimately the factors most likely to affect our lives. Not coincidentally, they are also what we value morally. Psychologists Martin Seligman and Christopher Peterson studied how different cultural traditions around the world define character, and found that there are six moral virtues at the core of all of them. Half are forms of strength, and half are forms of warmth:

- *Courage*: the force of will to act in the face of danger
- *Temperance*: the principled exercise of self-control
- *Wisdom*: intellectual competence in its highest form
- *Justice*: a commitment to fairness for humanity
- *Humanity*: a deep and abiding concern for people's well-being
- *Transcendence*: looking beyond day-to-day concerns to achieve a sense that we are all connected.

Different Strokes . . .

It is important to note that as with beauty, strength and warmth exist in the eye of the beholder. For the most part we all recognize the basic signals of strength and warmth. They are like a shared language, easy to identify in others because they are rooted in our shared culture and biology. But the judgments each of us makes are also colored by our own idiosyncrasies. As we mentioned earlier, some people are skeptical of traditional displays of strength, suspecting weakness behind the bluster. Faced with a friendly salesperson, some people will appreciate the cheerfulness, but others will feel put off and prefer to be left alone. In either case, everyone recognizes the traditional strength and warmth signals, but some people do not see the salesperson as particularly strong or warm.

Not only do our interpretations of standard signals sometimes vary, but we all also see strength and warmth signals in different places. A rough-looking man wearing a beat-up black leather jacket and a vacant look might project high strength and no warmth to someone afraid he might beat them up. Or neither strength nor warmth to someone who dismisses him as a loser. Or low strength and high warmth to a professional counselor who suspects he needs help. Or both strength and warmth to a rock 'n' roll fan who recognizes him as Gene Simmons.

The ultimate measure of whether someone projects strength or warmth is the feeling they evoke in others. When you feel respect for a particular person, you see a kind of strength in them. And when you feel some kinship or affection for someone, you see them as warm.

Aiming High

Turning the lens the other way, we can begin to see how we could be more effective in dealing with people. It shows us why a lot of our life experience depends on whether we hit that quadrant of high strength and high warmth—or if we miss, in what direction we fall short.

The upper-right corner is clearly the place to be. People there are on our team, and they are the best players. This is where the people we call "charismatic" hang out. There is not a lot of company up there, because it is not obvious how to master the tension between strength and warmth and project enough of both simultaneously to earn both great respect and great affection.

Think back to Martin Luther King's speech about power and love. The upper-right quadrant is where he operated. The source of his charisma was the extraordinary depth of both strength and warmth in his public persona. His strength was seen in his unyielding commitment to his mission. And that mission was fairness for all, which is a consummate expression of warmth as shared concern. As a preacher, he understood both the power of language and the dynamics of performance, and used his body and voice as an instrument that gave his words force and passion—strength and warmth, at the same time.

Few people will ever hold a candle to King. But we know what this looks like in everyday life too. If you watch just a few seconds of a silent video clip of a teacher at the front of the classroom, research shows you can tell right away how students will rate that teacher at the end of the year. Since all of us have spent years in classrooms watching teachers, both great and less so, we quickly recognize which ones kids would pay attention to and do their homework for, and which ones kids would tune out and blow off. The teachers we remember fondly years later are the ones who got us to focus and learn while always making clear how much they cared about us.

Echoes Everywhere

Once you realize how central strength and warmth are to how we judge each other, you suddenly see the strength-warmth duality all around you. In the corporate world, the soft-skills curriculum runs from assertiveness training (strength) to sensitivity training (warmth). In church, the Old Testament calls God Elohim when He dispenses punishment (strength) and Adonay when He shows mercy (warmth). The daily news tells tales of "mamma grizzlies" (warm + strong) and "tiger moms" (strong + warm). In the food court at the mall, a server wears a T-shirt that sarcastically declares, "I will try to be nicer if you try to be smarter" (warmer, stronger), while the hippie who orders a veggie wrap from her wears a T-shirt with the ancient Chinese symbols for yin (warmth) and yang (strength). And out in the parking lot, there is a Hummer parked next to her VW Beetle.

Whether we are judging people, organizations, objects, or abstract concepts, we are judging character. And whenever we are judging character, the basic strength and warmth calculus is at work.

The Hand You Are Dealt

Quick and Dirty Judgment

Among the first things people learn about you are the physical basics: gender, body type, looks, ethnicity, age. As quick and superficial as this initial glimpse is, these attributes already convey the silhouette of a strength and warmth profile.

Your gender, ethnicity, and looks are the hand you are dealt. Whatever that may be, you can play that hand well so others recognize the great qualities of your character. To start, though, it helps to understand what you are working with.

We humans have evolved a whole lot of neural circuitry for making split-second judgments based on basic physical factors. These rapid-fire calculations happen automatically, below our conscious awareness, with very little effort. Being thorough and precise are not the top priorities; making good enough assessments quickly will do. Psychologist Daniel Kahneman calls these fast-thinking processes "a machine for jumping to conclusions."

Jumping to conclusions about people makes us feel more confident and less uncertain about the world around us. But once we start to think we understand someone, we filter incoming information and tend to dismiss things that do not fit in our hastily drawn picture as meaningless aberrations. We become prisoners of our preconceptions. And so do the people we stereotype.

It is possible to resist being slotted into someone's preconceived notion of "people like you" by doing things that do not fit the stereotype. This is best done early on, both because first impressions formed tend to last, and because people often do not like it when you upset their expectations later. The technical term for this upsetting of expectations is a "stereotype violation." When you show them something that makes them reconsider their comfortable worldview, you make their life a little bit harder, and that can leave you seeming less warm. And when people are emotionally invested in a particular view of the proper social order, if you show a lack of appreciation and respect for that social order, they lose respect for you, see you as less strong, and regard you with contempt.

Since strength and warmth perceptions are in the eye of the beholder, people's judgments of you depend on where they sit in the social hierarchy. Even after a half century of social upheaval and evolution, straight white guys are still what social scientists call the "in-group," which means they (the two of us included) are accorded higher social status than other groups. As a general rule, people in higher-status groups are seen as competent, while those in lower-status groups are assumed to be less competent. But the full story is more interesting than that, and there are plenty of stereotypes to go around—including unflattering caricatures of straight white guys too. Everybody stereotypes, and everyone is stereotyped. It is just how our brains work.

Gender

Gender is almost always the first thing people look for when we size someone up. We all instantly recognize the distinctive shapes of male and female bodies, even from a distance. The differences are sometimes subtle, but we are very attuned to them, because so much about our experience depends on gender.

Men

Men are presumed strong. Not all men are especially strong, of course, but on average, they are built slightly bigger and stronger than women. There are any number of recognizable archetypes of male strength, from gangsters to good ol' boys, prizefighters to fathers.

Judgments of men are closely tied to stereotypical views of family roles. In American culture, this is perhaps best captured in the title of the 1950s TV show *Father Knows Best*. This paternal stereotype casts men as heads of families, providers, and protectors. The metaphor of father-as-protector dates back at least to the book of Genesis, with God as the father of creation anointing Abraham as the father of his people. The association between men and strength is rooted in the division of labor in hunter-gatherer times, and transcends cultures. Numerous societies have had rites of passage in which boys attain manhood by proving their strength through physical contests, deprivation, or other trials.

Just as men are presumed strong, they are also presumed a little cold. Women, conversely, are presumed warmer but weaker. There is some biology behind this as well: Hormonally speaking, men have more testosterone in their systems and women have more estrogen. Higher testosterone is correlated with physical strength and determination, but also social and emotional detachment. This is the strong, silent type. Conversely, estrogen is correlated with being more in tune with others' feelings.

Since men are expected to be strong, they not only can get away with dominant behavior; they are often rewarded for it. For instance, anger often works fine for guys. Anger is an extreme emotional expression of strength that is all about imposing one's concerns and will on people within the blast zone. It makes people sit up and take notice, if not cower and obey. It can be an appropriate and effective way to display strength, but when it does not seem warranted it definitely undermines warmth. It is also important to note that while the whole point of anger is to display strength, excessive anger can also signal weakness: Angry people are by definition upset, and can easily seem out of control, unable to handle the challenges of their environment in a functional, clearheaded way.

Anger increases a man's status when it shows his determination. Research shows that men who show anger when they fail to achieve a goal are perceived as more competent, higher status, and deserving of higher salaries than men who accept failure calmly. There is logic to that: Anger represents disappointment at failing to meet high standards, and presumably angry energy can be channeled toward doing better next time.

Because they are presumed strong, men are not expected to project much warmth or weakness. In many cultures men who defy this expectation with displays like crying are roundly mocked. Men who fail to project strength are labeled cowards, wimps, sissies, and any number of other names that cast doubt on their masculinity. The absence of strength is stereotypically synonymous with "unmanly" behavior, which can mean anything that falls outside the father-protector-hunter-provider role.

That said, plenty of successful men do not fit the standard model. Pop culture icons like Mick Jagger and David Bowie traded on androgyny decades ago, and this did not diminish their strength or appeal. If anything, their willingness to defy cultural taboos and norms won them admirers and added to their perceived strength. Gay culture has also entered the mainstream, and there are now both male and female public figures who embody every conceivable combination of masculine and feminine traits. People who hold a paternalistic worldview may still judge nontraditional men as lacking in strength because they do not fit the provider-protector type, but for the rest of us, our working definition of strength encompasses far more than 1950s stereotypes of manliness. Assertiveness, competence, and physical power can take all sorts of forms.

But men are not just seen as stronger than women—research suggests they are also seen as having the better balance of strength and warmth overall. Where women are generally seen as warm but weaker, men are seen as stronger and less warm, but not problematically cold. This plays out differently in different cultures. For instance, if a culture values ambition (an expression of strength), men get higher marks for ambitiousness. If instead the prized trait is sociability, which has a skill component but also aligns closely with warmth, then men are seen as having more of that. Amy Cuddy and her colleagues describe this phenomenon as men embodying the "cultural ideal," regardless of whether that ideal leans more toward strength or warmth. Maybe this is just because in most cultures men are still mostly in charge, so they get to choose what counts most. Whatever the reason, when it comes to projecting a balance of strength and warmth, men just have it easier.

Women

Strength and warmth for women is a longer story. Recall our friend Emily, the awkward young woman who answered the door at the party. We described her as someone who brings to mind an eighth-grader trying to blend into the gymnasium wall at a school dance: nice as can be, but zero self-confidence or assertiveness. She represents a shy version of a classic paternalistic female stereotype of women as warm but not strong: "nurturant but naive," as psychologists Susan Fiske and Peter Glick put it.

There are some positive or benevolent feelings we associate with these sorts—"She is such a sweetheart!"—but the overall effect reduces them to kindly comforters whose virtues are only social and emotional. Intellect and ambition are not part of this picture, and even basic competence is suspect. While this stereotype is fading, it is far from gone. It keeps women from being offered positions that require high competence, and contributes to the systematic underrepresentation of women in leadership and management positions. Even among professional scientists, where one might expect that a Spock-like devotion to evidence would carry the day, female job applicants are viewed as less competent than men with equal qualifications.

Another famous female stereotype is that of the woman who rebels against those expectations. This is the strong, cold woman. She does not "know her place"—subordinate to men, at home raising kids. Her strength and ambition threaten the social order and lead her to neglect her family. She is portrayed as angry, resentful, cunning, and generally unpleasant. Here the hydraulic effect and the stereotype violation penalty combine in an especially vicious and unforgiving way. Against the backdrop of the traditional female stereotype of warmth and weakness, a woman who displays strength in areas that are not socially sanctioned not only loses warmth from the hydraulic effect, but is hit with an extra warmth penalty for violating the stereotype. In unscientific terms, she is seen as a bitch. This is especially likely when a woman is perceived by others—particularly men—as a competitor.

Professor Frank Flynn illustrated this with a case study about the challenges faced by Heidi Roizen, a Silicon Valley entrepreneur and venture capitalist, as a successful woman in the male-dominated high-tech industry. When Professor Flynn assigned the case to his Columbia Business School students, he conducted a little experiment: For half the class, he changed Heidi's name in the case to Howard. The results were stark: Male and female students alike judged Heidi and Howard to be equally strong, but they judged Heidi to be much less warm. "Students were much harsher on Heidi than on Howard across the board," Flynn writes. "Although they think she's just as competent and effective as Howard, they don't like her, they wouldn't hire her, and they wouldn't want to work with her." We root for the fictional Howard when he demonstrates strength because he is the protagonist of the story. But when Heidi demonstrates strength, she is undercutting her warmth and upsetting our expectations, which makes us regard her as even less warm.

Note that even though everyone agrees Heidi is highly competent, the social punishment she receives can actually make her less effective. To overcome this, she actually needs to have more strength, skills, and drive than a man in the same position. In some extremely male-dominated professions, the competence threshold is pushed even higher for women. Research looking at women working in roles such as police chief found that women can be judged successful in these jobs—as long as they are *perfect*. When they make a single mistake, however, they pay a steep price in perceived competence and status. This one-strike-and-you're-out strength dynamic means that women who make it to the top against overwhelming odds in these fields are constantly in a precarious position.

None of this will come as news to women in the modern workplace, but the social penalties for strong women and the depths of the catch-22 are remarkable. For instance, highly competent women are seen as lacking in warmth even when warmth is one of the requirements of the job they are clearly good at. In hiring decisions, decision makers sometimes shift the hiring criteria to emphasize social skills and penalize highly competent female candidates, who are viewed as cold. When women negotiate for a higher salary, they become less likable, though the opposite is true for men. When working women have children, they are perceived as warmer, but professionally they project less strength—presumably because their loyalties are now divided between work and children. This is not the case for men: When they become dads, they get a bump in warmth but are not penalized on strength, possibly because it is assumed child-care responsibilities will fall primarily to Mom.

Men do suffer collateral damage from archaic female stereotypes as well: Those who work for female bosses are seen as less masculine—and end up getting paid less—than men with male bosses. One study even found that men who worked for women were seen as less masculine than women with bosses of either gender. This becomes yet another challenge for women leaders, making it harder to recruit talented men to work for them. Despite all of this, most female leaders seem to be doing a remarkably good job. People see women leaders as more organized, more responsible, with better people skills. One study found that women leaders got better scores than their male counterparts on fifteen out of sixteen leadership competencies. As the old problematic stereotypes fade and are replaced with increasingly familiar images of effective female leaders, those perceptions will translate into more acceptance of, if not preference for, women at the helm.

The Case of Hillary Clinton

One of the most fascinating case studies of how women leaders are perceived is Hillary Clinton. When Hillary first came to national attention during Bill Clinton's run for president in 1992, she had a number of attributes on paper that might suggest a very warm image: woman, liberal, child advocate, First Lady of a southern state.

And yet if you know anything about Hillary Clinton's public persona, you recognize that is completely backward. As the first woman to be made partner in a powerful Arkansas law firm, she spent decades outearning her husband. Her remarks during the 1992 presidential campaign about how she didn't stay home baking cookies provoked a media storm that forced her to come to terms with the public's traditional image of First Ladies—and to participate in a cookie "bake-off" with

First Lady Barbara Bush (which Hillary won). She provoked strong reactions from a lot of Americans who disliked her strength, triggering the hostile sexism stereotype that we described earlier. Once her husband was elected, her failed health care plan, dubbed "Hillarycare," raised concerns that she was a cold, scheming technocrat. She became a staple of late-night TV comedy routines. She was even branded with nicknames like "Chillary," which says it clearly: strong but cold.

It was only after the Lewinsky scandal that her public approval rating shot up, because a significant part of the public sympathized with her as an aggrieved yet loyal wife, even if she did not outwardly radiate warmth. When she first ran for Senate, she began her campaign with a "listening tour" to demonstrate how tuned in she was to other people's concerns. These factors warmed her up enough that the people of Democratic-leaning New York State elected her to represent them in Washington.

There she went back to amassing strength, serving on the Senate Armed Forces Committee and earning the respect of many generals along the way. When she ran for president in 2008, she presented herself as the stronger, more experienced candidate than Barack Obama, even running a famous TV ad making the case that she was the better candidate to handle a 3 a.m. national security emergency and keep the country safe.

But after unexpectedly losing the Iowa caucus to Barack Obama, she had a moment right before the New Hampshire primary that forever altered the way people see her. A woman at a campaign stop asked her how she kept up the pace on the road. "It's not easy. It's not easy," she started. As she went on, her voice choked up: "You know, this is very personal for me. It's not just political, it's not just public. I see what's happening. And we have to reverse it. And some people think elections are a game, they think it's like, who's up, or who's down. It's about our country, it's about our kids' futures, and it's really about all of us together." She never quite cried, but the emotion was unmistakable. "So, as tired as I am—and I am," she said with a smile, "and as difficult as it is to keep up what I try to do on the road, like occasionally exercise, and try to eat right—it's tough when the easiest food is pizza—I just believe so strongly in who we are as a nation, so I'm going to do everything I can to make my case, and then the voters get to decide. Thank you all." In that moment, her mask of strength cracked, and she showed herself to be a genuinely warm, sympathetic person, running for the right reasons. And she took us behind her formal facade to share her daily struggles with exercise and sleep and food, things everyone could sympathize with.

The next day, the voters of New Hampshire sided with Hillary. She went on to win a string of big-state primaries and almost take the nomination. Though she did not win in the end, her campaign did achieve something truly historic: No one doubts anymore that a woman can be tough enough to be commander in chief. There will still be questions about whether particular women are strong enough, as there will be with particular men. But Hillary made it easy for many Americans to imagine sleeping easy with her in charge.

Hillary's story illustrates the conflicting dynamics women have to navigate to establish their strength while not provoking a negative reaction. It also shows us that our strength and warmth are not set in stone: We can and do change the way people perceive us through this lens.

Backwards in High Heels

Successful women can and do overcome the social challenges they face. It is just not an easy thing to get right. The tricky bit is not just how to project strength, but how to project strength without losing warmth. When a woman displays strength, it can easily trigger negative stereotypes, both because strength generally seems cold, and specifically because these displays violate stereotypes.

Having worked with all different kinds of people, we can say for certain that everyone's challenges are unique. But when it comes to women in the workplace, we see our clients facing the same challenges time and again. The best way to understand these difficult dynamics is to look at what it takes to navigate them.

Strategy #1: Assertive, Not Angry

Anger generally does not work well for women. Given the basic challenge women have projecting strength without seeming cold, it will come as no surprise that an extreme strength display like anger would bring women even more negative reactions from both men and other women. Women who voice anger risk being defined solely in terms of the emotion: They are judged to be angry people, not likable, and potentially too unstable to warrant respect. Women are not the dominant social group either, so when they show anger, a dominance move, they are breaking unspoken rules. This stereotype violation has its own name—researchers call the social penalty attached to it "anger backlash." Angry behavior can count against women in many realms: perceived warmth, competence, status, and wages.

Women can express disapproval without triggering the "angry woman" reaction by making clear that they are in control of their feelings and are choosing to express their disapproval, as opposed to having their anger burst forth unbidden. This is the difference between responding and just reacting. If there is an opportunity to send this signal without having to abandon warmth entirely, that is always the best first option; a well-timed humorous one-liner can work wonders, winning points for likability and unflappability. Not every situation lends itself to humor, though, and sometimes women have no choice but to play the strength card. The outer limit of this kind of disapproval is a stern tone and a serious look, the tried-and-true trick used by mothers and teachers the world over to bring unruly children into line. By contrast, if a woman seems "out of control" or "upset" in expressing disapproval, the anger backlash will kick in.

Strength is not necessarily about being angry or mean. It is about being assertive and firm, stern and determined, but also calm and in control.

Many of our female clients face the challenge of figuring out how to raise an issue that other people do not see as a problem without activating the hostile stereotype. For example, if you are a woman, suppose a male coworker takes credit for your work, and nobody else knows this but you. Anger is a perfectly natural first response to theft, but leading with anger is not likely to get the response you want, which is respect for a job well done. If you raise the issue calmly, and maybe even use humor, you are more likely to win the respect you deserve.

Occasionally, you may also face a personal attack in which someone publicly questions your integrity or your professionalism. This is a direct challenge to your character. It must be met with strength: To retain the respect of your colleagues, you must express clearly that you are not going to accept what your attacker is suggesting about you. Showing anger is definitely an option here, as it is clearly explained by the circumstances and does not suggest that you are just an angry person. Still, even in these situations, it does not hurt to show control.

It is not easy to keep that kind of behavior from getting under your skin, but when you feel the confrontational energy getting turned up, remember that the person attacking you is the one with the problem. In fact, if you stay calm as they get riled up, that shows your strength. Just be sure you make it clear that you do not approve of or condone what's going on. (If you react with anger, that takes care of itself.)

One client of ours faced a situation like this at work and handled it perfectly. She was on a conference call when a colleague crossed the line from criticizing her team to insulting her personally. She heard him out, and responded calmly, "That's not going to work. When you are ready to have this conversation, let us know." And with that, she hung up.

Note that if she had just hung up the phone without saying anything, she might have left the impression that she was too upset to talk, or fleeing in fear. Her brief, calm statement cast her as the adult in the room and her assailant as the child throwing a tantrum.

Strategy #2: Getting Tough for the Good of the Group

While showing anger is generally a losing strategy for women, research shows there are certain situations where women can display anger without getting hit by backlash. And while this does not mean women should look for opportunities to be angry, it does suggest that people are more open to women showing strength in some circumstances than in others.

First of all, if genuine harm to a loved one is at issue, anyone can express anger without being branded as an angry person. For instance, if an older kid is physically threatening a younger child, no one will hold it against Mom if she yells.

But women's latitude seems to stretch a little further than just imminent bodily harm to immediate family members. A study by Victoria Brescoll and Eric Uhlmann at Yale looked at reactions to women expressing anger in different scenarios. When a woman displayed anger because she and a colleague blew an important account, people saw her as less competent and less deserving of status than if she reported the loss of the account calmly. But when a woman expressed anger at blowing the account specifically because her colleague lied about getting directions to the big meeting, people did not penalize her. In fact, in that case, she was actually seen as more competent and deserving of higher stature. In other words, she was accorded higher status and seen as more competent for showing anger about her colleague's lack of honesty and teamwork.

In strength and warmth terms, she paid a penalty for showing anger in response to a lapse in strength (losing business), but was rewarded when she showed anger over a lapse in warmth (lying). This suggests that women may have broader latitude to express themselves on issues linked to warmth, which are more traditionally associated with women.

This idea that there are realms where women are more trusted, respected, and heeded shows up in other research too. For instance, when a group faces an internal conflict that requires management mediation, women are seen as more natural for the role, while men are preferred when a group faces an external threat. Women are presumed to be better able to handle warmth issues and are seen as worthy of deference there.

Recall the importance of constantly maintaining warmth so as not to run afoul of the tomato rule, where one cold moment ruins you forever. The key to projecting warmth is demonstrating your intentions. If you show that you share the concerns and interests of your colleagues, that you are working for the greater good of the group, that projects strength while also projecting warmth. It does not matter what the shared goal is—it could be increasing ROI or putting bad guys behind bars or getting the boss to ease up about the TPS reports. As long as the group can see that you want what they want, you are projecting warmth.

That helps explain why both men and women react so harshly to a woman perceived as selfish or opportunistic: She exercises her strength on her own behalf—which, of course, men do all the time—rather than on behalf of some group. If she is instead seen as acting out of concern for her team or family, then all of that strength she shows can also be interpreted as an expression of warmth. Women have more latitude to be strong if the strength is seen as selfless.

Making sure people do not lose sight of your warmth can be as simple as clarifying your motivations. When issuing a warning, a command, or a reprimand, cite the interests of the group as your reason for showing that strength. That can keep you looking warm as well.

Strategy #3: Dial the Warmth Up, Not Down

If the key challenge facing a woman is to project enough strength to balance her presumed warmth, one strategy would be just to turn the warmth displays down. According to this thinking, less warmth tends to project more strength, so being serious and businesslike should do the trick.

But the women who truly succeed at transcending the stereotypes project both strength and warmth—actively and a lot. When we ask people to think of public figures who project high strength and high warmth, Oprah Winfrey's name comes up more often than anyone else's. Oprah turned her warmth into strength. The empathy she showed presenting her guests' stories made her a huge success. At the same time, she would also identify the villain in each story, and she drew clear lines between right and wrong. With an arched eyebrow here and a stern look there, she made her disapproval crystal clear without ever letting anger get the better of her. The runaway success of her public persona also gave her strength as a businesswoman unparalleled in the entertainment industry. (Take that, Ayn Rand.)

Ann Richards, former governor of Texas, also projected tons of warmth, but from a very different place: She was funny and sassy, a wise Southern woman in a world of overgrown boys. To succeed in the cutthroat world of politics, she had to deal in strength, but she did it with a quick wit and a big smile that made her likable rather than cold. When she spoke about the challenges she faced in a world dominated by men, she came armed with one-liners that made the men chuckle and the women nod in recognition—like the old saw that Ginger Rogers did everything Fred Astaire did, only backwards and in high heels. Her demeanor made it clear that despite those challenges, she was happy to claim her place on the political stage, and she was ready to give as good as she got.

The winning formula that we see with both Oprah and Ann Richards is not to dial anything down, but to turn both strength and warmth up: strength to be taken seriously, and warmth to keep that strength from coming off as cold.

Where We Are Today

Gender stereotypes have always been with us, and your gender will always send important signals about your strength and warmth. But the world is changing. The further we get from hunter-gatherer days, the more civilized we become, the more warmth becomes strength, and the more women's contributions are valued.

Women are getting the job done, winning due respect, and changing the rules. When the presence of strong women in a workplace becomes the norm, women face fewer penalties for being strong. Discrimination does not end quickly, and sometimes it gets more subtle and insidious before it goes away, but it does become gradually harder to get away with.

Having more women in positions of leadership also gives both men and women more latitude for warmth. As we write this, Facebook chief operating officer Sheryl Sandberg and Yahoo CEO Marissa Mayer represent the latest women in the public eye defying expectations for successful executives. Sandberg talks openly about her commitment to spending time with her family, which just years ago would likely have been held against her as evidence of her lack of fitness for the demands of the executive suite. And Mayer surprised the business world by announcing that she was pregnant as soon as she took the job of CEO. As women continue to move into positions of power that were previously off-limits, old stereotypes fade, and warmth increasingly seems more like an asset than a liability.

Ethnicity

The short black man and the tall white man looked at each other warily. They stood just a few feet apart, but their contrasting skin colors opened a yawning gulf between them. The black man had a question for the white man: How was it that he was always saying "N—r this" and "N—r that" when all of his favorite stars—Magic Johnson, Eddie Murphy, Prince—were black?

"It's different," the white man protested. "Magic, Eddie, Prince, they're not n—rs. I mean, they're not black, I mean . . ." he trailed off, then collected himself and tried again. "Let me explain myself. They're, they're not *really* black. I mean they're black, but they're not *really* black. They're *more* than black. It's . . . it's different."

Spike Lee and John Turturro's classic scene from *Do the Right Thing* perfectly captures how stereotypes work. When we spend time getting to know people as individuals, they have the opportunity to demonstrate their character as individuals. If they do not fit their group's stereotypes, those category associations just fade away. This is different from stereotype violation, where people we do not know well violate our preconceived ideas of how the world works. When we get to know people, if they project strength and warmth, we admire them, no matter what other stereotypical notions we otherwise associate with their demographic group. Twenty years after *Do the Right Thing* left theaters, Barack Obama was elected President of the United States, at least in part by people who still subscribed to some negative stereotypes about black people.

Many Different Boxes

Like gender or age, ethnicity is one of those visible markers that offer a clue to what a person's life experience might have been. We discern a person's ethnicity through a complex combination of signals: Mostly we look at skin color, facial features, and hair, but we can also use vocal cues like accent and diction, distinctive words and phrases ("Hey, y'all!"), and sometimes personal choices like clothes. Some folks look like they might fit in several ethnic categories—light-skinned African-American, Pacific Islander, Middle Eastern, or maybe just deeply tanned southern European. These people are often highly sought after by advertisers as models and spokespeople because people of many backgrounds can see them projecting the warmth of shared ethnicity.

Racial or ethnic groups often have more than one stereotype associated with them. As we get to know more people from a group, we are more likely to have a mix of positive and negative associations with that group. To untangle the interplay between strength and warmth in ethnic stereotypes, think back to our four quadrants and the emotions that accompany each.

Stereotypes about black people in the United States, for instance, fall into several quadrants. A paternalistic stereotype suggests that poor black people are pitiable because they suffer the injustices of living in a racist society. This is a warm but weak lower-right-quadrant stereotype: Being black is a sympathetic but helpless condition. Picture an elderly black man working as a porter at a hotel, scraping by on tips from younger rich white patrons.

A harsher stereotype depicts poor blacks as lazy freeloaders—neither warm nor capable, banished to the lower-left quadrant. This is the idea of the "welfare cheat" who collects a check for doing nothing and then squanders that money on liquor or drugs. There is also an upper-left-quadrant stereotype of black men as dangerous, strong, and fearsome—cue a pop-culture image of gun-toting thugs wearing gang colors.

As other ethnic groups become more prominent in American society, they also acquire multiple stereotypes. Among Latinos, for instance, one stereotype is of humble people who work long hours for low pay and live in cramped quarters to be able to build a better life for their families—definitely warm, not necessarily strong. There is a stronger stereotype of Latinos as "hot-blooded" and intensely passionate. Jews and Asian-Americans are thought of as smart and therefore successful, which makes them economic competitors with other groups, so they are often stereotyped as cold and untrustworthy. Studies have even found Asian-Americans viewed as "unfairly competent" in realms of academic and financial performance, while lacking in warmth. But just as Jewish stereotypes extend beyond competent and cold—consider the lovable loser Catskills comedian, or the overbearing mother—conceptions of Asian-Americans are also broadening as pop culture figures from Margaret Cho to Aziz Ansari to Psy have punctured this narrow stereotype. As American society becomes more multiethnic, stereotypes for these and other groups continue to evolve.

Within racial and ethnic groups, there are further social distinctions that serve as markers of status and power. Within the black community, having lighter or darker skin can be a big deal. Black people with lighter skin tones are generally thought to face less discrimination from whites and to move more easily in white-dominated circles. This is a form of social strength, and historically within the black community people with lighter skin were accorded higher social status. The flip side is that light-skinned black people are sometimes criticized as being "not black enough," on the grounds that they do not wholly share the defining experience of oppression that darker-skinned black people have endured. These perceptions are also deeply intertwined with class distinctions. For example, Newark, N.J., mayor Cory Booker is a light-skinned black man who grew up in a nearby suburb and attended the best universities in the world. When he first ran for mayor, unsuccessfully, Booker faced a smear campaign that raised doubts about whether he really shared the interests of the city's poorer, darker black majority. In short, they questioned his warmth.

The broader point is that there are in-groups and out-groups at multiple levels throughout society, and the judgments that separate them still revolve around strength and warmth.

White people are generally treated as the in-group and the universal, neutral reference point in American culture, but they also get the stereotype treatment. A recent study showed that college students from other ethnic groups hold at least three common stereotypes of white men. In the strong-but-cold upper-left quadrant is the Gordon Gekko type—highly competent, but selfish and mean. In the warm-but-weak lower-right quadrant are the nice guys—warm and friendly, but weak willed and deferential. And down in the weak-and-cold lower-left quadrant are the "frat boys"—basically selfish idiots.

There are stereotypes within the white world as well. This is most obvious in Europe, where the cultural differences across countries yield well-known strength and warmth profiles. The stereotypes about which nationalities are warmer and stronger in which areas are probably best illustrated by an old joke: In heaven, the lovers are French, the cops are British, the food is Italian, the cars are German, and the whole thing is run by the Swiss. In hell, the lovers are Swiss, the cops are German, the food is British, the cars are French, and the whole thing is run by the Italians.

While people tend to prefer to socialize with people from their own group, there is actually a fair degree of agreement across cultures about which cultures are generally warmer and which are generally stronger. Belgians rate Brazilians as warmer and less competent than themselves, but judge Japanese to be more competent and less warm. People from middle-income countries generally rate higher-income countries to be stronger but culturally less warm than their own.

When Stereotypes Collide

While it is not necessarily the most common black stereotype, as soon as black people start competing with white people for power within an organization, the strong-but-cold black stereotype shows up. This can be seen in the phenomenon of the black baby-faced CEO. Generally, having rounded facial features—a "baby face"—suggests feminine warmth, and can make someone look less strong and authoritative. But Robert Livingston and Nicholas Pearce, of the Kellogg School of Management, found that for black male executives, having baby-faced features works in their favor, because it softens their appearance and keeps them from being perceived as threatening. That is reflected in the corporate world, where a disproportionate number of the black men who run Fortune 500 companies have round faces and soft features.

Not surprisingly, black women in positions of authority have little margin for error, because there are so many negative stereotypes that can be attached to them. Professor Livingston and colleagues Ashleigh Shelby Rosette and Ella Washington found that black women leaders are often judged more harshly than white women or black men, especially when their organizations have stumbled.

But it turns out that there can also be an upside when ethnic and gender stereotypes collide, specifically with regard to using an all-strength "dominant" leadership style that motivates people through fear by doling out punishment and threats. When white guys use a dominant leadership style, it costs them warmth but is considered appropriate, and it generally earns them respect. For white women in authority, using a dominant style violates the stereotype of women as nurturing—so projecting strength by acting dominant can actually end up costing white women strength as they lose respect. For black men in America, a dominant style is also not acceptable, but largely for a very different reason: It reinforces a view of black men as strong and cold, echoing historical white fears of black men overturning the existing social order.

But when black women adopt a dominant leadership style, the research suggests that the stereotypes balance each other out: Black women leaders do not suffer any greater social penalty for dominant behavior than white men do. This demonstrates that stereotypes do not just get piled on top of each other. Different strands of stereotypes combine in unpredictable ways, and can even open up new space to operate. Acting dominant still costs warmth and is generally not optimal. But the research suggests black women are not feared the way black men can be, nor are they expected to operate within the same social boundaries that white women are. Like any other group, black women's leadership challenges and opportunities are unique.

Talking Across the Divide

Imagine a block party on a summer afternoon in a city neighborhood that has a mix of black and white families. Neighbors who usually only pass each other briefly on the street are now meeting each other more formally for the first time. What do those conversations sound like?

When people of different races talk, each group is often concerned about addressing their stereotypical shortcomings. White people want to be viewed as likable and moral, while people of other ethnicities want respect. White people understand that their socially privileged position generally checks the box on strength, so to make a good impression they want to project warmth. Some also worry about appearing prejudiced, so they want to be seen as open. People who are not white want to project warmth too, but they also want to project strength to earn respect. The groups also prefer different conversation topics. White people tend to focus on commonalities among groups, hoping to foster good feelings that will enhance their likability. Black people, on the other hand, prefer to acknowledge and talk about power differences.

This played itself out recently at a block party in John's rapidly gentrifying neighborhood in Washington, D.C. Young white residents admired the gardening skills of their black neighbors and everyone played with each other's kids and had a good time. In the conversations that ran long enough to get past the basic pleasantries, black residents would often steer the discussion to the impacts of rising property values and the dynamics between the police and the black teenagers who hung out in the park.

When white people miss these dynamics in interracial conversations—when they talk only about common ground and tiptoe around power dynamics—the outcome can be precisely the opposite of their goal: Instead of demonstrating warmth, the white folks demonstrate just how little they understand other people's experiences, creating frustration and disappointment on all sides. Real dialogue involves give-and-take, and that includes giving others the opportunity to put uncomfortable topics on the agenda.

Overcoming Anger

In the summer of 2010, Americans' frustration was mounting as oil continued to gush into the Gulf of Mexico from BP's Deepwater Horizon disaster. President Obama had campaigned in part on a promise to respond more forcefully to emergencies than President Bush had when Hurricane Katrina hit New Orleans, yet he had not issued any urgent declarations or publicly castigated those responsible at BP. In that moment, CNN ran a story with this headline: "Why Obama Doesn't Dare Become the Angry Black Man."

Anger triggers negative stereotypes, and "anger backlash" is a concern for pretty much anyone outside the socially dominant category of straight white guys. For everyone else, projecting anger means stepping out of line. Black people who voice anger risk finding their identities defined solely in terms of the emotion: They are judged to be angry people, not likable, and potentially too unstable to warrant respect.

This issue is especially acute for black people because of the tortured history of slavery and Jim Crow and the continuing debate about present-day discrimination and who is at fault for perpetuating it. Against that backdrop, the angry black person stereotype can provoke not only fear but also sometimes resentment in white people. So powerful is this effect that even the President of the United States, arguably the single most powerful person in the world, is potentially subject to it.

But not expressing anger has its costs too. When we know something hurtful or unfair has happened to people like us, we have no trouble imagining how angry those victims must be. For people outside of our ethnic group, however, we tend not to empathize as much. White people express higher levels of anger when they learn about a white person in an unfair situation than when they hear the identical story about a black person, and the same is true when the roles are reversed. This is called "anger denial": The less we identify with someone, the less we see their misfortunes as legitimate cause for them to be angry.

This is a big deal, because we are more likely to help people whose anger we appreciate than those whose anger we fail to recognize. But as we have seen, if someone from a lower-status group expresses anger about an unfair situation, this provokes a backlash, resulting in a loss of sympathy instead of an increase. This tension between anger denial and backlash creates a classic case of damned-if-you-do, damned-if-you-don't.

So how do people who are not in the in-group make themselves heard? We looked earlier at one person who figured out how to break out of this bind: the Reverend Dr. Martin Luther King Jr. One way to understand the genius of the nonviolent civil disobedience strategy used by the civil rights movement is to recognize how it overcame the anger denial–anger backlash bind. All the protesters knew that any direct expression of anger by black people would likely have provoked far-reaching backlash effects that would have eroded white support for their cause. But nonviolent boycotts, sit-ins, and marches offered a way for black people to make the depth of their dissatisfaction clear without projecting anger. The protesters were solemn and dignified, wearing their Sunday best—strong but calm. Time and again, they faced angry white mobs yelling and threatening them, and they stood silently, refusing to take the bait, letting their mere presence speak for itself. Even when police and dogs attacked them on Bloody Sunday on the Edmund Pettus Bridge, the protesters did not respond with violence or anger. The emotional discipline they showed to remain so calm in the face of such hatred and violence is almost as impressive as what that discipline was able to achieve.

Today, women, black people, and other groups being stereotyped are still expected to respond to adversity with great self-control, to keep the expression of anger in check while still making clear what lines should not be crossed, to show strength calmly, as well as warmth if they expect to win any sympathy. This is a lot to ask of anyone, and trying to clear this high bar can cause serious emotional and mental strain. Recent research has even found that black men who repress their emotional responses to everyday racist incidents are more prone to symptoms of depression.

In most cases, we counsel people to avoid projecting anger in a professional context regardless of ethnicity or gender, in large part because showing anger means revealing that you are upset and possibly out of control, which can project as much weakness as strength. But not showing anger does not mean being passive. Anger is not necessary to show determination to tackle challenges or to explain or deliver consequences for misbehavior or subpar results. Being assertive or even stern is almost always all the strength you need.

Age

At seventy-three years old, President Reagan was the oldest president in United States history, and to many, it was starting to show. Increasingly as he campaigned around the country in 1984, he looked tired. His opponent, two-term senator and former vice president Walter Mondale, looked comparatively spry at fifty-six. Sure enough, at a debate that fall, Reagan was asked directly if he had any doubts about his ability to handle the rigors of the presidency. "Not at all," he replied. "And I want you to know that also, I will not make age an issue of this campaign. I will not exploit for political purposes my opponent's youth and inexperience." Even Mondale cracked up laughing.

There are two sides to age: We grow more experienced and presumably wiser with it, but at some point we also start to become less capable. Age is one of the first things people notice and describe about each other. It also provides some clues about life experiences, both recent and distant.

The basic relationship between strength, warmth, and age in American culture is pretty straightforward: Both young children and senior citizens are generally seen as less competent but warmer than adults in the prime of life. As to competence, both the very young and the very old need varying levels of assistance with basic functions in everyday life. The warmth aspect also makes sense—we have a natural human sympathy for the infirm. Kids are built cute exactly because they depend on our help to survive. In between, strength follows a bell curve, peaking earlier for athletes and later for professionals.

The senior stereotype turns out to be resilient, or at least the incompetence part of it. Nearly all of us have had a parent, grandparent, aunt, or uncle who began regularly struggling to recall names or driving erratically, and suddenly that person seemed not quite so capable of navigating life's everyday challenges. We often see that first sign of frailty not as an isolated issue, but as the onset of a downward trend, which means we tend to discount other signs that older people are still capable.

The harshness of this judgment begs the question: What, exactly, tips people over this threshold and marks them as "old"?

We are all familiar with the physical signs of age: Skin wrinkles and sags, hair loses pigment or just disappears, hearing diminishes, posture droops, gait slows toward a shuffle, gestures get stiff, the voice grows lower and then acquires a quaver. Interestingly, we do not assess someone's age as an average of the ages suggested by all of these cues. Instead we go with the most advanced age cue, and assume the person just got lucky on the others. Imagine being at a restaurant and noticing a well-dressed woman seated at a nearby table, a somewhat lined face suggesting late-middle age. She still has the upright posture she learned in ballet class long ago, and at first glance it is hard to read her age. When she stands up, though, the stiffness of arthritis is unmistakable, and your estimation of her age is revised up instantly.

The incompetence stereotype does not kick in until we see noticeable changes in someone's level of energy, alertness, and engagement with the world. The energy level is most damning in terms of social perception. There is a common expression for this: We say someone "lost a step." John's hound dog just passed this threshold. In some ways it is subtle, but if you know him, the little changes in energy feel like a big deal. He runs less and less, and starts dragging his paws more, not just on hot days. He is rounding the last turn, into the home stretch now.

Before we reach that point, there are many other visible signs of aging we accumulate. Some of the variation is due to how people live: Exposure to sunlight, and to a lesser degree cigarette smoke, will age skin more quickly. Stress can leave its mark, most noticeably in hair color, as recent U.S. presidents have demonstrated.

Genetics also plays a role in determining how quickly and visibly people show signs of age. Some faces stay younger-looking longer than others. That brings us to the broader—and possibly even more fraught—subject of looks.

A Closer Look at Looks

Your face is how people identify you, the most important visual manifestation of the unique person beneath. A police report might describe you as a six-foot-tall Caucasian male or a five-foot-six Latina female, but if you want to board an airplane you have to show a photo ID. So does your face merely identify you like a fingerprint or a Social Security number? Or does it also suggest something about your character?

The short answer is yes—but that answer comes with a big asterisk. Most of what others can tell about you by looking at your face has to do with the expression you are wearing at any given moment, which is closely linked to your emotional state. Most of us do not usually walk through the world wearing a blank expression, yet we only dimly notice that our faces are broadcasting emotions much of the time. If a friend or colleague has ever surprised you with the question "What's wrong?" on a day when you felt just fine, that person was probably reading facial cues that you were not even aware of.

We all perceive strength and warmth in facial structures in two distinct ways: First, we assess particular facial features directly for these qualities. Second, we also assess how good-looking a face is, whether it is aesthetically appealing or not, and that also shapes our strength and warmth judgment.

We all know there are plenty of angelic-looking people who are mean, and coarse-looking people who are big hearted. But is there still some connection between looks and character? Is the shape of a face somehow connected to the shape of the soul behind it?

The Expression Connection

At the heart of the connection between face shapes and character judgments is a simple insight: Facial structures sometimes resemble facial expressions. The size of your nose will not make you look happy or sad, but if your mouth is built in the shape of a smile or a frown, you convey the emotions associated with these facial expressions without moving a muscle.

When someone is born with a facial shape that resembles a common emotional expression, there is no organic connection to the person's character, at least to start. But when someone's mouth naturally forms a frown, that can have understandably serious effects on that person's social life unless they get in the habit of actively smiling a lot to counteract the effect. Bad moods are socially contagious, so people walking through life with unhappy expressions on their faces may be avoided or approached with some trepidation. If the world consistently reacts to someone in a negative way, that will inevitably shape that person's character.

A familiar verbal expression—"Why the long face?"—points to a similar effect: On a face where the features are more spaced out vertically, a neutral facial expression can seem sad. That tracks a common sad facial expression, in which your lips are closed but your jaw hangs slightly open, pulling your mouth down slightly. Conversely, compressing your facial features vertically can make you seem mad, because this mimics a Popeye-like angry face with the furrowed brow lowering the eyebrows and the lower lip raised in a pout. If you are not aware of them, these expressions can also make social interactions harder.

Social feedback loops can also have happier effects: People with naturally smiley faces will tend to have more positive interactions with other people, and that will shape their character accordingly. Research suggests that extroverts tend to have slightly wider cheeks on average—just like we all do when we smile broadly. It is easy to imagine how social feedback could account for this: People with wide cheeks tend to be greeted more openly because people see their cheeks and associate that with positive feelings, so wide-cheeked people learn that social interactions are easy and fun.

Hormones at Work

Some facial features are directly linked to perceptions of character because they are shaped by hormones. When our faces are developing in the womb, we are awash in a rich cocktail of hormones, including testosterone and estrogen, and the ratio between them varies for every individual. Each hormone tends to encourage the development of particular facial features. More testosterone typically produces a slightly heavier brow, a shorter forehead, a slightly wider nose, and a chin and jaw that extend slightly farther south of your mouth. More estrogen leads to slightly bigger eyes, a higher forehead, shorter chin, and a slightly wider mouth relative to the overall shape of the face.

Traditional nonverbal strength displays include facial expressions like furrowing our brows, clenching our teeth—which flexes the jaw muscles out to the sides slightly—and even flaring our nostrils. These expressions are all visually mimicked by the effects of testosterone on a developing face. A prominent brow resembles an angrily furrowed brow; a chiseled jaw, particularly at the back corner under the earlobe, mimics the look of angrily clenched teeth; and a wider nose looks like angry nostrils flaring. Warmth expressions often involve opening the eyes wider, and raising the eyebrows is a signal of submission; both of these are paralleled by estrogen's effect on developing faces.

We are all wired to think baby mammals are adorable, but the most adorable ones have extra-big eyes and extra-smallish noses and jaw-bones. While most of us get less cute as we grow up, some people's faces retain childlike features well into adulthood. People with a particular constellation of these features—roundness through the lower cheeks, a larger forehead and ears—are said to have a "baby face." This looks relatively normal on women, but is more conspicuous on men. Research shows that baby-face features make a person seem more warm but less strong, and the lives of baby-faced adults can be profoundly shaped by people's reactions. Unsurprisingly, baby-faced adults are overrepresented in caring professions where warmth is perceived as a critical virtue. Moreover, baby-faced adults are more likely to lose lawsuits when they are accused of negligence, because juries generally see them as less competent and so more likely to commit sins of negligence. But juries are much less likely to convict a baby-faced defendant of a crime of intent, because juries find them warm.

As with other stereotypes, there is a steep penalty for violating this one. When someone with a baby face admits to intentionally committing a crime, they get significantly harsher sentences than other defendants. These baby-faced criminals seem extra deceitful and dangerous because their criminality is hidden behind a warm, trust-inducing face, and their crimes seem more shocking because they betray that implicit promise.

With all of these striking biological connections, it is easy to start to conclude that your genes are your destiny. But there are many other signals that shape strength and warmth judgments, and facial structure is not the most important among them. Moreover, your facial structure is not limited to what your genes say it is: Your character can also shape your face. George Orwell once remarked, "At fifty, everyone has the face he deserves." If you have spent years smiling crow's feet around the corners of your eyes, or scowling a deep groove into your brow, you did that yourself.

Lookin' Good

We cannot talk about looks without talking about good looks. Looking physically attractive is only part of the story of what makes someone attractive, but it definitely counts. And physical appeal shapes so much of how we interact with the world that it becomes an important part of the story of character too. This is especially true for women, who because of their traditionally less powerful roles in society are judged more, and more harshly, on their looks than their male counterparts.

The French musician Serge Gainsbourg once remarked that ugliness is in a way superior to beauty, "because it lasts." It is true that in addition to all the other indignities of aging, the beautiful have to deal with losing the luster of their looks over time, which can have a profound psychological effect, particularly if they have relied on their looks to feel good about themselves.

There are other downsides to being conspicuously good-looking, especially for women. Pretty girls and women get a lot of attention, which is often unwelcome, especially if they are shy. Being persistently encouraged to focus on appearance can distract from more satisfying experiences. And in some cases they may be presumed vapid and incompetent—after all, why would they bother getting good at anything when the world falls at their feet? The more homely among us are spared such troubles.

On balance, though, beauty is usually the better deal. Beauty has a kind of blinding effect on our judgment. For instance, research shows we judge writing more favorably if we find the author attractive. This could be because of the halo effect we discussed earlier, where someone with one positive quality—beauty, in this case—is assumed also to have others. Or in some cases people may rate beautiful people highly on other attributes just to curry favor with them. One study found that we respond to small favor requests from winsome strangers much more willingly than from less attractive strangers—in fact, we respond just as eagerly as we do for old friends.

Many benefits flow to the beautiful. Attractive children get more attention from parents and teachers, who perceive them to be more intelligent. Attractive people make more money. Good-looking women are more likely to marry into a higher social class, and to have many healthy children. Kate Middleton was no doubt among the most attractive young ladies in Prince William's class at school, and it served her well.

Good looks have also been found to correspond with actual strengths. Some of the same internal chemistry that makes women attractive also makes them more fertile. They have even been found to be better lovers (as measured by their ability to help partners to achieve orgasm, if you must know—academia is not all boring).

In strength and warmth terms, if you think back to our four quadrants, we admire beauty—it lives in the upper-right quadrant of high strength and high warmth. Why is that? Beauty has warmth to it. Not only are we drawn to it because it pleases us, but we definitely share a common interest with beautiful strangers: At a minimum, we want them to continue being beautiful and making our world more enjoyable. There is also undeniably a strength dimension to beauty. It affects people, moves them to action, and conveys a social power that its possessor can wield, for good or ill. Beyond that, there is also the strength-as-warmth effect: Their beauty is strong, and we are drawn to it in part because we want people like that to be on the same team (if not in the same bed) as us.

But this dynamic does not necessarily mean that we admire everyone we find attractive. Competitive reactions can develop, making attractive people the envied enemy. For example, research has found that when corporate job applicants submit pictures with their resumes, attractive female applicants can be at a disadvantage if women in the human resources department do not want to add more attractive women to the office social dynamic. We also often resent people we find attractive when they are not as friendly toward us as we feel toward them: It does not seem fair of them not to reciprocate our positive feelings. And attractive women are often assumed dim and shown disrespect because it seems like they can get by on their looks. Actress Charlize Theron is classically pretty, but she did not win an Academy Award until she made herself as unattractive as possible in the role of prostitute-turned-killer Aileen Wuornos. In real-world social contexts, looking good can be a mixed blessing.

The Magic Formula

What exactly do we mean by "good looks"? Is there even such a thing as one objective standard for ideal beauty that almost all of us fall short of to lesser or greater degrees? The answer turns out to be complex. Yes, there are shared ideal standards for physical beauty—but at the same time, our perceptions of beauty still vary a lot based on other factors.

For starters, except in the occasional close case, there is a general consensus about how attractive different people are. In studies, infants shown a pair of faces will reliably gaze much longer at the more attractive of the two. We know beauty when we see it.

But explaining exactly what it is we find beautiful has proved difficult. The ancient Greeks were enamored of the mathematical notion called the "golden ratio" and thought it might describe the geometry of the ideally beautiful face: the distance between the eyes and the width of the face, or the distance from the eyebrows to the lips, and so on. More recently, researchers were hopeful that facial symmetry might help account for the mystery of beauty. It is true that most of the time asymmetrical features lessen attractiveness. But there are many attractive people with asymmetrical facial features and lots of less attractive people with perfectly symmetrical features.

What baffled the ancients is finally beginning to yield to modern computer imaging technology. Researchers can now easily isolate, re-create, exaggerate, and otherwise manipulate facial images to figure out what makes the beauty detection circuits in the brain light up. While they have not yet come up with a single gold standard of aesthetic perfection, they have teased out a lot of the key ingredients.

The Golden Mean

The most important thing shaping our idea of who looks beautiful is what everyone looks like—everyone, as in an entire population. The truly average among us—people who have the average nose plus the average cheeks, eyes, mouth, and so on—turn out to be strikingly attractive. This is easily demonstrated with computer imaging: If you blend all female faces together, you get an attractive woman, and if you blend all male images together, you get a good-looking guy.

It makes sense on several levels that the "average" face is the ideal. If someone tells you to think of a bird, the archetype that pops to mind is probably a robin-like critter, not an ostrich, a hummingbird, or a penguin. The same is true about people. If you scrutinize the average face feature by feature, each one looks very familiar, and that familiarity may also bring a pleasant sense of comfort with it.

Biologically, matching the archetype is probably a good sign that a person is healthy. There is also the concept of hybrid vigor, the idea that offspring of animals who do not have many traits in common are likely to be healthy and biologically fit. You can think of this as the opposite of inbreeding. (This may help explain why the children of parents of different ethnicities are often so gorgeous.)

Pretty Girls

But as tidy and sensible as it sounds that the ideal is just the average, there are some faces that outshine even the perfectly average ones. So what could be more beautiful than the Platonic ideal? For women, the answer is to tweak a handful of features, mostly to make them more feminine. If you start with the average-ideal face and then turn the dial up on those few key features, you get the slender nose of Natalie Portman, the oversize eyes of Zooey Deschanel, the dramatic cheekbones of Olivia Wilde, the broad mouth of Rashida Jones, the swollen lips of Angelina Jolie. You also shift the features down within the frame of the face, creating a higher forehead and shorter chin, which subtly shifts the whole geometry of the face so that the eyes seem relatively farther apart. The result is a universally recognized, if generic, pretty face.

Be careful with that dial, though: If you crank it up, you will quickly create a freakish-looking elfin monster. The differences between the features of the perfectly average face and an even more attractive face are extremely small and subtle, and they are very hard to pick out consciously in pictures. But because we are armed with a head full of neural circuits dedicated to processing facial geometry, we can see these differences clearly, and easily distinguish the young Keira Knightley from the young Natalie Portman.

But the story has one last wrinkle: In the most attractive female faces, not every typically feminine facial characteristic gets dialed up. As with babies' faces, feminine faces are on average slightly rounder through the lower cheeks, and also have a higher arch to the eyebrow. These feminine features are actually slightly dialed down in the most alluring female faces, which feature tapered or even slightly concave cheeks dropping below prominent cheekbones and eyebrows that come in close over the brow toward the bridge of the nose. A sculpted cheekbone with a concave cheek underneath definitely projects a certain sleek strength, as does an eyebrow coming in low above the eye. Once again, the most admired form has strength signals balancing warmth signals.

In fact, research suggests that having some masculine aspects to their facial structure makes women seem more emotionally stable, more "down to earth" than women with especially feminine features. This is because more feminine-looking women can sometimes trigger archaic stereotypes of women as emotionally volatile. Similarly, feminine facial features make men seem warmer, while men with lots of prominently masculine facial features can seem overly domineering.

Pretty Boys

To get the most attractive male faces then, you start with the average guy and then follow the same directions as with female faces: Dial up the same, mostly feminine features. Research participants agree that this makes guys seem less masculine, not more, but also that dialing up the warmth adds more aesthetic appeal than dialing up the machismo.

As for the lower face, as with women, people prefer slightly sleeker-than-average cheeks. Rounder, more feminine "baby face" cheeks make guys seem weak, while a heavy protruding jaw makes guys seem too menacing. Most of the time, then, what is judged the most attractive is what is sometimes called a "pretty boy" face. If you wonder what this looks like, think Zac Efron or Rob Lowe. For a slightly tougher, more masculine ideal, think George Clooney or Robert Redford.

In general though, neither men nor women are as uniform in their preferences for male faces as with female faces. Once again, guys have more latitude: They are not judged as harshly on looks in general, and their character counts more toward their overall attractiveness. That said, there are still plenty of beautiful men out there, as well as women who appreciate them for their looks alone.

The big picture here is that feminine features are closely associated with warmth and masculine features are closely associated with strength, and once again what we admire most has elements of both.

An Average of One's Own

While we all recognize beauty standards that can suggest both strength and warmth, their tyranny is far from absolute. If you are worried that you are not the most aesthetically blessed, there is plenty of good news too. Experience and research confirm it: The old saying about beauty being in the eye of the beholder is true.

First of all, while there may be only one perfectly average face, every one of us actually has a slightly different vision of what that is. We each gauge our own averages based on what is familiar, so our friends and family have an outsize influence in setting our personal standards of beauty.

Moreover, when you meet someone whose features remind you of strong or warm or attractive or unattractive people you have known in the past, a little bit of those associations transfers to the new person with similar features. If someone's nose looks like that of someone you used to love, a little of that feeling will seep into how you see this new person, even if the nose in question is not so lovely on its own. Our individual experiences mean we all develop a slightly different ideal of physical attractiveness.

Also, unlike in the research, we do not experience each other as still images of expressionless faces in a computer lab. A jaw that looks vaguely menacing in a picture with no other context could look quite handsome on a real guy with a comfortable manner and a warm smile. The same goes for female features too: An awkward feature might actually look kind of cute on a smiling face. We do not judge each other on our mug shots alone.

Moreover, the beauty that we initially find so striking fades quickly, not just over years as age takes its toll, but in just the few minutes it takes to start to get to know one another. Looks have their greatest impact when we first see someone. As soon as we watch them move and hear them speak and read their emotions and judge the quality of their decisions, all of these other strength and warmth signals affect our judgment of how attractive that person is. This is very similar to the way our impressions based on demographic stereotypes fade as we get to know people as individuals. Superficial signals count initially and from afar, but once we interact with someone, those signals diminish in importance quickly. When we meet someone who is objectively physically attractive, at first we are struck by how remarkable this person seems. But after a few minutes of conversation, our judgment of them depends much more on how they act and interact with us.

Research shows this clearly. For instance, one study asked people to rate the attractiveness of the people they went to high school with, and then asked strangers to rate the same people based on yearbook pictures alone. These more objective but limited ratings were significantly at odds with the impressions the students had made on their peers as live, flesh-and-blood members of their high school community. We find people attractive for a whole host of reasons; having a nice-looking face is only a part of the story.

Ultimately attraction is not just about looks; it is a much more complex emotional phenomenon. We begin with aesthetic judgments, both about what a face suggests about a personality and about how attractive it is. But while these aesthetic judgments are important, they do not necessarily translate into an emotional response of attraction—romantically, carnally, or platonically. We can be unmoved by people we recognize as aesthetically appealing, and we can also find ourselves powerfully attracted to people who are not. You can get along fine without good looks, even in the romantic department, if you have other strength and warmth signals working for you. And you can also easily end up miserable with good looks if you do not know how to work with them.

Body Type

The physical basics tell a lot about people. When a man shows up at your door with the physique of a sumo wrestler, you jump to different conclusions than if he is built like Woody Allen.

We all take stock of whether people are tall or short, fat or thin, fit or flabby. Our first reaction is an immediate friend-or-foe calculation (Do I have to worry about this person harming me?), followed by broader assessments of competence, vigorousness, and attractiveness.

Our views on body type are tangled up with stereotypes and other cultural information, including biases and expectations based on gender and ethnicity. For instance, the adjectives "hulking" and "petite" refer to body type but also have strong gender implications. Some of the ideals for body type vary according to cultural norms. The visual cues that indicate good health in one country may be perceived differently in another. In a country where food is scarce, for instance, a few extra pounds can be a sign of wealth (strength), whereas in industrialized countries where food is abundant, the same cue may be read very differently.

While some ideals are culturally specific, others cross boundaries. Even though norms for beauty are different around the world, there are universally favored proportions, such as the shoulder-to-waist ratio for men and the waist-to-hips ratio for women, which psychologists link to judgments about biological suitability for mating. These serve as a shared international language for attraction.

The other basic dimensions that matter most are height (tall or short) and the balance between muscle and fat (skinny, medium, overweight, and ripped). In general, we equate a big physique with strength, until it shades into obesity and a lack of fitness. Big can mean tall, broad, or both. There have been lots of studies showing relationships between tallness and leadership and even a "tallness premium" for men in terms of salaries. Tall people are considered more confident and competent, unless they slouch and throw away their advantage. Similarly, people with rippling muscles and broad shoulders signal that they are physically vigorous, even if they do not win the height competition. One caveat here concerns women who are tall or have large, muscular physiques that are traditionally associated with men: Physical strength may also trigger the hostile stereotype we discussed in the section on gender.

Conversely, small people run the risk of being discounted because of their size. This is true for both women and men—remember, men are presumed strong, so a lack of physical stature goes against expectations. Short, skinny, or otherwise slightly built people can be perceived as weak, wimpy, or inconsequential.

Being aware of this stereotype, some small people display high levels of aggression to project strength; this is known informally as the Napoleon complex. Russian president Vladimir Putin (5'7" according to some reports) fits this description. His penchant for being photographed shirtless or while performing athletic feats highlights his obsession with projecting strength. Actor Danny DeVito has made a career of playing the Napoleon complex for comic effect. The downside of this approach speaks for itself.

The good news is that there are ways to deal with having a small physique without going to the Napoleonic extreme. One client of ours is roughly 5'5" with a slender build, but he projects strength by dressing sharply all the time. His appearance makes it unmistakable that he means business, which gives him the confidence to be himself without worrying how his height might affect others' perceptions. He then balances the seriousness of his look with an ever-present smile, and nobody pays much attention to his height.

With awareness of obesity raised to the level of a public health concern in the United States, heavyset people face stereotypes about being lazy or unhealthy that are not unlike those associated with smokers. Many people perceive obesity as a problem with behavioral roots—they believe people who suffer from it lack willpower—and make character judgments accordingly. There is evidence of hiring discrimination against obese people, which suggests that obesity can hurt perceptions of professional competence. There are other factors that may weigh into this discrimination, such as concerns about obesity-related health conditions, but these also may serve as rational justifications for emotional responses.

Sexual Orientation and Identity

Like gender, sexual orientation plays a huge role in shaping character. And it is no surprise that there are plenty of strength- and warmth-related stereotypes that go along with being lesbian, gay, bisexual, or transgender.

Sexual orientation is not usually one of the first things we notice about other people. Playing the averages, we assume people are heterosexual until it is established otherwise. The reality can be hard to discern, but that does not mean that sexuality is invisible. Gay people can choose how overtly they want to signal their membership in the club, and folks who know the signals—those with good "gaydar"—will know how to interpret them. How gaydar works is a perennially popular topic of argument. Gay people can signal with nonverbal cues, with men using more feminine cues and gay women using more masculine. Gaydar also works through cultural clues: That well-dressed guy with the defined muscles talking about his love for show tunes could be straight, but chances are he is not.

Many of the cues are deliberately subtle, as unfortunately many gay people feel pressured to hide their identities and "pass" as straight. Being gay is itself a kind of stereotype violation, because it means bucking basic gender expectations. Beyond that basic issue, there are many crosscurrents of strength and warmth associated with being a gay man or woman, and these vary widely from one sociocultural setting to another. Gay women are generally perceived to be tougher and more masculine than straight women—and therefore less "in need" of men. Gay men, on the other hand, are generally stereotyped as more feminine than their heterosexual male counterparts. Note that this can have some upside too. Just as we saw with looks, even the most feminine-seeming men and masculine-seeming women can also benefit from being seen as combining strength and warmth in one character: the more levelheaded woman, the more sensitive man.

As gay culture has become more mainstream in America, gay stereotypes have also multiplied. Researchers have now formally identified ten different gay male stereotypes, including warm-and-weak flamboyant and effeminate types, strong-and-cold hypermasculine biker types, and even a somewhat admired stereotype of the gay artist. It is almost a cliché to point out that many straight women find gay men make the best friends, as they seem to have an uncanny understanding of both sides of the straight gender divide. Being openly gay means dealing with all of these stereotypes one way or the other, embracing them, playing with them, or challenging them. Ultimately each person has to figure out what works best.

Transgender individuals also face special challenges in terms of social judgments. Often the biggest difficulty is that the visual cues from trans folks are not clearly either male or female. Male and female are such ingrained categories of social perception that when someone does not fit neatly into either box, people sometimes respond in all kinds of crazy ways. Straight people seeing both male and female cues can sometimes feel deceived and have strongly negative reactions. Research and common sense both tell us that when we see a man saying, "I am a woman," most of us believe the visual cues, not the words. Transgender individuals face this reality constantly, even when they use style cues to clarify what they want people to see.

Then again, as generation after generation of pop music stars attest, gender-bending, convention-defying pansexual rebels have a strong appeal within certain cultural contexts. As society's awareness grows, transgender men and women may even be seen as both stronger and warmer because they possess special insight into the experiences of both genders.

Disability

Our friend Daniel might be the most charming man in New York. He is a brilliant guy who has traveled the world investigating and writing great stories about sports heroes and war villains. When you meet him, though, the first thing you see is his great smile—he radiates "happy to be there." You might actually speak with him for a few minutes before you notice the way he is standing, or see him shift awkwardly or take a few steps with his effortful, loping gait, heaving forward the leg that was smashed in a car wreck along with his own dreams of sports stardom when he was ten. He is neither perfect nor endlessly sunny—he gets grouchy and sarcastic and argumentative—

but his baseline demeanor is a joy in being alive that shows on his face.

For all of his warmth, though, how could Daniel be so compelling if projecting strength is half the battle and he has a conspicuous disability? It does not hurt that he has a successful career, or that he is a great storyteller. But the point is that his disability is not a social liability; he has made it an asset. Not by playing it for pity to help get information for his stories, though he is not necessarily above that. He is more compelling, more admirable with his injury than he would be without it, because it shows character.

A disability is a weakness, by definition. But presenting oneself with a disability does not necessarily show weakness—it can show strength. Not bodily strength, of course, but strength of character. And ultimately that's how we judge each other. We all know strength of will trumps bodily strength anyway.

When people without a major physical disability see someone who evidently has one, they experience a few things in quick succession. First, they tend to wince. Sensing that something is not right with a human body is unpleasant, aversive. For most of us, a sense of empathy then follows: "That must be hard, having to deal with that constantly."

So our initial reaction is some combination of discomfort and warmth. If the person is elderly, some of us may be uncomfortably reminded that our own bodies will fall apart someday. As we are imagining what that might be like, we are also reading this person's nonverbal signals for clues to their attitude.

If we sense little or no positive emotion, then our overall reaction will likely remain whatever blend of aversion and pity we first felt. If this person projects a lot of active bitterness at their circumstances, that additional unpleasantness will make us less likely to empathize with them, however understandable their feelings may be.

But if instead this person wears a big, pleasant smile and projects positive feelings, that immediately stokes our feelings of empathy. This effect may have more to it than just pity: Since we were just thinking how miserable we might feel in such circumstances, we might even credit this person with impressive strength of character to be able to smile through adverse circumstances and forge ahead with life.

And if in addition to a warm smile, we see traces of confidence and comfort, suggesting that this person is truly fine with his or her circumstances, those signs of strength are even more impressive. Not only do we doubt our own ability to display this kind of fortitude and acceptance under the circumstances, we also now let ourselves off the hook: If everything is fine, there is no need for us to feel bad—our pity is unwarranted. This comes as a relief, absolving us of any guilt we might feel for our own relative good fortune, and we have their strength of character to thank for it.

If the disability in question directly impairs the person's mood or basic communication skills, there may well be very little upside at all in terms of character projection. Then the reaction others have is pity, aversion, or both.

But researchers working with trauma victims find that "post-traumatic growth" is as common as post-traumatic stress disorder. Trauma survivors often report a renewed appreciation for life, new energy to explore new possibilities for their lives, and more satisfying relationships and spirituality. All of this goes directly to confidence and strength.

This connection between physical disability and strength of character supports the view of people who suspect that traditional strength signals mask weaknesses in character. Post-traumatic growth presents an interesting twist: Real physical weakness may lead to real strength of character.

None of this is to say that a disability is a great gift, or that all disabilities follow the same dynamics as those brought on by traumatic experiences. It does mean that by focusing exclusively on the obvious downsides, it is possible to miss social upsides for those in a position to capitalize on them.

Adversity builds character. Someone who manages to project even a moderate level of warmth and strength in the face of it is someone we can all admire.

Playing the Hand

The Choice Is Yours

The signals you send with your gender, ethnicity, looks, and age are more or less fixed: Short of surgery, you cannot do much about them. But that is exactly why these physical attributes are far from the last word on how people judge your character. At the end of the day, character is a matter of who you choose to be, not the way you happen to be born. People judge your character by the way you act, and especially by the way you interact with them.

Not all behavior is conscious. If you are lost in thought, for instance, you may be walking around with a puzzled look on your face without realizing it. We even sometimes say things that we do not mean to say aloud, such as Freudian slips. This may get us into trouble, but that is just how our brains work. All of us often speak without paying close attention to every word.

But even if a lot of behavior is unconscious, nearly all of it can be subject to conscious choice. You can choose not only to behave differently, but to learn how to behave differently: You can take steps that change the way you react unconsciously in the future. Some of these changes require a lot of practice, but others just take a little imagination.

In this section, we explore all the different ways you can project more strength and more warmth to balance out the signals you send just by showing up. In other words, this is how to play the hand you have been dealt.

Nonverbal Communication

"The body does not lie."
—Martha Graham

As far back as Charles Darwin, researchers have recognized the connection between social power and demeanor. Our partner, Seth Pendleton, familiarized us with a famous (and often misinterpreted) series of studies about emotional communication by UCLA professor Albert Mehrabian in the 1970s. He postulated that there were several factors we use to interpret the feelings of someone speaking to us: their tone of voice, visual cues like facial expression, posture, and gestures, and the actual words they use.

To figure out which was most important, Mehrabian's experiments pitted these factors against one another: Where the words and tone of voice conveyed one thing—"I am very glad to meet you," for instance—the visual cues of flexed neck muscles and a lowered brow said something very different. When the emotional signals from these three different channels were in conflict, people believed the nonverbal cues much more than the words, leading Mehrabian to the specific formulation that 55 percent of the cues we use to interpret how a speaker is feeling are visual, 38 percent come from the speaker's tone of voice, and a mere 7 percent are derived from the words themselves.

These numbers are not precisely accurate in every case—a poet's words carry more emotion than your average prose, and some speakers have more powerful voices than others. But the general point is clear: How we *feel* is conveyed more by nonverbal behavior than by the words we choose. The lizard brain circuitry is running the show, not the fancy parts of the brain that spent years learning to "talk good."

Nonverbal communication goes directly to the issue of trust. When all the signals—facial expressions, posture, gestures, vocal tone, and the actual words—line up to tell a consistent story, then we can be confident those signals are an accurate expression of how that person feels. By contrast, when different signals are telling different stories at the same time, we suspect that a person is conflicted, uncomfortable, or maybe even trying to hide something. Without consciously thinking about it, we notice nonverbal inconsistencies and use them to sniff out insecurity, uncertainty, and weakness. They are how we know when something is not quite right.

Here's a party trick to try with your friends . . . or your clients, as our partner, Seth, often does when working with groups. "Everybody make an okeydokey sign," he says, forming a circle with his thumb and pointer finger and holding his hand out. "Now go ahead and put that on your chin," Seth says—only as he does, he moves his hand slowly up to his face and presses the circle to the right side of his face, against his cheek. And so does everyone else in the room. A moment later, the room cracks up, as people realize he said "chin" but they put their hands to their cheeks. Some burst out laughing, others quickly move their hands to their chin, hoping no one will catch them, while the last few to catch on look frantically around the room trying to figure out what just happened.

The point is simple but powerful. We are visual creatures, and we react to visual cues. Monkey see, monkey do. When what we say to the world conflicts with what we show to the world, our words lose nearly every time. No matter what else you may say or do, the way you present yourself serves as the shortcut others use to understand you.

Space

Around the same time we started exploring nonverbal communication in depth a decade ago, we discovered a rising pop culture phenomenon named Cesar Millan, better known as the Dog Whisperer. His work involved helping people sort out behavioral issues with their dogs, and more often than not the problems began with the two-legged creatures. Right away we noticed that Cesar carried himself with a sense of purpose that reminded us of a martial arts expert or a dancer. His body was integral to his work, and he used it like an athlete.

Even though Cesar worked with dogs, the behaviors he used to project strength and warmth visually bore a striking resemblance to those used by great speakers and performers. It turns out that dogs and humans respond to some of the same basic nonverbal cues. (Think back to our yawning example earlier.) And when Cesar coached dog owners, he stressed that they needed to serve as pack leaders for their dogs. That is exactly what he did when he walked into a room for the first time; within seconds, he owned the space.

Owning space is more about strength than warmth, so we will start there. The way you use space in a room says a lot about how much strength you project. In general, strong people make themselves at home anywhere, occupy a lot of space, and move about freely rather than getting locked in one place. When engaging with another person, sometimes they close distance to assert dominance. (If you search online for "LBJ treatment," you will find photos of Lyndon Baines Johnson doing this to his political colleagues.) Other times they use space in exactly the opposite way: They create distance and set themselves apart from others. Above all, they exert control over space, making it clear who is in charge.

Closing distance is also what we typically do when projecting warmth. This happens in all sorts of ways, from confiding secrets to huddling in cold weather for physical warmth to getting down between the sheets. We even use the word "close" to describe our relationship to dear friends. Conversely, keeping your distance from someone almost invariably comes off as a lack of warmth, even if it is done out of respect.

Posture

Good, upright posture projects strength. This also is about owning a lot of space, only vertically: Standing tall demonstrates confidence. At an elemental level, taking up physical space with your body sends a nonverbal message that's not so different from having a big car or a big house: *Look at me. I am important.*

There's a reason new military recruits learn to stand at attention on day one: In the heat of battle, men and women in leadership positions have to order fellow troops to dive in front of bullets. The military calls the ability to get people to follow orders under even the most perilous conditions "command presence." The correct posture for projecting command presence is not the almost cartoonish formal posture referred to in the military as standing "at attention," with chin up, shoulders back, chest out, and stomach in. That posture is good for instilling discipline and creates a powerful visual effect when reviewing troops in formation, but actually standing that way feels awkward and makes it hard to react quickly to changes in your environment. Functional command presence starts with what the military calls the "at ease" posture: The spine is straight, the head held high, but the chin is level and the chest is relaxed. Physically, this means actively using the muscles in the back to straighten the S curve in the spine, going for maximum altitude. This projects plenty of strength, and is appropriate not just in the barracks and on the battle-field, but in most business and personal settings as well.

Projecting strength is not just about stereotypically macho activities like military service. Another community that understands the importance of posture is the ballet world. Dancers rivet our attention because they often appear to have an invisible string pulling them upward from the crowns of their heads, keeping them perfectly perpendicular to the ground. Projecting strength in a poised manner, whether in the line of fire or on a stage, is truly a matter of walking tall.

Our third partner, Seth Pendleton, is a longtime actor, and he often recounts the story of an exercise his acting teacher used to make their class do. First they would curl up in the fetal position on the floor, and after a couple of minutes the teacher would come around and ask each one how they felt. The responses were invariably grim: "I feel small," "I feel sad," "I feel lost," and the like. Then the teacher had everyone jump up and stand tall with their arms spread out above them—the classic Yul Brynner pose from *The King and I*, later reprised by Leonardo DiCaprio in his "I'm the King of the World!" scene in *Titantic*. When a few minutes later the teacher came around again to ask the class how they felt, they were transformed: "I feel great!" "I feel powerful!" "I feel ready for anything!"

The key behind this effect is the deep connection between nonverbal behavior and character. Our feelings and our physicality are hardwired together, which is why our nonverbal behavior is such a reliable indicator of our emotional experience at any given moment. Usually, we think of our perceptions and thoughts about the world shaping our feelings, and then those feelings shaping our nonverbal expressions—posture, gestures, facial expressions. But it turns out that connection is so strong that if we consciously force ourselves to adopt certain postures, our emotions change to align themselves with that posture. When people win big competitions, they feel powerful and elated, and they naturally get big, raising their arms in triumph, sometimes jumping, sometimes raising their heads and puffing out their chests as well. This is consistent across cultures. If you want a little shot of that feeling, all you have to do is adopt that posture and wait a minute or two for the hormones in your blood to catch up.

How powerful is this effect? Our friends Amy Cuddy of Harvard Business School and Dana Carney, now at the University of California, ran a very clever study to find out. They had one group of people spend two minutes in constricted poses—not the fetal position, but sitting with their hands clasped or standing with arms folded and legs crossed—and another group spend two minutes in expansive poses, either stretched out in a chair with their arms behind their heads and feet up on a desk, or standing over a table with their hands spread wide on it. A few minutes later, these groups were put through three tests: a gambling test, a deliberately stressful job interview facing a camera and two stony-faced people, and a saliva test. In the gambling test, the expansive, high-power pose group was much more willing to risk money for a chance at a big payoff than the low-power pose group, so high-power warm-up poses might not be the best strategy if you are heading to the casino or doing other things in which excessive optimism could lead you to take dumb risks that get you hurt. But with the interview, impartial judges who watched the tape found the high-power posers to be far more engaging, persuasive, and compelling interview candidates than the low-power posers. The saliva test revealed why: They had much higher testosterone and much lower cortisol levels than the low-power group, so they felt a surge of confidence, while the low-power group felt butterflies in their stomach. All this from just a couple of minutes of standing still—in the right position.

The moral of the story is that high- and low-strength postures are so closely tied to the attitudes they reflect that you can run the circuits in reverse. Psychologists call this "embodied cognition," when your body shapes your thinking processes. Whereas usually the posture we show the world reflects our internal attitude, by intentionally altering our posture we can drive internal hormonal changes and create greater feelings of confidence. It is like dressing up more than usual to make yourself feel good.

The findings of this study are also very practical. Anytime you are heading into a situation where you want your body and mind to feel powerful, adopting strength poses a few minutes in advance will help make that happen. Whether it is a date, a doctor's appointment, or a tough conversation with a coworker or a friend, a little less cortisol and a little extra testosterone will help you steer things to the conclusion you want. Just like teaching military recruits to stand at attention helps them internalize the feeling of power and develop their command presence, you can develop your confidence for the long term—and you can turn it on at will. You really can "fake it till you make it"—in fact, you can fake it till it's real.

Putting this into practice does not require any imagination at all: Just stretch and hold a big position for a minute or so to give your glands time to adjust your blood composition—you can often feel a tingle as it happens. Stretching across the chest seems to be especially helpful, and stretching out your limbs and shoulder and neck muscles in general to release tension is also a good idea. There is even some evidence that you can achieve the effect just by imagining that you have extra limbs stretched powerfully into the space around you like some giant mythological creature. Many people find this leads to similar feelings and a deepening of breath, and it has the advantage of looking a lot less funny when you are sitting in a meeting.

Sated Strength

There is an entirely different way of projecting strength through posture, one that also reflects confidence by taking up lots of space, but does not look anything like our poised friends in uniform or in toe shoes. Imagine a young entrepreneur who, having just sold his first multimillion-dollar company and bought a swanky spread in Malibu overlooking the ocean, is now sprawled out on his new ostrich-leather sectional couch, arms and legs akimbo, supremely confident and supremely relaxed, without a care in the world, like a lion resting lazily after devouring his kill, or a king slouched on his throne. We call this the relaxed manner of strength, or "sated strength." It's the slouch of someone who is perfectly satisfied, at ease with his surroundings.

There is a basic trade-off here: less height for more width. Instead of standing straight for maximum altitude, you may spread your legs and arms out in several directions. If the stance gets any wider than shoulder width, it reduces altitude up top, but the increased width down below takes up additional volume.

Be careful with this relaxed manner. Its informality may seem warm to you, but by using it you risk giving the impression that you are not taking the occasion seriously. Like many strength gestures, it risks undercutting your warmth—in this case, by exhibiting disrespect for those around you.

First Things First

The volume of space we take up is not the only way our posture signals strength. Consider what part of your body you lead with when you move through the world: If you were crossing the finish line of a race, what part of you would break the plane first? There are three candidates:

Head first

This pose has the head extended at least slightly forward instead of upward, with usually stooped shoulders, so the forehead is the first body part into every room. This fits with the stereotype of a doddering old professor, perhaps holding a book up to his face to peer over his glasses to read it. The nonverbal message this conveys is of someone lost in thought. Despite the implication of mental activity, this pose does not project much strength. Physically, with the head extended forward, it is at best slightly off-balance, and at worst, with the face tilted toward the ground, it is difficult to even see the world, much less react to it. Moreover, a slightly bowed head is a classic signal of deference ("Right away, my lady").

Hips first

Hips-centered posture is sated strength in motion. It is all about the pelvis, and it's sexy: Imagine a fashion model sashaying down the catwalk. Weight is supported by a back leg, while the hips project forward and the torso reclines slightly backward. Hips-centered posture is always informal, but it can project a lot of strength. With the chest open—the shoulders not hunched forward, in other words—hips-centered posture is the classic languid pose of sated strength.

Heart first

Heart-centered posture means leading with the chest slightly forward and the shoulders slightly behind, as with the military and dancer postures we discussed earlier. It projects poised strength: It occupies vertical space, with the head erect to survey the environs, and the body balanced so it can easily move in whatever direction might be required. In our party scene, both no-nonsense Kurt and center-of-attention Cheryl exhibited heart-centered posture. It suggests openness, confidence, and a willingness to engage. Leading with the heart is the most fundamental way to project strength through posture.

At the same time, the heart is the warmth center of the body. Baring your breast to the world and exposing your vital organs to potential threats is a way of making yourself vulnerable. While this is also the most common center of gravity for projecting strength, the difference is principally in the shoulders, which are relaxed slightly forward and lower than in a high-strength pose. In combination with the right gestures, a heart-centered posture suggests a sense of openness to the world.

Breasts First?

Understandably, adopting strong posture creates a conundrum for many women, particularly in professional settings, because in practice heart-centered posture means leading with their breasts. Especially for women with curves, it can be hard enough to maintain eye contact with straight male colleagues without making their bustlines even more prominent. Conspicuous sex appeal can also distract or detract from women's efforts to project competence by leaving people suspecting they might have been hired or promoted for the wrong reasons.

None of that changes the rules of projecting strength, however: Good posture projects confidence and competence. It is definitely true that some women will have their breasts noticed more often than others. But trying to hide breasts with bad posture does not improve things; it just projects a lack of confidence. It is much better to project strength with good posture and then dress in ways that downplay physique in professional situations where sexuality can be a distraction. Unfortunately, this is just one of the countless ways women in our culture currently have it a little harder than men.

Excesses

Very few people present themselves in public at attention like a soldier, but there are a few common postures involving exaggerated strength that are worth noting, not only to appreciate them on others but also to avoid using them yourself.

The Nose Thinks It Knows Better

One such maneuver is known as "looking down one's nose" at people. This literally means raising your chin so as to tilt your head back, which raises your eye level slightly so you feel taller. It also leaves you looking at people down the bridge of your nose like you are sighting a target down the barrel of a gun. Research by a team including our friend Dana Carney found that people see this sort of behavior as reflecting high social standing, a form of strength. But it's not just generic strength or confidence; it specifically projects the related sentiment of pride. This is fine for peacocks, but is usually dubious among us humans. It can work well for people we are already strongly inclined to root for: someone defying social expectations to become the first person from the family/hometown/demographic group to achieve something great, or an acclaimed hero with an audience, a cute kid getting a good citizenship award for saving a playmate in a harrowing ice-skating misadventure, or any other kind of acclaimed hero with an audience behind them. The rest of us would do well to remember that pride is a sin for a reason. Looking down our nose at folks is a signal that we think we are better than they are. It may project strength in the moment, but it also demonstrates the hydraulic effect, freezing out any warmth. Barack Obama has been guilty of wearing this expression on many occasions, and when he does, his demeanor goes from cool to cold.

Knuckle Dragging

An exaggerated strength posture that got a lot of attention in the first decade of the century was the Texan-style pose of President George W. Bush. He used a simple trick to project more strength standing still. Instead of letting his arms hang naturally, he swiveled them so that you see the backs of his hands facing frontward. This turned his elbows out slightly to the side, which then turned his upper arms so his triceps extended out slightly to either side. This projected extra strength two ways: First, if you were facing him, you couldn't see his palms at all, just his knuckles. Second, the triceps trick effectively made his upper torso wider.

If all of this seems a bit over the top, it is. Both the chin-up posture and the triceps flare are purely ornamental. Both project strength by taking up a little extra space, but neither position actually adds to your capacity for action. Having your chin up lets you see the sky, but it also keeps you from seeing the ground in front of you. Turning your palms to face behind you does not ready you for action either, unless that action is sitting down abruptly.

The Head Tilt Trade-off

If you are more concerned with projecting warmth than strength, tilting your head slightly to the side projects more warmth than keeping it straight up and down. We associate this with warmth because it literally exposes the side of your neck to someone who could potentially harm you, thereby sending the message that you are not a threat. In everyday life, we associate this with listening sympathetically to someone. A tilt of the head can also be a flirtatious signal. At its warmest, the head tilt evokes the image of someone saying, "Aww, what a cute puppy!"

But the added warmth of a head tilt comes directly at the expense of projecting strength. We have worked with scores of clients who were unaware that they were undermining their strength with a head tilt, and for most, it was not the best choice. In most cases, simply pointing this out was enough to help them self-correct. To be clear, there is nothing wrong with expressing warmth this way; it can be utterly charming and endearing. The important thing is to know that you're doing it.

Gait

If posture is how you hold your body when you stand in one place, gait is how you hold it as you walk. A short, quick gait with the head angled down sends a very different message than a gait with the head level, the chest open, and the stride long. A runway model's strut (usually hip centered) can project lots of sexual power, but it can also project unsteadiness—with every step, the body is ever-so-slightly off balance before the center of gravity shifts back to the center line.

Spring, Swagger, and Goose

A common way to project strength with stride is by having a "spring in your step." By bouncing up and down on the balls of your feet as you walk, you can gain an inch or more of extra height at the highest point in your stride. Note that even as this takes up more space, the bouncing around detracts from whatever sense of poise you might otherwise manage, and excessive bounciness can leave you looking pretty goofy. This gait conveys excited energy. As long as it's not too bouncy and uncontrolled, it conveys strength, in the form of a jaunty confidence. Closely related is what is known as "swagger." This can also involve a bounce in the step, and often involves hip-centered posture as well. The key moment in the swagger stride is when you put your next foot forward—at that moment, you push your chest slightly forward in a miniature strength pose, like a rooster strutting around the barnyard.

Once again, the military provides the extreme vision of strength: the goose step, wherein soldiers in formation walk by swinging each leg out straight in front of them with every step. (This is often accompanied by a wide swing of the arm reminiscent of the Who's guitarist Pete Townshend windmilling a power chord.) The goose step is still used by military all over the world to project strength in formal parades. It has fallen out of favor in many countries, as during World War II it came to be associated with the fascist Axis forces. To an American eye, it now seems buffoonish, indicative of an unbalanced perspective, worshiping strength at the expense of all that is warm.

Gesture

We have talked about the legs and torso. How do we project strength and warmth with our arms? First, let's consider strength.

Volume

First of all, the key principle we saw with posture—volume projects strength—applies to arm gestures too. This means you project strength by moving your hands and elbows, literally getting them farther away from your torso. Think of a sixth-grade dance: The kids who stand stock-still—like Emily from our party scene—are rightly assumed to be shy, while the kids whose limbs move freely and easily project more strength. If you clasp your hands in front of you and keep your elbows pressed to your sides, people will justifiably assume you are either cold or anxious. You might not get in anyone's way standing like that, but then again, mice do not take up a lot of space either.

Control

But when pushing hands and elbows out in order to command more space, be careful, because the next rule for gesture is equally important. The key to projecting strength with gesture is not to flail around excitedly, but to move deliberately, discreetly, gracefully. That presents poise; random dynamic energy bouncing in all directions does not. The aim is to demonstrate complete control of where your body is in space. Imagine the quality of movement you would expect from an expert in martial arts, or (again) classical ballet. As with music, the pauses between the gestures themselves are important: You gesture intentionally, and when you are done, you are still. That stillness demonstrates your physical control as much as the motion itself does.

Speed

Your gestures also convey a sense of your overall energy level: whether you are lethargic, relaxed, alert, or jittery. Relaxed and alert are good for projecting both strength and warmth. When your energy seems too high or too low, it can detract from both your strength and your warmth. Lethargic energy seems weak and disengaged, while jittery energy seems anxious, which is neither strong nor warm. A useful analogy here is the difference between big animals and small animals. A giraffe walks in long, graceful strides that look almost like it is moving in slow motion, while a hummingbird flits from spot to spot like a movie on fast-forward. Flitting is great for a hummingbird, but that kind of twitchy energy makes a person seem nervous.

Hands

On a smaller scale, the way in which one holds one's hands also sends a signal. If you curl your fingers into a fist, or straighten them flat out to form the blade of a karate chop, you convey strength, not least because these gestures suggest you are contemplating hurting somebody. Pointing with the index finger similarly comes off as strong—too strong, in fact, which is why politicians contort their hands into such odd shapes as they try to avoid making this gesture. Bill Clinton popularized the "thumb point," which looks as if he's casting a spell with an invisible wand, or perhaps changing the channel with an invisible remote. (Just about the only time he pointed the regular way in public was while denying his indiscretions with Monica Lewinsky.)

Fingers

Beyond those few stark positions, you are most likely to project strength or weakness simply by how relaxed or tense your fingers are. If your fingers are relaxed, they will generally have a gentle curl and spacing to them, which is neutral at worst. Fidgeting and clenching, on the other hand, always betray anxiety, and anxiety reads as weakness.

Similarly, Dana Carney and her colleagues found that we perceive touching one's head, face, or hands as low strength gestures. They are seen as signals of anxiety, and project weakness. This is most pronounced with the hands, especially with gestures that give the appearance of self-comforting, such as gently rubbing the back of one hand with the other. The emotional message it sends is that you are giving yourself a tiny reassuring hug. In short, it does not inspire a whole lot of confidence.

Wrists

People also often unwittingly project weakness through the angle of their wrists. Bending the wrist too far forward looks "limp-wristed," which is associated with being effeminate and physically weak ("limp-wristed" has also been used as a slur against gay men). Bending your wrist too far backward, on the other hand, unless you are actually in the middle of a push-up, also reads as weak—others see it as a defensive position. Hands bent back at the wrist is the position we instinctively assume when fending off something dangerous hurtling toward us. It is also the position we assume when we put up our hands in surrender, or when defending ourselves against an accusation. Even if your hands are kept down at your sides, that wrist angle still signals profound discomfort.

Strong Lines vs. Warm Curves

If strong gestures are defined by sharp, deliberate movements, warm gestures are soft, flowing, slow movements that emphasize curves rather than perpendicular lines. They do not cut the air—they move languidly through it like a swimmer doing the breast stroke. The emphasis on connecting with others rather than controlling one's body in space means there is more informality and leeway for gestures that are the equivalent of nonverbal chatter, which can project friendliness. This has its limits. Nonstop gesturing can be just as distracting or annoying as nonstop talking. The starting and stopping points are not as pronounced as with strong ones—sometimes there is a barely perceptible wiggle at the end of a gesture rather than stopping with martial arts precision. Warm gestures can also be small, because there is nothing gained by taking up lots of space. Imagine a person placing his hand slowly over his own heart to signal sorrow or compassion. We read warmth in gestures when they evoke common feelings and emotions.

The grandest warm gesture is with the arms curved open on either side, with the fingers similarly curved and open rather than cupped. Think of an Italian Renaissance painting of Jesus talking to his disciples, and he is probably in a pose like this. This gesture, paired with heart-centered posture and a compassionate facial expression, is how we actually welcome someone "with open arms." We see it all the time when a parent reaches out to a young child, or when we go to hug a long-lost friend or relative.

The Magic Ball

So enough about what not to do. Here is a surefire tip you can fall back on to project strength with your hands without scaring off small children. Call it "the ball" (or the energy ball, or the invisible ball, or the magic ball if you prefer). Imagine holding a volleyball with both hands between your waist and your hips, slightly away from your body. Curl your fingers as if there were actually a single sphere there, and hold it with your fingertips, not your palms. Now check yourself out in a mirror. From here, you can have the ball grow larger to the size of a beach ball you hold with your arms out, or smaller to the size of a marble you hold in one hand, the other hand falling to your side. You can hand the ball to the audience in front of you as you talk and give it a little shake to emphasize your point. As odd as this may sound, you have seen countless public speakers do it before you, and it looks as natural as can be. Should you ever find yourself in an awkward moment wondering what you ought to be doing with your hands, keep this ball in mind. The ball provides an infinite number of ways to make warm, round gestures with one or two hands. Generally speaking, palms are open, fingers curved, elbows free to extend away from the torso. Since there is an element of surrender in warmth, the wrists can bend slightly backward toward the "Put your hands up where I can see them" position. Remember, the wrists should not extend farther forward than the curvature of the ball—that looks awkward regardless of whether you are aiming to project strength or warmth.

Gestures and Character

There is a broader point about projecting strength with gesture, though, one that goes to the heart of why we use nonverbal signals to judge character. One might think the reason taking up more space projects more strength is that larger creatures have more physical power. After all, they have larger bodies under their direct control. Smaller people, according to this theory, can still project strength by taking up space to make themselves look bigger, like a blowfish or a cobra. But there is more to it. The more space we occupy and move through, the more attention we call to ourselves, and the more new things we encounter. When we feel strong and confident, we project our physical presence into space with ease. When we feel less strong, less confident, we are more reluctant to take up space because it makes us more vulnerable to hostile forces we might run across. Thus taking up space is a reasonable proxy for how confident you are feeling.

Both posture and gait are to a large degree under your conscious control: You can force your muscles to do whatever you tell them in the moment, no matter how you are feeling. Gesture is significantly more subject to the dictates of your own anxiety level, and facial expression is more susceptible still. Taking up more space only projects more strength if you appear comfortable doing it. If you appear to be anxious and trying too hard, you telegraph weakness. With posture and gait, you can fake it relatively easily just by deciding to, even if you are feeling anything but strong and confident. With gesture, and even more with facial expressions, that is a very tricky business.

There are specific gestures that hurt the ability to project warmth. Researchers from MIT, Northeastern, and Cornell have identified four behaviors that trigger concerns about trustworthiness: leaning away; crossing arms; touching, rubbing, or grasping hands together; and touching the face, stomach, or other parts of the body. To varying degrees, these demonstrate anxiety, self-protection, and avoidance, all of which are at odds with the openness associated with warmth. While no single gesture clearly corresponds to untrustworthiness, our brains recognize these four behaviors as warning signals. This ties back to our earlier point about the importance of having all of the nonverbal signals telling the same story as the words. When someone is lying, their inner emotional state is affected by their knowledge of the truth and their awareness that they are lying, and those emotions lead to nonverbal behavior inconsistent with their story.

Touch

Gestures are closely related to touch, which is integral to warmth. We mentioned earlier that the warmth-as-affection primary metaphor is shared by many cultures because the experience of being held by our parents as newborn infants is also our first encounter with affection. We use touch to express warmth in a variety of contexts, including joy, attraction, familiarity, and sympathy. Touch activates the orbitofrontal cortex, the same part of the brain that responds to tastes and odors. Our sense of it is so finely tuned that one study found that two people can accurately communicate love, gratitude, and compassion silently with blindfolds on, only touching hands.

People who are touch-averse in settings associated with warmth are perceived as cold. When we meet people who shrink when hugged by a close relative or friend, or who give a cursory little wave rather than shaking hands when introduced, we attribute those behaviors to a lack of social skills. At the far end of the scale are individuals with autism or Asperger's syndrome, who can have extreme touch aversion and react very negatively to unexpected contact, particularly from strangers.

Touch can also project strength. People in dominant positions at work or otherwise are more likely than subordinates to initiate touching, and those touches are often not reciprocated. (Imagine a stereotypical male boss backslapping his way through a room of underlings.) This makes sense intuitively—strong people have less reason to be concerned about the reactions they might provoke. In the reverse situation, it could be potentially risky for someone lower in the pecking order to make uninvited physical contact, since there could be adverse consequences. (At the extreme, the rich and famous employ bodyguards and entourages to prevent this from happening.) The connection between touch and strength brings us to the uncomfortable territory of power dynamics. There is a fine line between using a great handshake to project strength and touching people in a way that makes it clear you are asserting your dominance over them. The former is fine, whereas the latter is creepy.

Touch can take all sorts of forms, of course, from a tap on the shoulder to a bear hug. We'll stick to the most common ones used to project strength and warmth.

Handshakes

In a professional context, the handshake is your physical business card. Handshakes can tell us all kinds of things about people that go beyond what we can discern from appearances: assertiveness, physical strength, sensitivity, comfort level, and even class. (A bricklayer and a surgeon have very different hands, and you certainly feel a difference in the handshake of each.) While there are cultural exceptions (for example, Orthodox Jewish women do not shake hands with men who are strangers), handshakes are the most fundamental and widely accepted form of touching for people in a business setting. When we talk about making a deal on the basis of a handshake agreement, we are interpreting the handshake as a physical manifestation of a person's good word— a nonverbal expression of trust.

Getting this right takes some conscious focus, because you cannot be sure what kind of handshake you are in for, and it is important that your handshake match that of the person you are greeting. When you extend your hand, before you make contact, you want the muscles in your fingers already firing, both the flexors and the extensors, so you are ready to squeeze back as hard as you have to if this other person tries to crush your hand bones. If instead you get the dreaded "dead fish" handshake, you want to apply only a little pressure. You also have to be careful not just to leave your hand out for the other person to seize as he or she sees fit, lest you end up with just your fingers grasped and your thumb flailing helplessly alongside. To avoid this, be sure to push your hand forward as your hands meet so the web between your thumb and forefinger touches theirs and you can both get a good grip.

Sometimes you may encounter someone extending a hand at an unusual angle, with the palm facing either partially up or partially down. As with other gestures, palm up is warm and also submissive. You can shake it as is, or turn their hand up to an equal position, with your hands facing each other sideways. More important is the downward-facing palm. This is a dominance display, and it behooves you to meet the challenge it presents. You can meet this gesture where it is, offering your palm facing slightly upward, but squeeze a little harder than you get squeezed and use a firm pump of your arm to turn your palms back up to even the angles.

Eye contact is expected while shaking hands. This is a case where all the nonverbal signals have to align to send a congruent message. The value of a good handshake will be lost if you fail to match it with appropriate eye contact.

One piece of advice gleaned from hard-won handshaking experience: Watch out for big men and small women. There are large men out there who dearly miss playing high school football and will relish shaking your hand as a chance to show off their great physical strength. On the other hand, many petite professional women have also adopted the hard handshake as a discreet way to convey that although they are of smaller stature and may not naturally project much strength, they are not to be messed with. Keep those hand muscles flexed as you go in, and you will be ready for any grip strength you come across.

There are all kinds of variations on the theme, ranging from fancy two-handers that include using the left hand to grab the forearm just below the elbow to ever-changing street greetings that signal social exclusivity. (Either you are cool enough to know them or you are not.)

Fraternities and social groups like the Masons have had secret hand-shakes for centuries. People who master them project strength by possessing insider knowledge and warmth by sharing it with others who are in the club. Suffice it to say that high fives, fist bumps, and other pop culture staples all started out as expressions of cool before being co-opted by the mainstream.

Hugs

Hugs are obviously more intimate than handshakes, and for that reason they are more rare outside of settings with family and friends. A hug expresses more warmth than a handshake, but also carries more possibilities for misunderstanding, particularly in a professional setting. Hugging brings with it a host of gender issues and social expectations. As a general rule, if men are exchanging handshakes, women can rightly expect to do the same—and no more. Men who shake hands with male colleagues while soliciting hugs from female ones set up an uncomfortable double standard that reinforces presumptions about strength and warmth.

Man hugs (or "bro hugs") are a relatively new phenomenon, though they are now almost required among powerful politicians in social settings. The man hug is a handshake-hug combo that is less intimate than a full bear hug, but it projects both warmth and a comfort with one's masculinity ("See, I can hug a man and be straight") that reads as social confidence, or strength.

Cultural and Social Sensitivity

Cultures have different norms regarding what is acceptable or expected in terms of touch. Just as with gestures or eye contact, some are more touch oriented than others. For example, the air-kiss on both cheeks, which is French in origin and common among many cosmopolitan Europeans, is far more intimate in terms of closing distance than a simple hug—you are literally cheek-to-cheek with the person greeting you. In other cultures, male-female touching is a clear red zone that can put you and the person on the other end of the exchange in a difficult position.

There are clearly social and even legal lines that should not and cannot be crossed in terms of when it is appropriate to touch someone. In an American business context, for instance, handshakes are almost always appropriate with colleagues, but anything more intimate requires a careful reading of both the person involved and the prevailing social and cultural norms. A pat on the shoulder or upper arm (assuming it is clothed) is also generally acceptable as a way of showing support or positive good feeling, but remember that projection is in the eye of the receiver. Will he or she think you are making an unwelcome romantic advance? Expressing dominance? Acting like an attaboy glad-hander? These questions are doubly important in mixed-gender, mixed-status, and multicultural settings. Do not expect that your good intentions alone are enough to ensure that an unsolicited touch will not cause someone discomfort. The consequences of misjudging this can range from inadvertently creating distance and awkwardness to being slapped with a harassment charge. Emotional intelligence and keen attention to a person's words and nonverbal cues are essential to determining how your touch will be interpreted.

Face

The hiring process for career diplomats in the U.S. Department of State is an arduous one by design. The most famous hurdle is the Foreign Service exam, which is legendary for the breadth of topics it covers. But those who pass then face a different kind of challenge: a full day of interviews and simulations, where the interviewers are trained to show as little facial expression as possible. It is a thoroughly unnerving experience to try and project an appropriate level of energy and emotion in response to impassive interviewers whose faces are still as stones. We all look for cues in the faces of others, and they do the same with us.

The past few decades have brought a wealth of new science about facial expression and emotion, primarily pioneered by psychologist Paul Ekman and his cast of academic colleagues. Their research has proved not only interesting but useful—for example, by measurably improving law enforcement agents' lie-detection abilities. It has even penetrated pop culture, inspiring the TV crime drama *Lie to Me*, which featured a fictional Ekman-like scientist whose infallible lie-detection skills helped him aid the FBI in foiling bad guys.

Ekman and company found that humans convey basic emotions through facial expressions in the same way everywhere in the world. Each emotion has its own characteristic facial muscle movements that naturally and directly follow from the emotion's underlying physiological chemistry, and so our interpretation of them is not dependent on cultural context. This is profoundly different from our interpretations of gestures, which in some cases are very culturally specific (e.g., the okeydokey sign). Ekman first demonstrated this cross-cultural consistency in the 1960s by showing that tribesmen in Papua New Guinea who had never before encountered people from other cultures recognized basic emotions in pictures of foreigners' faces.

The Face of Strength

If you compare the full facial expression of three emotions—anger, disgust, and happiness—you will notice one consistent aspect across all three expressions. The brow is lowered in anger and disgust, but not in happiness. The mouth is different in all three. But in all three emotions, the lower eyelid is flexed slightly upward in a half-squint. To your conscious mind, this feature may seem tiny. But the large occipital lobe at the back of our brains is full of highly specialized neural circuitry dedicated to spotting these tiny differences and interpreting them for you at a subconscious level. We may not be able to explain what we are seeing, but we understand the expression without any explanation.

The emotional effect of flexed lower eyelids with the rest of the face relaxed is somewhat ambiguous, but what comes across clearly is an intense interest, a sharp focus and determination. For our purposes, this flexed lower eyelid is the purest form of facial projection of strength. Colloquially, we speak of this expression as showing "steely" eyes, or sometimes "flinty" eyes, to reflect the unyielding will beneath. Sometimes we say this look seems like the person is boring holes into you with their eyes. In fact, in some cultures this look is called the "evil eye."

The patron saint of this expression is one Mr. Clint Eastwood. In roles like Dirty Harry and in his Westerns, Eastwood famously wore it with flexed eyebrows to convey intense disgust. But even in pictures of him smiling, or not making any particular expression at all, his lower lids are always flexed, always signaling intensity.

The Face of Warmth

The best place to begin decoding the visual elements of warmth is the face, and the number one way we project warmth is by smiling. Smiling is a fundamental means of nonverbal communication that is deeply rooted in human behavior around the world. Babies everywhere bond with their mothers through smiling. We effortlessly understand smiles from people who don't speak our language. Cultural norms regarding smiling may differ, but it's still a universal form of expression.

We attribute all kinds of good things to people who smile at us, such as happiness, attractiveness, sociability, flirtatiousness, and success, among others. Smiling can even create a halo effect, which causes us to make a wide range of positive associations with people who smile at us. Teachers are more likely to call on students who smile at them. Restaurant waitstaff and bartenders know this as well as anyone: They get better tips when they smile at customers.

Smiles are also contagious. If you look at a picture of a smiling person, you know how to mimic the expression you see. When someone smiles at you, your brain remembers what it feels like when you wear that expression, and it makes you happy to remember that feeling, even if just a little bit. So you're inclined to smile back. This reciprocity happens without even thinking about it. To put this simply, we tend to like people who smile at us because they make us feel good. When Louis Armstrong sang, "When you're smiling, the whole world smiles with you," he knew what he was talking about. It's not just a greeting card platitude—our brains actually do some very rapid processing that enables us to recognize smiles and get that good feeling.

It is one thing to experience another person's smile, and it is another to have a smile on your own face. Smiling elevates your mood and affects your mental function, in part by increasing your sense of cognitive ease. As psychologist Daniel Kahneman notes, you can actually trigger this feeling by putting a pen between your teeth and forcing the facial muscles around your mouth into a smiling position. In this case, just as with power poses and strength, you can run the warmth circuits in reverse.

So smiling is a very good thing for many reasons, but all smiles are not created equal. It's important to understand which smiles help us project warmth as opposed to those that do other things. In order to do that, we need to get under the hood and look closely at how smiling actually works.

There are more than three dozen muscles in the face, most of which are paired symmetrically on the left and right sides. The primary muscle around your mouth that makes the shape of a smile is called the zygomaticus major, which does the work of pulling the other muscles around it into place. That is only half the deal, though, because a genuine smile happens in two places: at the corners of the mouth and around the eyes.

This real smile, sometimes called a Duchenne smile (after French researcher Guillaume Duchenne, who identified it in the mid-nineteenth century), uses both the zygomaticus major and the orbicularis oculi muscle around the eyes. The so-called twinkle in the eyes is actually a squinty expression that happens from contracting muscles around the eyes. A fake smile, on the other hand, only raises the corners of the mouth, with nothing happening in the upper half of the face. Even little kids are not fooled by this. In fact, babies become adept at forming both Duchenne and non-Duchenne smiles pretty early in life. Research even suggests that when people routinely fake smiles, it makes them feel not only inauthentic, but stressed and fatigued.

A smile has a few aspects to it: how quickly it emerges, how long it lasts, and its actual shape on your face. Each of these tells us different things about the feelings behind it. For instance, a deliberate smile shows up more quickly than a voluntary smile. We are all very good at spotting this. Imagine meeting someone in a social situation whose smile turns on and off like a light switch. That has a very different emotional resonance than when you say something amusing that brings a smile to the same person's face. The latter smile happens more slowly, and you perceive it as more genuine. It projects more warmth because you shared a good feeling in that moment together.

Similarly, we learn a lot from the duration of a smile. A smile is like a story: It has a beginning, middle, and end. The expression spreads across your face, gets widest in the middle, and then gradually recedes. We perceive more warmth from long smiles than from quick ones, but we also perceive that someone is faking it when they maintain the widest part of the smile for too long. The warmest smiles last a long time and have a natural transition between beginning, middle, and end.

It's important to point out here that we don't smile only to project warmth. We also smile to express joy, politeness, dominance, anger, ridicule, concern, and a host of other emotions. Some of these project strength rather than warmth. We even use smiles to deceive people, whether it's to lure someone into trusting us or to say yes even when we don't mean it. ("Your new haircut looks *great*.") Where warmth is concerned, think of smiles that demonstrate agreement, familiarity, empathy, concern, and attraction. It's relatively easy to imagine a range of facial expressions that convey each of these emotions.

There are also polite smiles that make the pretense of expressing warmth. In certain parts of the American South, for example, smiling when greeting someone in public is a social convention, regardless of how a person feels. The resulting expression is a jack-o'-lantern grin that pulls the corners of the mouth up and flashes the teeth. It's just for appearances—nobody is fooled—and as a result it does not actually project warmth.

A fallen figure from the past decade of American politics who often wore the southern smile was Senator John Edwards. We had an opportunity to see Edwards up close in the autumn of 2003 when the news program *Hardball with Chris Matthews* did a series of live broadcasts from Harvard Kennedy School featuring a different Democratic candidate each week. Those of us in the studio audience saw something that the viewing audience could not: As soon as the red light went on, so did Senator Edwards's smile. When the segment ended, his face went completely flat, registering no emotion whatsoever. He did not interact with anyone—not Matthews, the host, not the crowd of college students surrounding him (who were potential supporters he could have been courting). We knew everything we needed to know about Edwards at that moment: He was highly skilled at faking it.

Don't Worry About Me

Another smile we run across frequently in our practice is what we refer to as the Gomer Pyle. (If you prefer a more current pop culture reference, see Kenneth on *30 Rock*.) In this smile, the eyebrows are raised about halfway up the forehead. If we cover up the mouth of someone making this face and just look at the top half of their face, we see something else: From the nose up, this looks like surprise, maybe with even a hint of panic in it. As very few people walk around looking surprised or frightened on a regular basis, that is not a big concern. But a common facial expression involving those same raised eyebrows and upper eyelids is central to our story. Imagine you are meeting a cute child for the first time, and the child is related either to you or to a friend of yours, so you want to make a good impression. The problem is you are a complete stranger, and you are five times the kid's size, so you are at risk of scaring the kid. What face do you make? On your mouth, you definitely wear a big smile, signaling that you mean well, as we will talk about more when we discuss nonverbal warmth. But you might also raise those eyebrows high and open your eyes wide. Why is this? You are not surprised, and you are certainly not afraid of the kid physically. But you show a look of surprise anyway, because by signaling that you are off guard—by projecting low strength—you convey to this much smaller creature that you are not a threat to them and there is no need to fear you.

A very similar signal is used among our primate cousins to facilitate social relations. Certain primate societies are very hierarchical, with the alpha male on top and all the other males waiting to depose him in order to gain the right to mate with the local females. When the alpha saunters by a subordinate male, the subordinate will offer a smile with eyebrows raised high, doing everything he facially can to convey that he is a friend, not a threat, and that there's no need for the alpha to beat him up to show who is boss.

That is all well and good for adults trying to befriend babies and primates trying to avoid getting pummeled. Problems arise when adult humans use this expression with other adults in an attempt to be ingratiating. Opening the eyes wide, raising the brows, and leaving them high with a smile on the mouth signals "not a threat" very effectively—so effectively that it seems weak and naive, which people do not respect.

The Strong Smile

Smiling does not have to project weakness. There is such a thing as a strong smile, and it may well be the most powerful single technique we know. We have already talked about flinty eyes, a.k.a. flexing the lower eyelids. Pair flinty eyes with a smile around the mouth—it can be open-mouthed or closed. And finally, don't stop: Leave that look on your face as your regular, default expression—wear it permanently, except when you have a specific reason to make a different face.

You will find this facial expression wherever you find remarkably and annoyingly charismatic people: It is common among top salespeople, captains of industry, acclaimed classroom teachers, notoriously successful daters, and two-term presidents. It is the small smile of social success. Wear it habitually and you might not get elected president immediately, but good things may begin to come your way. Paired with a smile, the strong eyes are often said to have a twinkle in them, or a mischievous look to them. And people who wear this look on their face—they are called cool.

Remember our central riddle: We want to project strength to be respected, and we want to project warmth to be loved—so how can we do both when most everything we do to project strength hurts our warmth, and vice versa? This expression—the flinty smile, the twinkle in the eye—projects both at once: strength and warmth together.

Smiling with an Accent

As biologically basic as smiling is, it does vary across cultures in frequency, meaning, and even shape. As Yale psychologist Marianne La-

France explains in *Lip Service*, a British smile shows the lower teeth more than an American smile. (Take a look at a picture of Prince Charles.) Americans are far more likely than Europeans to smile at strangers. Some Europeans read this as a sign of naïveté, which speaks to a lack of strength rather than a projection of warmth. Within the United States, southerners smile more than northerners, as we noted above. And sometimes it is difficult to interpret the smile of a person from a foreign culture. For instance, LaFrance notes that many Americans have a hard time reading Japanese smiles, particularly those that express something other than a good feeling inside. Smiling to project warmth may be universal, but as she points out, each culture does so with a different accent.

There are also gender differences worth noting. Women smile more than men, which fits with our presumptions about strength and warmth. Women are also *expected* to smile more than men, and are viewed more negatively when they do not. Since men smile less than women, their smiles can be perceived as saying more about how they feel, or can be interpreted as expressing greater intensity of happiness.

Smiling Lessons

In our client work, we often end up talking with highly intelligent and accomplished people about when and how to smile. One such incident happened in the summer of 2006. A campaign manager working a long-shot congressional race realized his candidate had a problem. The candidate, a smart, hardworking state senator, had the right resume and the right background. He was a family man with a squeaky clean past. He also had the discipline to succeed, and was willing to take direction, unlike many of the egomaniacs who fancy a run for Congress. In all these respects, he was a dream candidate.

This exceptional professionalism came at a price. The candidate was genuinely fired up about the problems he saw in the country, and he could articulate his arguments with machine-like precision. But he could not shift gears easily and show voters that he was also a father, a husband, a son, a friend, a neighbor—a regular person, in other words, and not just an ambitious politician.

When we and Seth met with the candidate, the first thing he did was describe his strengths and weaknesses. He understood the problem, which encouraged us right away. We watched a campaign video and asked him to note each time he smiled. Then we sat in silence and waited as the minutes ticked by. Finally, during an attack on his opponent, there was a quick flash of a tight-lipped grin. We paused the video. The point registered immediately: He could not expect to win friends by grinning as he blowtorched the opposition. We needed to find a way to help the candidate share a wider range of emotions with his audiences.

How do you teach someone to smile? The short answer is that you do not. One of our core convictions is that a genuine smile can only come from a genuine emotion that you feel on the inside. It cannot be manufactured. An actor with years of classical training may be able to gin up a smile on command, but the rest of us lack those skills. We call these two opposing methods "inside-out" and "outside-in." As we saw earlier, you can either fake strength or use techniques like power poses to trigger genuine feelings of strength. But fake smiles do not fool anyone. The best way to project warmth is the inside-out approach: If you feel warmly about something, you will smile naturally.

One thing we had noticed about our candidate was that he beamed when telling us about his son, who was about to start his senior year of high school. This gave us an opening. We suggested that he begin one section of his stump speech with a sentence or two about his son's future, and then connect that to his position on a specific issue. After some gentle persuading, he decided to give it a try. We turned on the video camera. As he said his son's name, his brow and jaw loosened, and he broke into a proud father's smile. He was no longer just a candidate. He was also a regular guy who conveyed real feeling when he talked about his family. This little touch did not instantly convert him into a lovable teddy bear, but it gave him a way to connect with the emotional concerns of the people in his district. The angry fire breather could also convey a positive vision of the world he wanted for his children.

The Phone Booth

More broadly, the practical challenge of projecting your strength and warmth to others is to get yourself in the right mood at the right moment. You want to get into a frame of mind beyond your anxieties, where you are using appropriate signals to express genuine feelings of strength and warmth that you have conjured within yourself. Most of us get to this place once in a while, often when things are really going our way, and sometimes for no apparent reason at all. Afterward, we remember how that felt: like anything was possible and everything was all right. One of the most powerful things you can do to get yourself in the state you want is just to step away from whatever company you are in and take a moment on your own to remember what that feels like, to conjure up the memory as vividly as you can, and bring that feeling and attitude into the present moment. Some of our clients even carry a picture or video clip that reminds them of their perfect moment to help bring it back to them. Like Clark Kent ducking into the phone booth, after a moment's reflection, you emerge with the poise and energy of your more confident alter ego.

Eye Contact

We're not done with the face just yet. Eye contact is a crucial way to convey visual warmth. Imagine a first date over dinner at a restaurant. We expect lingering gazes when it is going well, and, conversely, we know something is not quite right when a date spends more time looking at the food (or the iPhone or the person at the next table) than at us. Even beyond romantic attraction, eye contact is essential to warmth, whether you're wooing people to your side or establishing mutual understanding. There's a reason for the old saying about seeing eye-to-eye: It means sharing a common perspective.

Good eye contact is also critical for projecting strength. Dominant people typically make a lot of eye contact, and it can be highly aggressive: Picture two men standing nose-to-nose in a staring contest. At the other end of the spectrum, a lack of eye contact can signal weakness or a lack of confidence, especially when someone looks down toward the ground. That is not a universal rule, though: A high-status, dominant person might also choose to avoid making eye contact as a way of signaling disrespect.

We also interpret the absence of eye contact as an indication that someone is not sharing with us. You wouldn't lend money to a friend who couldn't look you in the eye when explaining why he needed a few bucks until his next paycheck. We don't need social science to tell us what every parent knows when a child won't make eye contact after telling a whopper of a lie. Averting your gaze from someone certainly diminishes warmth, even if you look away because you're embarrassed to have been caught staring into the eyes of someone you find attractive. In that case, looking away signals vulnerability, but it does not score you any points for warmth unless the person you're with feels the same way. As with smiles, we are all intuitive masters at spotting inauthenticity with regard to eye contact, and we notice the same kinds of things as with smiles: quickness to connect, intensity, and duration. And we read nervousness and social discomfort in people who are uncomfortable with eye contact.

One caveat about eye contact: The rules for it vary widely around the world. In some Asian cultures, for instance, direct eye contact can be perceived as a form of aggression or disrespect. When Matt taught grade school many years ago, he had a Chinese-American student whose parents were immigrants, and this boy had a great deal of difficulty making eye contact with teachers. At school, he faced an expectation that he would look adults directly in the eye, while at home his parents and relatives read this as a sign of disrespect. Similarly, the rules for eye contact between men and women who are not family members are different in many Muslim societies than in the United States. We do not pretend to understand all these subtleties, and the guidance we have given is based on our experience advising people in American business culture. Being mindful of local customs is critical for getting nonverbal cues right, and this is particularly true with eye contact.

Voice

A few decades ago, a young woman named Karen began a job as a receptionist at a law firm. She became familiar with a few dozen people who called the office on a regular basis, including a lawyer named Phil who worked at another local firm. He had a deep, resonant voice that sounded confident and relaxed, and he always asked questions about her day in a way that suggested he really cared about the answers. Over time their exchanges stretched from thirty-second handoffs to conversations lasting several minutes. Karen started to look forward to his calls, which were increasingly frequent. She realized she had developed a phone crush on Phil.

Finally the day arrived when Phil had to come to Karen's office for a meeting. She fussed over her appearance while getting ready for work that morning, wanting to look good for her first real-life encounter with her phone pal. That morning, she watched anxiously from the reception desk as two men approached the front entrance a few minutes before ten o'clock. One was a dark-haired, tall, athletic man in his thirties. Her heart raced. She was so certain this must be Phil that she hardly noticed his companion, a thickset fiftyish man. As the door opened, she felt a big smile radiate across her face, her gaze fixed on the younger man. Before she could say a word, she heard the unmistakable voice that she had come to know over many months.

"Karen," the older man said, beaming at her. "I'm Phil. It's wonderful to meet you in person."

While visual signals are the most powerful means of communicating emotion, the voice also conveys a great range and depth of feeling. For nearly a hundred years, radio broadcasts have served as a testament to the voice's ability to express everything from astonishment ("The Giants win the pennant! The Giants win the pennant!") to sorrow ("It is with great sadness that I bring you the news that . . ."). Much as Paul Ekman's work identified facial expressions that are universally recognized across cultures, researchers have found the same is true of vocal expressions. While there is some notable variation—emotions such as joy and sadness are more accurately identifiable than lower-energy states such as shame and disgust—we are generally very good at figuring out how someone feels based on vocal cues.

Our ability to identify emotions in voices has been well understood for decades by telemarketers, who rely on a technique known as "smiling and dialing"—literally smiling as they talk on the phone—to boost sales. Studies show that people can accurately "hear" a smile in your voice through the phone, and they picture that smile on your face as they listen.

On the other hand, people can also hear stress in your voice, and that sounds neither warm nor strong. Computer software can hear that stress too: Duke University professors William Mayew and Mohan Venkatachalam have developed a program that can detect stress in the voices of CEOs during investor calls with a high degree of accuracy. In other words, we know warmth and strength—or the lack thereof—when we hear it.

Many clients tell us they hate the way their voices sound. It is jarring to hear a recording of your voice if you are not accustomed to it. There is a straightforward reason for that. When we hear our voices in our heads, the vibrations travel from our vocal cords directly through a couple of inches of neck flesh up to the tiny bones in our ears. When someone else hears your voice, they hear how it vibrates through the sinus cavities around your nose and then out through the air to their ears. That is what accounts for the difference between the extra-nasal version of your voice you hear on tape and how you think you sound. What you hear when you play back a recording of your voice is how you sound to the rest of the world.

The basic elements of vocal delivery include pitch, volume, rate, and tone. A metaphor for thinking about the different parts of the voice is a synthesizer keyboard, which allows you to manipulate each element in isolation and change the blend among them.

Pitch refers to how high or low a note someone's voice sounds. A low-pitch delivery conveys strength, while a high pitch can signal excitement ("We won!"), uncertainty, or nervousness. For men, having a deep voice can project a sense of dominance among other men and attractiveness among women. The voices of professional announcers and advertising pitchmen are nearly always deep and resonant. When we ask our clients to think of someone who projects vocal strength, the name that comes up more than any other is James Earl Jones, the voice of Darth Vader. Having said that, this does not mean your voice has to be in the basso profundo range to project strength. Vocal range works much the same way that height works with posture. Just like being tall, having a naturally deep voice helps project strength, but you do not need a deep voice to be taken seriously. Each of us has our own vocal range, and others can tell from our tone whether we are speaking from a high or low pitch within that range, regardless of gender, age, or other factors.

While strength corresponds with low pitch, warmth is not simply the opposite. Instead, we recognize warmth through variation in pitch. Imagine the melody to a lullaby or a sentimental song like "Somewhere Over the Rainbow": It goes up and down in pitch before resolving somewhere in the middle. At the other end of the spectrum, the vocal delivery that projects the least warmth is a monotone. (Remember, warmth and strength are not opposites.)

Volume is generally connected with strength, as we expect loud voices from traditionally strong figures, such as members of the military or police. Loudness is manly, and research shows that volume corresponds with attractiveness. (Note: Guys, please do not shout at your date—we will discuss courtship later.) There are exceptions to the link between loudness and strength, but as a rule that works only for people who possess so much authority or influence that others feel compelled to listen closely to their voices. If you are not already the Godfather or E. F. Hutton, good luck with that.

Softness can signal either compassion or timidity. It can be soothing (think of a parent with an infant), which we perceive as warmth, or it can simply come across as a lack of strength. If someone is too timid to speak up clearly or forcefully, we judge that as weakness or ineffectiveness. Context is critical, of course, to interpreting how volume will be judged. In a potential romantic situation, for example, the inability to turn down a loud voice could be a deal-breaking turnoff.

Rate refers to how quickly a person speaks. It is more than simply a measure of raw words per second, because it also includes the use of silence or pauses, and fluency. As the late pianist Arthur Rubinstein once said, "The notes I handle no better than many pianists. But the pauses between the notes—ah, that is where the art resides."

The way we perceive rate of speech is complex, because a rapid-fire delivery can demonstrate either high verbal competence (think of a college debate team) or nervousness ("I don't know, officer, I was just mind-ing my own business when . . ."). When we describe someone as a fast talker, we also associate that with con men or swindlers who are trying to put something past us. On the other hand, a slower, more deliberate rate of speech can suggest either confidence ("The state of the Union is sound") or the inability to think on one's feet.

In other words, rate of speech by itself does not necessarily project strength or warmth. Together with using low pitch and good volume, however, adopting a slower rate to deliver a key point is very effective. If you are zeroing in on something important, the technique of slowing down while speaking loudly and clearly creates a sense of drama and adds emphasis to critical words or phrases.

When working with clients, we often talk about the technique of "landing the punch"—using vocal pacing to stick a key point. We advise doing any needed explanation first, then ending with a short statement that sums up the key point. By delivering this last line at a measured pace and then pausing afterward for effect, you underline the important bit, and your pause lets the audience contemplate that for a second before you move on so it really sinks in.

Tone is perhaps best understood as the musical quality of a voice. This can vary widely. Think again of a synthesizer: It can make a note sound brassy, muted, smooth, choppy, or any number of different qualities. Is a speaker barking his words like a seal, or is he employing a breathy delivery that suggests a candlelight dinner for two? Control over tone of voice comes from understanding the different acoustic qualities associated with delivery from the diaphragm, chest, throat, or nose (sinus cavities). Projecting from the diaphragm makes the fullest use of the breath, giving it the most resonance, whereas talking through the nose makes the thinnest, least resonant sound.

Finally, related to both tone and rate is a quality known somewhat alarmingly as "attack." Technically, this means how quickly the sound reaches its full volume. Does the speaker spit out words abruptly, in stac-

cato fashion, or do words flow together smoothly? Imagine the difference in delivery between a drill sergeant and a schoolteacher. Even if the
volume, rate, and pitch were the same, the clipped tone of the drill sergeant would be much different than the softer one of the teacher; faster
attack conveys more strength.

While each of these elements contributes to the strength or warmth
of our voices, there is more to it, because most of the talking we do is in
dialogue with others, not monologue. Working with Alex Pentland of
MIT's Media Lab, Tanzeem Choudhury, a former MIT graduate student
now teaching at Cornell, developed a wearable device called a "sociometer," which measures vocal signals and behaviors, such as turn-taking
in conversation. By collecting massive amounts of individual data from
the sociometer, they and their colleagues have identified distinctive patterns of vocal variation, such as influence, mimicry, and consistency,
that serve as social signals in a conversation.

Influence in this context can be thought of as control of the conversation. Who sets the pace and dictates the direction? Is turn-taking equal?
Who asks the questions and who gives the answers? How long does each
person hold the floor? Is one person pushing or using short pauses to
drive the speed of the conversation? The person who sets the agenda in
this regard is exercising a form of strength through vocal tone.

Mimicry is just what it sounds like: copying the patterns of another
person. In this case, we are not talking about blatantly copying a person's accent and diction like a comedian. This is more subtle (and less
obnoxious). This conversational pattern will often include both vocal
and visual cues, such as nodding. Mimicry is a means of establishing
empathy, by literally sounding similar to our conversational partner.
This is a very practical warmth technique. For instance, research shows
that waitstaff at restaurants get better tips when they mirror the patterns of the guests they are serving. American teenagers are masters of
vocal mimicry, as any parent of one can attest. They pick up speech pat-

terns and inflections from their friends and end up sounding just like them, thereby signaling membership in their chosen tribe.

Consistency refers to how much a speaker sticks to a single pattern of tone, rate, pitch, and volume variation throughout a conversation. If you are completely clear on your point, and not listening to other people, you will generally speak with great consistency. This projects strength: You may or may not be influencing your conversation partners, but you are giving no quarter to them. At the other end of the spectrum, vocal variability signals openness to others' ideas—warmer and less strong.

The energy level in your voice generally tracks your overall physical energy level, and being either too lethargic or too jittery works against you. If you sit on your hands and constrict your movements, it is hard to manufacture a high level of energy with your voice. When working with clients on how to conduct good teleconferences, we encourage them to move and gesture a little more than usual on the phone to keep up their vocal energy, since they do not have a visual.

There is no one ideal combination of vocal elements; the best approach depends on how much strength and warmth a particular situation calls for. In a phone sales setting, Pentland found that low consistency—lots of variability in emphasis, which creates a sense of openness to the person on the other end of the line—coupled with active listening is a good predictor of sales success. This speaks once again to the importance of establishing empathy, or warmth, rather than delivering a canned pitch. Similarly, people negotiating their salary and benefits were found to do better when they traded short utterances with their counterpart—"Yup" in reply to "Done?"—in the first five minutes of conversation. In a job interview setting, when a potential employer is making decisions about competency and fit within the organization, the most successful candidates displayed both strength patterns like high degrees of consistency and influence and the warmth pattern of mimicry.

Make It Stop!

In our client work, we encounter lots of bad vocal habits. Two of the most common are filler and uptalk. *Filler* is speech that fills in otherwise natural pauses, such as "um," "uh," "like," and "you know." Filler has an important conversational purpose: It is a way of saying, "I'm not done speaking yet—just hold on a second while I assemble my next sentence." Overuse of filler detracts from perceptions of strength, especially in, like, professional settings. While different workplaces have varying tolerances and expectations, we have found that heavy use of filler signals some combination of youth, inexperience, informality, and lack of polish.

Overcoming this habit requires becoming comfortable pausing between words or sentences. The trick is to practice leaving silences and notice the effect that these pauses have on the people who are listening. The point is not just to speak without the filler; it is to learn to replace it with pauses.

As a practical matter, the best way to rid your own speech of filler is to record yourself speaking in the offending manner and then force yourself to listen to it. It can make you cringe, but in this case that is a good thing: That squirmy, shameful feeling is your subconscious rewiring itself to stop doing that. This is the fastest route to ridding yourself of this sort of mannerism.

Uptalk is a relatively new term that describes a speech pattern that ends a declarative phrase or sentence by going up in pitch, as is typical when asking a question. (Some people still refer to this as sounding like a Valley Girl.) The emphasis on the final "up" syllable is usually a nonverbal way of checking on mutual understanding, as if you had finished your statement and then added a follow-up question: "Do you understand what I mean?" This rising final tone is an ambiguous signal, though, and especially when a speaker is not projecting much strength otherwise, it is often interpreted not as checking for comprehension, but as submissive approval seeking: "Is that okay with you? May I keep talking?" This creates the impression that the speaker is uncertain about things that should not be in doubt, and this undermines their strength. Uptalk is nearly endemic in certain circles among people under thirty-five, and is more common among women than men. We have worked with professionals from the best universities and most elite organizations in the world who consistently undermine themselves with uptalk. It is a definitive generational marker that pegs someone as young, informal, unsure, or inexperienced.

If you hear yourself doing it often, recording it and forcing yourself to endure listening to yourself is once again the best way forward. If you do hear yourself slipping into uptalk while you speak, the easiest way to recover is to end the next sentence with a solid period, lowering your vocal pitch on the final syllable and then adding a beat pause for good measure. This suggests that you deliberately used the uptalk to mark that idea as raising a question, and now you have supplied the answer. This is actually a perfectly respectable rhetorical device, using the question in your voice like a rhetorical question to pique your audience's interest. As long as you do not leave them hanging, you still look strong.

Many people have a lot of concerns about their accents. It is certainly true that an unfamiliar accent or regionalism immediately conveys that you are "not from around here." (*My Cousin Vinny* was essentially a feature-length gag based on this premise.) As far as strength and warmth are concerned, though, a strong accent can cut either way, depending on the situation and the associations that a particular accent carries with it. It can be interpreted as a mark of authenticity—you sound like a regular person, not a fancy-pants who puts on airs—which can add warmth. In another setting, particularly if accompanied by poor diction and lots of filler, it might be taken for a lack of polish, which can undermine perceptions of strength.

Some accents have inherently strong or warm qualities to them, at least to American ears. "Ahnold" Schwarzenegger made a living exploiting a strong-sounding Austrian accent that matched his bodybuilder physique. Posh British accents convey sophistication and intelligence that can bleed into arrogance. On the warmth side, Brazilian, Hawaiian, and some Caribbean accents have soft, lilting cadences that convey a sense of intimacy. If you are aware that your accent has a distinct strength or warmth to it, you may want to consider balancing in other areas.

Ridding yourself of an accent takes an immense amount of time and effort (and money, if you use coaching assistance). Unless you are deeply committed to that process, our general recommendation is to *own* your accent and your voice: Understand the associations it carries with it, for better and for worse, and incorporate them into the overall balance of the impression you make. Popular culture is full of people who have made unconventional voices work for them, from Bob Dylan to Ira Glass to Roseanne Barr. Filler, uptalk, poor diction, and halting fluency are usually more harmful than accents to your perceived strength, and more easily corrected.

As all of this suggests, the voice is a complex instrument, which is why it is capable of conveying so much emotion. When thinking about the role of voice in projecting strength and warmth, remember above all the importance of congruence: It should be sending the same signals as the visual nonverbal cues and the words.

By the way, there is a coda to the true story that kicked off this section. Karen and Phil have been happily married for nearly thirty years.

Mirroring

For all the visual and vocal cues we just covered, the big question is context: How and when should you use them? If you want to show someone how warm you are, it is important to realize there is more to that than just being yourself. That does not mean you should say or do things that do not feel right or honest—not least because your inauthenticity would probably show. But projecting warmth, showing that you care about how someone feels, means attending and responding to their signals too.

One way to establish warmth nonverbally is called "mirroring," which essentially means offering your conversation partner the same kind of nonverbal cues they are offering you. When we shake hands, for instance, we deliberately match the person we are greeting by making the same gesture at the same time. But that is not the only way mirroring works. Mirroring means tuning in to the signals this person prefers to use in conveying strength and warmth, and respecting their preference by using similar kinds of signals yourself.

Meeting strength with strength is straightforward: Stand a little taller and take up space, meet the gaze of the person you are addressing with a confident smile and level eyebrows—all the strength nonverbals we talked about earlier. Warmth too is easily dialed up: A genuine smile and more variety in your vocal inflection usually goes a long way. Offering small affirmative nods—occasionally, not steadily like a bobblehead—can also serve as a mirroring gesture to telegraph empathy.

If you find yourself with someone projecting less strength, the same principle applies, as long as you do not go so far as to appear weak. Ease off your strength and take up a little less space. Gesture less or less broadly, adapt your posture just a bit to match, and follow their vocal volume and tonal range.

Similarly, if someone is not very warm, do not reciprocate with coldness or rudeness, but respectfully remain a little more withdrawn. It is fine to be slightly friendlier if that comes naturally to you, but turning up gregariousness to draw out an introvert can have the opposite effect: Introverts are often skeptical of conspicuous displays of social skills that can be read as strength.

Remember, as simple as this sounds—mirroring strength and warmth, dialing each up and down—it can be hard to do in the moment because our natural instincts pull us the other way: We are naturally inclined to become more dominant around submissive people and more submissive around dominant people. The best way forward is to follow the lead of the person you are meeting—not to be manipulative or condescending, but to be respectful, with a goal of trying to make them comfortable with you.

One final note: If you happen to be a talented actor, amateur or otherwise, watch yourself here. The point of mirroring is to respectfully affirm the emotional state of the person you are with. That means adjusting your default tendencies in the direction of the person you are talking with. But if your mirroring is so thorough and spot-on that it starts to look like you are lampooning someone, you can get yourself in a lot of trouble very quickly. As we mentioned earlier, one particularly slippery spot is around accents: If the person you are speaking with has a pronounced accent, feel free to match the pace and tonal variation of your speech, but be careful not to start pronouncing your vowels differently or you will sound like you're doing a bad impression.

Style

"To rebel one must wear the right uniform."

—Devan Marques

After decades during which no respectable man would be caught dead outside without a hat, one man came along and changed that. His preference for two-button suits and Ray-Ban sunglasses demonstrated a conception of himself as modern, helping him radiate a sense of relaxed confidence that suggested his comfort with being the most powerful person in the world. His effortless appearance also helped mask problems that he went to great lengths to conceal: He suffered from constant back pain and a debilitating adrenal condition called Addison's disease.

John F. Kennedy and First Lady Jacqueline Kennedy were so notable for their personal style that they became enduring media icons. They broke long-standing conventions and forged new ones. Whatever they wore, they wore with confidence and grace, making every detail an expression of their personalities. Both understood how appearances shaped perceptions, and they skillfully used style to enhance their public images. (Mrs. Kennedy made such an impression during a visit to France in 1961 that President Kennedy joked, "I am the man that accompanied Jacqueline Kennedy to Paris.")

Fashion shapes the impressions we make in a number of ways. If you carry yourself with enough confidence, you can make whatever you wear seem fashionable. At the same time, when you wear the right clothes for the occasion, they make you feel ready to take on whatever challenges come your way. One study found that just putting on a white lab coat makes people start acting like rigorous scientific thinkers, so much so that they even make fewer errors on a test that measures sustained attention. But if people are instead told the coat is for painting houses, putting it on does not improve their test scores at all. The old cliché "the clothes make the man" has more truth to it than its author probably realized.

A client of ours recently had the opportunity to address the CEO of a global bank about an initiative she was working on for a nonprofit organization. It was her first meeting in a corporate boardroom, and though she had never worn a "power suit" before, she recognized the importance of wearing the right costume for the situation. When she suited up, she knew she would impress and felt ready to take the boardroom by storm. The experience of putting those clothes on helped transform her mind-set from that of outsider to that of someone who belonged in the corridors of power.

Because people choose what they wear, those style choices are reflections of character. When people notice someone's appearance, they draw on cultural associations ("That dress makes her look trashy") as well as more specific judgments about the fit between personal style and natural attributes ("Didn't anyone ever tell him that heavyset people shouldn't wear horizontal stripes?"). Style may strike some people as shallow, artificial, or otherwise unworthy of serious consideration, but there is plenty of evidence that it matters where judgments of strength and warmth are concerned.

A female friend of ours has a pair of boots that attract lots of admiring attention whenever she wears them. They are not flashy or bizarre or extra-sexy—they are just appealing, the kind of thing that people notice and feel moved to say, "I like your boots!" What is it about these boots that gets people talking? They are black leather—not shiny patent leather, but still dark—and tough like a motorcycle jacket, and they go up high, almost past the calf. On the other hand, they have a simple round toe like a child's Mary Jane shoe, and all the way up the side runs a row of big round buttons, each a perfect dollop of the same black leather.

In large part, clothes project more or less strength or warmth based on cultural associations. Mandals (sandals for guys) are associated with hippies, pastel-colored golf shirts are associated with well-off strivers, and work boots are associated with working-class guys. Our friend's boots don't fit with any one cultural type, but they mix and match beautifully. The black leather reaching up her leg is tough, intimidating, aggressive, like motorcycle or combat boots—very strong. But the cute buttons and little-girl toe are adorable and warm. Put all these things together in one pair of boots, and you have some sassy footwear.

Style has always been deeply wrapped up in class and status distinctions. For centuries royalty and nobility used style as a means of setting themselves apart from common folk. Wearing clothes, jewelry, or fashions only available to those with great wealth was a way of projecting strength. Certain luxury items still serve that function. Status cues today are also more nuanced than simple divisions between haves and have-nots. For example, thrift stores became hip years ago among artsy types, which led some designers to try and capture a secondhand look and feel in their clothes. And even people who hate the idea of fashion signal their status as regular folks who do not put on airs by wearing simple jeans and T-shirts everywhere.

Perceptions of personal style are more than a matter of aesthetics. Consciously or otherwise, we all use style as a way of signaling our membership in one tribe or another, and we have finely tuned visual processing mechanisms that enable us to recognize people from our own tribe as well as those from surrounding tribes. Whether in East L.A. or East Hampton, it can be relatively straightforward to pick out someone who is "not from around here" based on clothing, shoes, or hairstyle. Familiarity is a powerful warmth cue, so a stranger's style often acts as a signal to remain on guard until intentions can be determined. This is just as true for street gangs as for suburbanites.

Beyond status and familiarity cues, style works on yet another level. Let's say that in your relatively businesslike workplace, there are two white guys about the same age who are peers within the organization. (In other words, gender and ethnicity do not account for differences between them.) One of these guys seems to play by a different rule book, and always wears a black T-shirt and jeans. You could perceive this as a form of strength because it demonstrates the courage to buck social norms. You could even enjoy this guy's willingness to express himself, which would mean his style projected warmth from your perspective. Or if you are the kind of person who sees this as an affront to the group rather than as a statement of individuality, it would not project warmth in your eyes—it might seem downright cold, in fact.

The other guy dresses in standard business attire every day. He conforms to the social norm so much that he seems to embody it. You may interpret that choice as something you respect or even like about him. On the other hand, you may read that conformity as weakness or a lack of individuality.

This is the key to understanding how others see your style choices: People judge your appearance based on how much you meet or deviate from their expectations, and those judgments are influenced by their attitudes toward deviance or conformity. If they think deviance is a good thing, deviance will reflect well on you and conformity will not. Likewise, if they value conformity, deviance will reflect poorly on you, while conformity will add to your warmth as an expression of shared interests.

This played out in the business world when Facebook billionaire Mark Zuckerberg raised eyebrows on Wall Street for showing up at a big investor meeting in sneakers and a hoodie sweatshirt. His style choice announced that he was playing the game on his own terms. In a setting that prized conformity, his deviance did not go over well with the lawyers and investment bankers wearing expensive suits: His appearance projected arrogance, immaturity, or some combination thereof. When Facebook's stock began to tank almost immediately after going public, questions swirled about his readiness to manage a global corporation. (The *Los Angeles Times* ran a headline that read: "Is Mark Zuckerberg in Over his Hoodie as Facebook CEO?") There was not a cause-and-effect relationship between his dorm-room chic and the subsequent doubts about his managerial competence, but his style became part of an ongoing narrative about his character.

Clothes

Clothing is our number one signifier of style: It is our canvas to paint whatever picture of ourselves we would like. And while sometimes people just throw on whatever is at hand, clothing can carry with it powerful associations about who we are, not only for others but for ourselves as well, to the point that the clothes we wear affect how well our brains work. Remember the lab coat example: Like a superhero's costume, the right clothes make us feel like we are ready to take on whatever we are facing.

Generally speaking, more formal clothing projects more strength. Formal clothing makes the wearer seem intelligent, sophisticated, and generally worthy of respect. This can be helpful in getting others to go along with you, whether at the office or soliciting strangers in public to sign a petition. Formality means business, literally and figuratively.

We once worked with a former business executive in his mid-fifties who wrote an insider's tell-all account of the corruption in his industry. His story was fueled by moral indignation and outrage, but his demeanor was that of a courtly Southern gentleman. He had impeccable manners and a soft voice that retained traces of his childhood accent. Though he had severed ties with the corporate world a few years before we met, he looked the part of a company man circa 1960: dark suit, white shirt, crew cut, and thick-framed glasses. His sense of style worked for him with mainstream audiences because it affirmed his credibility— he was not a fire-breathing radical, but rather someone who had grown up inside the system.

Perceptions of informality are more nuanced. In settings where most people are dressed informally, wearing informal clothing projects warmth by expressing a similarity to those around you and validating their choice of clothing. This is why politicians periodically parade around in flannel shirts to telegraph their down-home bona fides. (This risks ringing patently false if this style does not match their words and other nonverbal cues.)

On the other hand, the informality of a fantastically wealthy movie star photographed with ripped jeans and a ratty T-shirt only adds to perceptions of strength: The message is that success brings with it the license to break the rules and dress however one pleases. Similarly, informality that conjures up cultural associations with a life of leisure—picture a ski bum—can be a marker of high status.

Men have fewer choices than women where clothes are concerned, and this makes it easy for lots of them to get dressed in five minutes for just about any occasion. On the other hand, the ones who get creative and expand their range of choices have it harder. They are likely to bump up against stereotypes of being effeminate, which translates as warm and weak, and this gets mixed in with preconceptions about gay men. Women have more latitude to express both warmth and strength through their wardrobes, but they also face more scrutiny.

Some people develop an iconic style that helps shape our perceptions of who they are. If you conjure up a still picture of Steve Jobs in your mind, chances are he is wearing a black mock turtleneck and jeans. PepsiCo CEO Indra Nooyi, a native of India, has developed a signature look that blends colorful elements from traditional Indian women's clothes with more conservative business dress. Johnny Cash was the Man in Black (and even wrote a song by the same name).

Color is the first thing we notice about clothing, along with the patterns that break it up, such as stripes, plaids, or other prints. In some cases, color alone serves as a personal signature. The color of our clothing also shapes our self-perception. As with the lab coat experiment, studies have confirmed that color affects the wearers as well as the people who see them.

It is tricky drawing conclusions about the strength and warmth of colors, because so much depends on context. It is a fashion cliché to refer to a red tie as a "power tie," but if red is so powerful, why don't men strut around in red suits? Why is solid tan popular for casual pants and field coats but completely drab for a woman's silk scarf? There are all kinds of different color wheels and theories tying color to mood, most of which do not hold up under close scrutiny. A few basics are worth noting, though. In broad terms, colors can be distinguished as either warm or cool. Dark, cool colors tend to project strength. Studies have found, for instance, that women wearing dark, conservative clothes are judged more competent in a professional context than those wearing lighter colors.

Black has a multitude of meanings and uses. It can suggest high formality (evening wear), solemnity (mourning clothes), austerity (clerical or traditional domestic service garb), sex appeal (lingerie or the "little black dress"), or a certain type of cool, echoing the mystery of the unknown dark (from bikers to artists). Depending on the use, its complete absorption of light can give it a severe effect.

Dark shades of gray are widely equated with business dress (*The Man in the Gray Flannel Suit*), but gray also has associations with dullness, lifelessness, and dreary weather.

Navy blue is synonymous with business and authority (think of formal military dress or police uniforms).

Color experts use the term "warm colors" to refer to the yellows, reds, and oranges found in sunlight from dusk to dawn. These do project warmth, as do brighter, lighter shades of so-called "cool colors" like blue and green. Bright colors are friendly and inviting to the eye. Colors that have low levels of saturation, such as pastels, also create a sense of visual softness that projects warmth.

Sometimes deeply saturated or rich colors can project strength even if they are not dark. The classic example is fire engine red, which is warm in its brightness and attractiveness—in fact, it is so powerfully attractive to the eye that it conveys a singular self-confident strength as well. It carries a variety of cultural associations ranging from romance to danger (e.g., stop signs and traffic lights).

In clothing, red is almost always the boldest, brightest color in an outfit. It draws attention to itself in clothing as it does in nature, as with the male cardinal. The power tie effect mentioned earlier, which suggests strength rather than warmth, is like a peacock displaying its plumage. The power of red also rubs off on those who wear it: Women wearing red or black are rated as more attractive than those wearing colors such as white, yellow, blue, or green.

Blue—the richer medium shades between dark navy and light turquoise—also warrants a mention, as it is the most popular hue. While not a warm color in the fiery sense, blue is generally calming and familiar, which projects soothing warmth. And unlike green, which flirts with frivolously happy yellow, blue still retains a solid, dignified quality that carries strength. It is not as in-your-face as red, but it has an admirable balance of strength and warmth to it.

The so-called neutral colors such as browns and tans are pretty much what they sound like where strength and warmth are concerned: They do not project much of either. White conveys lightness, brightness, and cleanliness. It can be warm in some contexts and formal in others. The wedding dress, the ultimate symbol of moral purity, is both highly formal and reserved for brides, who represent a cultural archetype of warmth. White loses its warmth when it tips into starchy formality or the clinical sterility of medicine or high tech.

It is important to point out that the general strength or warmth of a color in the abstract does not necessarily make it a good or bad color for a particular individual or in a particular outfit. Our skin tone, age, and body type have a lot to do with determining what looks good on us. While a red blouse may make one woman a knockout, it can make another look washed out and pale. Similarly, dark blue jeans do not project strength simply because they are dark blue.

Cut refers to the shape clothes take when we wear them. Generally speaking, well-fitted clothes, such as those common for business dress, are a symbol of strength. To a large extent this reflects the perceived link between strength and luxury: Custom-made suits are far more expensive than those bought off the rack, even though alterations can essentially make off-the-rack clothes look made to order. Conversely, ill-fitting business clothes that pull too tight, bunch up, or otherwise hang poorly take away from the appearance of strength.

Another aspect of cut is the way it emphasizes the shape of the body. Loose-fitting clothes suggest greater comfort, which typically corresponds with informality. As we said earlier, informality can send a number of signals, some of which correspond to warmth and others of which do not. Tight-fitting clothes draw attention to features such as the waist, hips, buttocks, and breasts, and can serve as a form of sexual signaling. As we noted in our discussion of attraction, this can project either warmth or strength, depending on the intention.

Clothes can suggest shape with line instead of structure. Pinstripes, for instance, have a slimming visual effect because the lines direct the viewer's eyes to follow them up and down rather than exploring out to the side. Ski jackets are often designed with colorful panels that accent the breadth of the shoulders and lines that taper down toward the waist to visually suggest a more dramatic shoulder-waist-hip ratio. This suggestion of strength makes the wearer seem capable of carving graceful turns down the mightiest mountain, even if the reality is much less impressive.

Cut also determines how much skin is showing. There is a long tradition of controversy around hemlines—are they going up or down this year?—though at this point it is common to see fashionably dressed women in everything from ankle-length dresses to micro-micro-minis. Legs, arms, shoulders, neckline, and cleavage are all in play with clothes that can be worn for work or a formal occasion. In informal settings from the bar to the beach, there are fewer taboos about having skin on display.

For women making decisions about cut, it is important to be aware of the connection between status and sexy style. Research has found that women in high-status positions are penalized for presenting them-selves in a sexy manner, but this is not true for women in lower-status jobs. We know a highly educated and accomplished female computer science engineer in her mid-thirties who is also incredibly fit and attrac-tive. Her preference for wearing tight clothes to work became an issue that distracted male colleagues—they could not concentrate on what she was saying—and prevented them from taking her seriously. She toned down her at-work attire and the problem subsided almost imme-diately.

Shoes

While some people are crazy about shoes, many others overlook their fashion function entirely. Research suggests that shoe-crazy fashionistas might have a point. People judge each other based on shoes, not because we are all bad and superficial, but because shoes turn out to be a pretty good gauge of a lot of things: Income, personality traits, and political attitudes are largely accurately reflected in our shoes. Work boots or wing-tip oxfords, purple platforms or plain pumps, it takes a certain kind of character to wear a certain kind of shoe. This is not the place to go into detail on the unspoken language of footwear, but the research suggests most of us recognize these signals well.

This is not a good reason to nurture a shoe obsession. But it does suggest that it is worthwhile to think about where you want to go and let your shoes help take you there—not just by protecting your feet, but by showing others what kind of person you aim to be. If you are headed for the corner office, you do not have to spend as much money on your shoes as you might if you were already there, but you want to wear dressy shoes and keep them in good shape.

Hair

Hair contributes significantly to the overall strength and warmth of our appearance. Even more than clothing, hair speaks to deep issues of identity and sends strong signals about ethnicity, status, cultural preferences, and even politics. Think of Don King or Donald Trump: The hair is the personal trademark. People like to talk about hair. In the span of a couple of days, sixteen-year-old Olympic gymnast Gabby Douglas's ponytail and NASA's "Mohawk guy" both became news items. Our hair is such a prominent feature that we collectively spend tens of billions of dollars cutting, coloring, and otherwise caring for it. And a bad hair day is something we have almost all been through at one time or another.

A hairstyle is a balancing act: It has to fit with the shape of the face, overall build and body type, and personality. Hairstylists think about strength and warmth in terms of bluntness and softness. An appearance that projects strength will highlight sharp angles and disconnected straight lines. Softness is suggested by an even density, an effect that can be achieved through layering.

In most business settings, as with clothing, understated hairstyles convey the most strength. "If someone in the business world has the appearance of being dominated by their hair, people aren't going to take them seriously," says Jordan Pringle, a Washington-based stylist who has been recognized by *Allure* as a rising star on the national scene. "In the case of someone with a small frame, you need to find a way to reduce the amount of hair. It has to be proportionate to the body and the face." By contrast, in more creative fields, a striking hairstyle can confer an advantage by attracting attention and making its owner memorable.

For most men, hair is relatively straightforward. Neat or well-groomed hair demonstrates a degree of self-control, which speaks to strength. At one end of the spectrum are members of the military or police, who are in the business of overtly projecting strength. Men working in professions that place a premium on meticulous appearance, such as corporate law, also tend toward short hairstyles. Regardless of a man's profession, less hair generally means more strength (at least as far as appearances go). A shaved head remains an intense look—strong, not warm—even a couple of decades after Michael Jordan made it mainstream. This is just as true for scientists as for skinheads. A shaggier look, by contrast, is more informal and can suggest either a warm free-spiritedness or a disregard for personal appearance. There are countless variations of beards, sideburns, mustaches, and other facial hair, but the basic judgment is the same: Either a man's look is intentional, or it is not.

On the balance, though, hair is not that big a deal for a lot of guys. If anything, a man may be penalized for a look that suggests spending too much time and effort fussing over his appearance. Unless the hairstyle is going for a specific effect that is particular to a certain subculture— like a true punk Mohawk, or the spiky gelled look of a Jersey Shore denizen—the result can trigger suspicions of narcissism.

Women face more choices when deciding on a hairstyle, and negotiating the balancing act can be tricky. A blunt cut with straight lines, for instance, signals a no-nonsense demeanor that can be strong on one woman but cold on another, depending on the shape of her face, her age, skin tone, and personality. "You don't want to put something sweet on a woman who already seems too soft, but on the other hand, you don't want to give her a look that is overwhelmingly strong and won't fit her personality," Jordan explains. After all, hair is enough of a personal matter that it does reflect character, and people judge hairstyles accordingly. And if you do not come out of a haircut with the effect you wanted, you may just have to live with it for a little while.

Own It

Style is a reflection of more than your tastes—it is a reflection of your attitude. Done right, your style complements the signals you send with your gender, ethnicity, age, and looks, allowing you to adjust the strength and warmth profile that comes as your birthright.

If we draw one overarching conclusion from the research, it is this: Pay attention to the way clothes make you feel when you wear them, because that will affect how you carry yourself and project strength and warmth nonverbally. Models stride confidently down the runway no matter how ridiculous the outfit, because it is their job to own it when they wear it. For the rest of us, our clothes affect how we feel, and what we feel affects what we project. No matter what you look like, those nonverbal impressions are still the most powerful piece of the overall impression you make.

Words

"The difference between the almost right word and the
right word is really a large matter—'tis the difference
between the lightning-bug and the lightning."

—Mark Twain

Just as your nonverbal cues signal warmth or strength, so do your words. The modern study of communications began with a 1951 paper by a pair of Yale professors who proposed that persuasion depended on two key elements: expertise and trustworthiness, a.k.a. strength and warmth. Whether we are soothing, swearing, or selling, the language we choose creates a verbal portrait of strength and warmth. We talked earlier about Albert Mehrabian's research demonstrating the dominance of visual and vocal signals over words in conveying emotion. Here is the other side of the coin: When your nonverbal cues align with what you are saying, the words can be incredibly powerful.

While nonverbal communication works largely on a subconscious level, language engages the entire mind. Words enter our consciousness like characters parading onto our mental stage to act out their play, triggering associations that resonate with us. In the language of brain science, words "activate neural networks" by bringing to mind visual and other sensory information as well as any related emotions. Though they take a little longer to process than someone smiling at you, words conjure up images and memories that can shape what we think or feel in an instant.

Verbal Strength

Nearly a century ago, one of the great legal dramas of American history played out in a country courtroom in Tennessee. A high school teacher named John Scopes was charged with violating state law for teaching evolution in a public school. Scopes's attorney, Clarence Darrow, faced off against prosecutor William Jennings Bryan, three-time Democratic presidential candidate and former secretary of state. Darrow sought to make a literal belief in the Bible look ridiculous, and he did so through his questioning of Bryan, a deeply religious man and legendary orator.

> **Darrow:** Mr. Bryan, do you believe that the first woman was Eve?
> **Bryan:** Yes.
> **Darrow:** Do you believe she was literally made out of Adam's rib?
> **Bryan:** I do.
> **Darrow:** Did you ever discover where Cain got his wife?
> **Bryan:** No, sir; I leave the agnostics to hunt for her.

Courtrooms are theaters for engaging in a highly specialized kind of verbal jousting. Lawyers get paid handsomely to represent their clients, and this requires both legal knowledge and the ability to articulate an argument convincingly within a prescribed set of rules and customs. The reason there is an entire genre of courtroom dramas is because speaking well is a performing art that is inherently dramatic. A stylized battle between two lawyers is a duel filled with tension, points for and against, and ultimately a winner and a loser.

The Greeks and Romans codified the skills associated with speaking powerfully and called the entire discipline rhetoric, deeming it an essential part of a liberal arts education. We attribute strength to people who master it; we consider them more believable and in command of the facts than those who lack it. We also find them more attractive and sociable. Sometimes we even fear people with highly polished rhetorical skills, calling them "fast-talking," "silver-tongued," or "slick" to signal our mistrust of their intent.

In a virtuoso performance, a speaker captivates an audience's attention, which is in itself a display of strength. It is not something that can be accomplished through sheer force of will or by saying, "Listen to me!" If a speaker is boring, inarticulate, or just plain stupid, the audience will tune out, even if trapped in a room. This brings us back to the idea of warmth giving rise to strength. Good speakers start with warmth—they establish an emotional rapport with the audience by connecting with shared concerns or interests. When the speaker seizes the audience's attention, that is also an exercise of strength: The speaker is now in charge, and has an opportunity to elicit emotions, change minds, and even stir some to action.

The Basic Elements

Verbal strength is something that we know when we hear it (or read it). Your high school English teacher probably emphasized the importance of active voice ("The president called the meeting to order") over passive ("The meeting was called to order by the president"). Direct, active verbs add force, clarity, immediacy, and vigor to speech. We also equate a rich vocabulary with verbal strength, though too much of a good thing with SAT words can cost some warmth points.

The absence of verbal strength has a different recognizable sound. For instance, hesitations or phrases like "kind of," "sort of," "like," or "you know" lead us to doubt the competence of a speaker. Qualifiers such as "I think" and "I believe" also diminish certainty and credibility, as do various kinds of vagueness. We also penalize deferential or polite speech ("Please, sir, may I have another?") and indirect speech like the passive voice.

Complex sentence structure does not necessarily translate as strength. For reasons having to do with cognitive ease, we do better understanding simpler sentences than complex ones, and positive constructions rather than negative ones. It may be tempting to show off with verbal pyrotechnics, but any points earned for strength will probably cost you in terms of audience comprehension. Needless complexity can also signal an effort to sound sophisticated, which can backfire by coming off as verbal pretentiousness. The resulting lack of clarity and logic diminishes strength rather than projects it.

Rhetorical Devices

The tried-and-true techniques of classical rhetoric are still very effective ways of bolstering verbal strength. This is not an all-inclusive list, but an illustrative sampling of some greatest hits.

Metaphor and Analogy

Metaphors are so ubiquitous that we unwittingly use them all the time. To cite a commonplace example, if we say things are looking up, we are employing the metaphor of up-as-good. James Geary, whose book *I Is An Other* offers a guided tour of the world of metaphors, notes that in everyday speech we use about six per minute. The ones that show off our verbal prowess reshape others' understanding of an idea, person, or thing. Tim Berners-Lee coined the term "World Wide Web" to describe a way of connecting computers, and in doing so also created a visual image that made it easy for non-geeks to understand. When John Gray wrote that men are from Mars and women are from Venus, there was no need to pull out the Roman mythology book and check that Mars was the god of war and Venus the goddess of love in order to understand what he meant. Like metaphors, analogies provide a way of classifying one thing in terms of another. For our purposes, it is helpful to think of analogies as more logic driven than metaphors: X is a letter *just like* 1 is a number. Analogies demand a tighter fit than metaphors. They are commonly used to interpret current events in terms of historical ones. (How many times have you heard that the financial crisis of 2008 was the worst since the stock market crash of 1929?) These comparisons are always somewhat imprecise since the present is never just like the past, and this can open the door for an argument.

If-Then

Deductive reasoning is the foundation of logical thinking. If all fish swim in water and a trout is a fish, then a trout swims in water. If-then reasoning is not only a powerful way of organizing facts to suggest a conclusion; it can also be a rhetorical weapon to take apart an argument or expose a logical fallacy within it. Used like this, it is not typically a way to win friends, but it is second to none as a knife for cutting through fuzzy thinking.

Repetition and Wordplay

There is a bagful of techniques that orators through the ages have relied on to move audiences. *Repetition* makes things easy to remember. The best-known example of repetition in modern rhetoric is Martin Luther King Jr.'s "I Have a Dream" speech. It can work when just a phrase or even a word is repeated, such as "all for one and one for all." *Alliteration* refers to pairs of words that use the same sound, making them easier to remember than words with very different sounds. It often employs two or more words in a row that have the same first sound (rock 'n' roll, land of liberty, sound of silence, friend or foe), but not always—Bounty paper towels have been "the quicker picker-upper" for decades. *Groups of three* are easy to remember (I came, I saw, I conquered), and we are accustomed to their rhythms. American civic language is filled with threes, from "life, liberty, and the pursuit of happiness" to "of the people, by the people, for the people."

Famous Quotations and Sayings

There is no easier way to flex your rhetorical muscles than to quote someone who found just the right words to say something. Quotations demonstrate that you are well read, fluent in ideas, and able to make connections between them. In this respect, quotations serve as a type of analogy—they are received wisdom about a familiar human predicament that somebody already figured out. (As Yogi Berra said, when you come to a fork in the road, take it.)

All of these techniques should be used sparingly, and some require plenty of practice. A clumsy attempt to use repetition, for example, can do more harm than good. Even so, they are the devices that powerful speakers have used throughout the ages, and when used successfully, they enhance our perception of a speaker's mastery of rhetorical skill.

Finding Your Voice

Even without any fancy techniques, whether writing or speaking, there is always a question of tone. Tone is the character of your writing, and it gets judged through a similar strength and warmth lens. A formal tone projects strength, as it demonstrates mastery of a set of conventions used and required by people with power. A more casual tone is generally warmer and more accessible. Then again, casual does not mean weak: Comedy routines, lyrics, and love letters can all pack a punch.

Whether you are writing or speaking, you need to get the voice right if you want to do it well. Sometimes the right voice will not be your natural voice. If you generally speak casually and use a lot of filler words, speaking in a formal setting might not come easily. If you write academic papers for a living, writing an action-oriented business memo may prove a challenge for you.

One way to make this easier is to adopt the mind-set of a more appropriate messenger, almost like playing a role. You can be creative with this, and the more thoroughly you imagine the character in question, the easier it is to speak in their voice. If you are speaking to a group of your grandmother's friends, imagine the nice, well-mannered, church-going young person they would like to think you are, and what that person's life might look and sound like, and you will make her proud. Or if you are trying to explain tech support to a Luddite audience, sprinkle your how-to advice with folksy words that make it sound more like you are talking with an old friend than reciting from a user manual.

We all do this naturally to some degree as we grow up, or whenever we enter a new situation that calls for us to act in a new way. When we first enter a formal business context, for instance, we don't just put on a suit; we adopt a demeanor that resembles what we see other people in that environment doing, right down to the speech pattern. It can feel a little funny at first, and it does initially create emotional distance between you and the people you are trying to project warmth to, even if the role you are playing is warm. But what generally happens is you gradually add your own personality back in: You stop pretending and drop some parts of the role, but you also keep the parts of it that seem to work well with your actual character and feelings in the situation.

Verbal Warmth: The Circle

"My uncle said there are two kinds of people in Barrington,
Rhode Island: those who belong, and those who don't."

—Spalding Gray

It was just supposed to be a short speech that night in Indianapolis, like many he had given before. Then he got the shattering news. He knew what had to happen next: This white man would have to tell the largely black crowd that Martin Luther King was dead. Stepping up to the microphone bearing that news felt like walking up to a powder keg with a lit match. The city police had said flat out that they would not be able to protect him if a riot broke out.

He got right to it. "I have some very sad news for all of you, and that is that Martin Luther King was shot and was killed tonight in Memphis, Tennessee." A chorus of screams erupted, and then the shocked crowd fell silent. "Martin Luther King dedicated his life to love and to justice between fellow human beings. He died in the cause of that effort. In this difficult day, in this difficult time for the United States, it is perhaps well to ask what kind of nation we are, and what direction we want to move in."

Then he looked at the crowd, at the many black faces looking back at him, and he spoke directly to them. "For those of you who are black, considering the evidence there evidently is that there were white people who were responsible, you can be filled with bitterness, and with hatred, and a desire for revenge. We can move in that direction as a country, and greater polarization, black people amongst blacks, and white amongst whites, filled with hatred toward one another. Or we can make an effort, as Martin Luther King did, to understand, and to comprehend, and replace that violence, that stain of bloodshed that has spread across our land, with an effort to understand, compassion and love. For those of you who are black and are tempted to be filled with hatred and mistrust of the injustice of such an act, against all white people, I would only say that I can also feel in my own heart the same kind of feeling. I had a member of my family killed, but he was killed by a white man."

Robert Kennedy spoke for another minute or two, and then everyone went home. Over the following days, riots erupted in more than a hundred American cities, killing thirty-five people and wounding several thousand more. But not in Indianapolis. Indianapolis remained at peace.

Words Redeemed

Robert Kennedy was an outsider delivering the worst possible news to a crowd—a scenario in which "shooting the messenger" was not necessarily just a figure of speech. The wrong word or phrase could have meant the difference between life and death.

It is true that nonverbal signals generally convey the bulk of a speaker's emotion. Yet without some words from you, your audience can only guess why you are feeling the emotions you project nonverbally—whether you actually share the same opinions they do, or just happen to be in a similar mood for a different reason.

When someone pays attention and hears or reads your words, you can paint pictures and experiences in their minds that evoke all kinds of feelings. Not every word moves people. But by using emotionally resonant language, you can change your audience's emotional reality. This is a demonstration of strength, for sure, and if done right—if you use your words to put you and your audience on the same emotional page—you can create warmth too.

The Circle

Exactly how did Robert Kennedy's words move his audience?

Did he argue that the crowd's anger was unjustified or unproductive? Far from it. Knowing that the announcement of Martin Luther King's death would create an instant wave of emotion, he realized it was critical to start by recognizing those feelings. This was no time for a logical explanation of the futility of violence. It had to be unmistakably clear that he understood the feelings of rage and helplessness that accompany an injustice of this scope.

He started by acknowledging the temptation to feel bitterness and hatred and to seek revenge. This was not the point he was trying to make, but it was that first step that opened the door for everything afterward. By connecting with his audience where he found them, he demonstrated that he was with them, on their side—the definition of warmth. Only after establishing this warmth would they consider what he had to say on its own merits, without reservation.

He evoked powerful, visceral feelings when he said, "I can also feel in my own heart the same kind of feeling. I had a member of my family killed, but he was killed by a white man." He knew that everyone in the crowd would recall images and feelings from the assassination of his brother, and he counted on its impact. This analogy enabled Robert Kennedy to transcend his obvious differences with the crowd and establish a connection with them: He understood how they felt because he had been there himself.

When we work with our clients, one of the first concepts we introduce is something we call "the circle." Imagine your audience as a person you are trying to persuade to support you in something. Not having much by way of art skills, we usually just draw a stick figure to help visualize this person. Next we draw a big circle around our little stick figure. This divides the world in two. People who understand the world the way your audience does belong inside the circle, next to the stick figure. They literally have common sense: They share in common the same sense of the way things are in life. People who don't understand the world the way your audience does belong outside the circle. They are out of touch.

What does this little doodle have to do with communication? It is a simple picture that reminds you what you have to do to communicate effectively with any audience: Your first job is to get in the circle. Because the circle is not just a Venn diagram of your audience's frame of reference—it is also the radius of your audience's hearing.

When someone starts talking to you, you are presented with two questions. One is whether what they are saying makes sense to you. But before you answer that question, you first consider a different question: Is this a person worth listening to? Do they understand how the world works—in other words, are they capable? And what is their agenda in talking with you—are they friend or foe? If you don't see that person as both strong, in the sense of having a grasp of the issue they're talking about, and warm, in the sense that they are on your side, you will discount everything they say accordingly, if you even bother to listen at all.

You face the same challenge with your own audience. You can talk all day long, but if your audience does not see you as belonging in that circle with them, they will not listen. They may hear you, but your words are just so much noise washing over them. They will not seriously consider adopting your point of view. You will remain an outsider who does not get it.

This circle is definitely not the most precise scientific representation of the process of interpersonal communication. But whatever it lacks in analytical rigor, it makes up for in universality. There is something about a circle—it is just such an archetypal image—that it resonates with us. And the idea behind this primitive little sketch is as powerful as it is simple: You are either inside or outside, and if you're outside, nobody will listen to you. That's why your first task when you open your mouth is to get yourself in that circle.

Finding the Way Inside

So how does one get in your audience's circle? By now we know lots of ways to project warmth: You can smile; you can do people favors. None of this is necessarily wrong, and all the usual ways of projecting warmth can certainly help. At bottom, though, what your audience is looking for is to know that you are on the same emotional page as they are. The key to getting in the circle, then, is simple: Show your audience that you feel the same way they do. Validate their feelings.

If your audience is frustrated about an issue and you are too, show your frustration. If your audience is happy about something and so are you, share your happiness. If you and your audience are ambivalent about an issue, show that you are torn. (If your audience is confused by the issue, you do not have to prove to them that you are confused about it currently, but you will help yourself if you acknowledge that the issue is a confusing one and that you felt that way too.)

If this sounds easy so far, it is. But it is also incredibly easy to overlook this step. Especially when you generally feel the same way your audience does, expressing that may feel like stating the obvious, a waste of time. It is not. The more you demonstrate your warmth first, the more believable you will be when you eventually make your point. What's more, if your point boils down to asking people to support a position they already know you hold, your argument may actually be superfluous. It may well do more to win an audience over to your position to show warmth and make them like you personally than to present a sound logical argument.

When you do not agree with an audience or even necessarily feel the same way they do, then getting in the circle is even more important, but definitely not so easy. The same basic concepts still apply: You still have to connect with your audience both emotionally and conceptually, even though you largely disagree with them. How does that work?

First and foremost, you need to empathize. You have to identify something that your audience is feeling that you can feel too, and then show them you feel it too. It is important to stay true to yourself and your views as long as you know they are correct. But it is also true that if you want to communicate effectively, you have to be willing to do the hard work of empathy. If you want people to take your point of view seriously, you first have to be willing to take their point of view seriously. That is the deal, and it is totally, brutally fair. So identify what kinds of emotions your audience is feeling, then put yourself in their shoes and ask yourself why they're feeling that way.

But what if you do not like the answer? What if they are being petulant, cowardly, inconsiderate, whiny, stubborn, intolerant, hateful . . . ? You and a colleague disagree about the direction of a new strategic initiative, or your uncle holds very different political views than you and likes to goad you at Thanksgiving, or your friend wants to invite someone to dinner that you don't like. Or perhaps it is more personal: You have a colleague who feels threatened by sharing credit, or your child wants something you cannot in good conscience allow, or your friend thinks it is no big deal that he has not paid for anything you have done together lately. This is where things get difficult.

Begin by asking yourself what it is about their circumstances that could legitimately make them feel just one of these feelings. If your audience is feeling hateful, you don't want to share that feeling, but you might empathize with the frustration that ushered in that hate. That was what Robert Kennedy did. You can empathize with their sense of being mistreated without agreeing about who is to blame. That's usually as far into their darkness as you need to venture. Just ask yourself: If you had walked the same path, might you feel the same way?

You have to meet your audience where you find them before they will walk with you. See what they see, feel what they feel, and then find some part of their emotional experience that you can genuinely empathize with.

You are not done yet, though. You still need some words to express yourself that both you and your audience can agree with. Unfortunately, even if you are clearly feeling the same emotions your audience is, you can't usually get away with explaining your feelings just by saying, "This issue is so frustrating!" What you are looking for is something more general than your audience's specific complaints—which you disagree with—that still speaks to the feelings behind their complaints.

For example, if you think your colleague is being unreasonable about getting sole credit for work he did with a group, you can both agree that it is good and important for him to get full credit for the good work he did. Saying that first avoids getting into the specifics of who else should get public credit for their work. That is not all your colleague thinks on the subject, but he does agree wholeheartedly with that part, and it's enough to demonstrate that you recognize his concerns. And that's enough to get a conversation going about what to do to fix it.

When people are unhappy, one approach you can use is to sternly declare that whatever basic good thing should be happening is not, and that is not okay. For example, even in places where tensions between ethnic groups run high, both sides want children everywhere—even across the fence—to be able to grow up happy and safe. Consider the statement "Children should not have to live in fear. Civilized people cannot stand by and let this happen." It is not clear what side of the argument this puts the speaker on, but it projects the frustration and anger common on both sides, and few people on either side will disagree with it.

The *Wall Street Journal* published a great description of how the circle technique works in February 2008. At the time, Barack Obama had just started winning presidential primaries, and people were puzzled at how the skinny guy with the funny name was charming voters in the heartland. *Journal* reporter Stephen Hayes followed Obama around and filed this report: "His rhetorical gimmick is simple. When he addresses a contentious issue, Mr. Obama almost always begins his answer with a respectful nod in the direction of the view he is rejecting—a line or two that suggests he understands or perhaps even sympathizes with the concerns of a conservative."

Hayes cited an example in which Obama was asked about the Second Amendment. He began his answer by saying that, having taught constitutional law for ten years, he believed that the Second Amendment granted individuals the right to carry guns—the conservative position—

and that he "respect[ed] the right of lawful gun owners to hunt, fish, and protect their families." (It is not clear he meant to say he respected fishing with a shotgun.) Only then—after he was in the circle—did Obama go on to talk about how he thought there should be new laws to help trace firearms used in crimes.

At the end of his answer, Obama employed one final circle move: kicking his opponent out. "The argument I have with the NRA is . . . they believe any constraint or regulation whatsoever is something that they have to beat back. And I don't think that's how most lawful firearms owners think." Obama is left standing next to the lawful firearms owners, his audience, inside the circle, while the NRA has just been declared bereft of common sense, not like us, cast out of the circle. In the last instance, then, the circle is not only a Venn diagram and the radius of your audience's hearing; it is also a sumo wrestling ring. Winning means not only getting inside, it also means pushing your opponent out.

This is an entirely different physics of persuasion than is suggested by the traditional model of argument. In that vision, each suitor stands his ground and tries to build a more glitteringly compelling case to draw the undecided audience in his direction. It is a tug-of-war, with the audience the prize in the middle. The circle vision suggests that to bring that audience over to your side, your first move should be to go where your audience is. Throw your arm rhetorically over their shoulder, make that connection, and then you can walk them back in the direction you come from.

Consider a practical application of this new angle of persuasion. There is a hard-won pearl of business wisdom about seeking support for a project: "Ask for money, get advice. Ask for advice, get money." This seems counterintuitive (which is why it is memorable), but circle logic explains why it makes perfect sense. When you ask someone for their money, you divide your interests from theirs: One of you will end up with that money, and one of you won't. By contrast, when you ask for advice on achieving your goals, you get in your audience's circle by validating their view of themselves as wise and worth listening to (yes, flattery will get you places), and they reciprocate by looking at your interests as their own. Once the two of you are on the same team, jointly facing down whatever challenges stand before you, they are more likely to offer you more than just advice.

When trying to get in the circle with someone, you first have to figure out how they feel, how they relate to the world, what makes them tick. You have lots of cues to work with—their fixed and nonverbal signals, the situation, etc.—but pay particular attention to their first few words, as they often speak volumes. We all use different words and phrases to express ourselves, even if we are trying to communicate the same basic idea, and our word choice and sentence structure reveal a lot about our personalities.

For instance, imagine proposing a new idea to your boss. Here are some phrases you might hear in response:

"What do the numbers show?"

"Wow, I love it."

"Don't stand here telling me about it. Go make it happen."

These three reactions suggest different orientations, toward ideas, emotions, or action. Psychologist Taibi Kahler devised a typology of six basic kinds of people—in addition to these thinkers, feelers, and doers, he also included dreamers, believers, and funsters—each of which has a unique style of speaking. These stylistic markers offer great clues about how to get in the circle with each kind of person.

Say that two people receive identical letters from their credit card company asking them to call a toll-free number to clear up a glitch with their respective accounts. The voice mail system then receives these two messages:

"Hello, I am calling in response to a letter I received in the mail about a problem with my account."

"Um, you guys sent a letter that said I should call about my card. I'm kind of confused about why."

The formality of the first message makes the caller seem very analytical, while the laid-back tone of the second one suggests a focus on feelings (confusion) rather than on precision. Customer service organizations have been making distinctions like this for decades, as Christopher Steiner explains in *Automate This*. When the voice menu asks you to describe the problem before connecting you to a real person, it analyzes your language in order to pair you with a representative who is a good match for your personality. Why? In the call center business, the faster you connect with a person who understands you, the faster your problem is resolved. That makes you more likely to feel good about the interaction, and it makes optimal use of the customer service reps. This is a clear example of the circle technique on steroids, and it has real implications for the bottom line.

Just as body language can tell you how someone feels in the moment, spoken language tells you how that person's mind works. Your ability to pick that up quickly based on speaking style and adapt accordingly will accelerate you into the circle. If the person you are trying to persuade has a "just the facts" orientation, start with the facts. On the other hand, if you are dealing with an indecisive dreamer, you can be the calm, Obi-Wan Kenobi guide who helps move that person to action. While we all vary our speaking styles somewhat for different settings—we use different language to talk to our doctor than to our loved ones, for instance—our default speech patterns are fairly deeply ingrained habits.

False Leads

To get a clearer understanding of how this circle works, it is helpful to distinguish it from several related but ultimately different concepts:

The circle ≠ sharing a background.

Having people, places, or experiences in common with your audience can definitely help, and it is often worth pointing out—recall how RFK drew on his own family's tragic history to establish his empathy with the crowd. Invoking those shared memories will remind your audience of their own similar experiences, and they will usually presume you reacted the same way that they did to whatever it is you have in common. On the other hand, if you went to the same school they did, and most people there loved it and went to all the football games, but the person you are talking to hated football and could not wait to get out of there, then just mentioning you went there does you no favors, because they will assume that like most people there you loved the school (and the football) too. Within every social situation, people have different experiences, and not everybody gets along. So to demonstrate you feel the same way your audience does, the shared experience can definitely help, but it is not necessary or enough to connect with them. The story is more complicated.

The circle ≠ having outstanding credentials.

One might reasonably think that one way to show your audience that you are worth listening to on a topic is to let them know that you are an expert. This is primarily about establishing your strength and competence, not warmth. Academic degrees and long experience and achievement in your field are certainly relevant and can definitely be useful to mention—but recognize their limits. First of all, some credentials can work against you. If you happen to have a fancy degree or corporate title but you are talking to an audience that has had less education and professional advancement, and maybe even associates those things with being out of touch with everyday realities, then you are not doing yourself any favors by calling attention to your degree or your business card.

Second, recognize that in the age of the Internet, experts are a dime a dozen. There may be a thousand Ph.D.'s who say our carbon emissions are causing global warming and making storms worse, but there's at least one somewhere who will say otherwise, and you can be sure that person will get some attention. That leaves all of us non-experts to arbitrate between two people who know more than we do. Faced with this conundrum, we go with what we know. If one of those experts agrees with us about things we are confident that we know about, we are likely to suppose she knows what she is talking about in general, and so we will trust her word about things we are not familiar with; this is the halo effect again. Showing your audience that you share their sense of how the world works is the most convincing credential of all.

That does not mean you should go out of your way to hide your credentials and experience. Instead of considering them symbols to be brandished and bragged about, think of them as material for stories. Telling an engaging story projects strength by taking command of your audience's attention, and projects warmth by compelling the audience to empathize with you. If you have experience with the topic at hand, describe to your audience what that looked like and felt like, and they will be right there on the same page with you.

Imagine a man telling you, "I am a retired naval lieutenant." Now imagine the same person instead saying, "After school I decided to join the navy, and spent the next eight years sailing the seas on a ship longer than a football field." In the first version, he tells you that he is something you are not. In the second version, he starts when he is finishing school, a moment that's probably familiar to you, and then paints a picture of his experience that lets you see it through his eyes, however dimly. (To project more strength while still connecting, one could say, "After high school I joined the navy and became a technician, maintaining complex weapons systems on destroyers.")

Don't tell your audience about your experience, like you are reciting your resume. Tell them about your experiences, like you are reliving them with your audience along for the ride.

The circle ≠ telling other people how they feel.

Let's say you have figured out your audience's feelings, made sense of them enough to feel them yourself, and found something concrete to talk about. You are almost there, but beware of one last pitfall: "You." It may be very tempting to say to your audience something like, "You're unhappy, and I don't blame you!" There is genuine empathy there, and you may even show your own unhappiness when you say it, and all of that is good. Unfortunately, "you" have just inadvertently separated yourself from your audience, just when their ears were almost open.

Remember your circle for a second. Initially it divides you from your audience: You are on the outside; they are on the inside. But when you're inside that circle with them, there is no more "you" and "they"—now there is "we," and you speak of your shared feelings and experiences using "we" and "us" and "our." These seemingly innocuous little pronouns are circle language. They group people, together or separated, drawing and patrolling the boundaries of the circle you are trying to get inside. The difference between "You're right to feel that way" and "We're right to feel this way" can easily be the difference between patronizing your audience and leading them to a new point of view.

Don't tell other people how they feel. Show them how you both feel, and tell them about the common ground you share.

The Magic Ingredients, Part 1

Why does all of this work? There are lots of reasons, each one a different psychological force pulling in the same direction, strengthening the power of that initial emotional validation that gets you inside the circle.

Because it makes you seem reasonable.

If you want to appear to be a reasonable person, the kind of person who usually gets things right, you are going to help your cause if the first sentiment you express (the only sentiment your audience has ever heard you express) is one your audience recognizes as being reasonable. All kinds of different people think all kinds of different things, but you can be sure almost every one of them thinks he or she is a reasonable person, and right most of the time about most things. So if you can express that you hold the same commonsense view of the world, you will appear reasonable too.

You have now set an expectation: You said something correct; therefore, you are the kind of person who says things that are correct. If you say something that is not immediately recognized as right, or that conflicts with something else that your audience believes, instead of writing you off immediately, your audience experiences what psychologists call "cognitive dissonance"—unpleasant mental conflict, in this case between their preexisting belief that you just contradicted and their expectation that what you say is true. They will be motivated to reconcile this tension one way or the other, probably not by rejecting their previous belief, but possibly by modifying it and accepting some of yours alongside it. This may not be total victory, perhaps, but it is far better than being tuned out, which is what would have happened had you not set their positive expectation of you by getting in the circle in the first place.

When you start by saying something that makes your audience respond mentally with a yes, you create what you might call "yes momentum"—the natural inclination for one yes to lead to another and another and another. It is similar to an interrogation on a cop show where they ask the suspect if his name is his name, and then if his home address is his home address, and then if he remembers killing the victim, in part hoping that the first two yes answers will lead to a third yes.

Because they like you!

This is different, but related: When you agree with people, you are confirming their view of the world, and that feels good to them. When you express familiar sentiments, you also seem more familiar and less likely to upset them or threaten their worldview, so their anxiety level goes down and they feel more comfortable. People like it when you make them feel good, and then they associate that good feeling with you, so they like you.

This is powerfully persuasive. Especially when the issue is complicated, sorting out all the competing considerations takes time and effort and skill that your audience may or may not have. Faced with that conundrum, it is tempting for your audience just to agree with whomever they like on a personal level, regardless of the merits of the case. This is cognitive dissonance at work again. We want to think being right goes along with being good. Agreeing with people we don't like requires a more complicated view of the world, which demands more work on our part. Agreeing with the people we like just hurts our brains less.

Because they owe you one.

Just as making people feel good makes them like you, it also makes them owe you. This is the basic psychological principle of reciprocity, explained masterfully by Robert Cialdini in his seminal book *Influence*: We keep track of favors like social accountants, and when you scratch my back, I understand that my role is to return the favor when the time comes so as to even up the ledger. As it is with watching a neighbor's pet, so it is in conversation. Your agreement makes them feel good, so it becomes their turn, and they return the favor.

The Magic Ingredients, Part 2

Sometimes, your audience is actively skeptical of you even before you open your mouth, or you have a persuasive opponent to contend with.

Here, using the circle strategy calls even more powerful forces to your aid. That is not to say that having a tough crowd makes your task easier—it does not. You would still prefer that your audience had no preconceptions about you or your topic. But facing a tougher persuasion task makes the circle strategy even better advice. Consider the following:

You keep them guessing.

Leo Tolstoy once observed, "The most difficult subjects can be explained to the most slow-witted man if he has not formed any idea of them already; but the simplest thing cannot be made clear to the most intelligent man if he is firmly persuaded that he knows already, without a shadow of doubt, what is laid before him." If you are introduced to your audience as coming from a foreign or hostile position—management talking to staff, country folk talking to city dwellers, substitute teacher talking to students—you start at a disadvantage. If you are to have any hope of getting your audience to consider what you have to say, you first have to prove that you are not what they think you are. Expressing agreement with them defies their expectations, and your audience suddenly realizes that their preconceived negative notions of you do not quite fit with this agreeable person they have before them, so they have to pay closer attention to what you are saying to figure you out. By breaking out of the box they had you filed away in, you earn yourself a fresh look.

They feel heard.

When you are speaking and your audience is listening, you are in charge. You control the parameters of the conversation, and you paint the picture in everyone's head. If you leave something out of that picture that your audience thinks belongs in there, they will not be happy about it. They may interrupt you and amend your picture. Then again, they may not bother, in which case they will probably just tune you out. By beginning with a vision of the world as your audience sees it, including accounting for the parts you disagree with, you reduce the likelihood that your audience feels something is being left out. Even though you are speaking and your audience is not, by giving voice to their feelings, you make them feel heard and respected.

You avoid the argument.

You also avoid another problem: the argument. When you talk about creating an argument, making an argument, or judging how persuasive an argument is, that's fine. But when you are *having* an argument with someone, whether it is happening out loud or even just in your audience's head, that is a potential problem.

Here's why: When an argument starts, persuasion stops. A group of researchers including psychologist Drew Westen conducted a revealing experiment, which Westen wrote about in his book *The Political Brain*. In the heated election campaign of 2004, the researchers found supporters of presidential candidates George Bush and John Kerry and took MRI pictures of their brains as they watched video footage of their favorite candidate completely contradicting himself. So what happened in people's brains when they saw information that contradicted their worldview in a charged political environment? As soon as they recognized the video clips as being in conflict with their worldview, the parts of the brain that handle reason and logic went dormant. And the parts of the brain that handle hostile attacks—the fight-or-flight response—lit up.

This is what happens when a discussion becomes an argument. It's no longer an exercise in logic and reasoning. It's just a fight. And being in a fight brings its own frame of mind, a whole set of attitudes, expectations, and conditioned reactions that go along with arguing. As soon as that happens, no one cares who is right and who is wrong. All that matters is who is friend and who is foe. So if you are trying to win over someone whose natural allegiances are not with you, getting into an argument is a sure way to fail.

Your best hope of persuasion is to keep things nonconfrontational, a friendly conversation about a shared problem. Do not let the other side turn it into an argument. Keep everyone's anxiety down and blood pressure low. Keep pointing out the common ground, expressing the shared emotions. Persevere in being pleasant. Because avoiding the argument is your best chance of winning it.

It is worth noting one final benefit. Unlike in the nonverbal realm, where projecting more warmth undermines your perceived strength, projecting warmth verbally by getting in the circle opens the door to projecting strength verbally by compellingly presenting new ideas.

Strength + Warmth, Word by Word

Building Blocks: Letters, Clusters, and Sounds

Strength and warmth even play out at the most granular levels of language. Words with a high degree of sonority—long tones in which the airflow is not broken by hard consonants—have a soft, feminine quality, which helps explain their popularity in women's luxury brand names such as Chanel, L'Oreal, and Revlon, as Christopher Johnson notes in *Microstyle*. He contrasts these with men's brands such as Craftsman and Black & Decker, which are broken up by hard sounds. These associations are an integral part of a brand's image, particularly for people who know a brand only by its name. Pharmaceutical companies spend gobs of money figuring out names that will suggest either warmth (Ambien) or strength (Viagra), depending on how the drug is supposed to make you feel.

Similar to the concept of high and low sonority, words with Anglo-Saxon roots are shorter, with fewer syllables and more hard sounds than those with Latin or Greek roots. For example, words like "gruff," "kid," and "tag" are of Anglo-Saxon origin, while "oval," "verdant," "morose," and "beneficial" are from Latin or Greek. If you pronounce the words aloud, you'll notice that those with Anglo-Saxon roots have a stronger sound, while the Latin ones are warmer. This is even true of the difference between the formal medical names and street slang for body parts. Just about every crude four-letter word has an Anglo root, giving it a stronger sound than the Latin version. The Romans said *fornicate*, we say . . .

We also read strength and warmth into the sounds of different letters and clusters of consonants and vowels. When children learn to read, the study of phonics emphasizes "hard" and "soft" sounds, which correspond with strong and warm associations. There is a reason that sharp attack consonants like *k* and *x* are used in the model names of sports cars: They're guttural sounds that evoke strength. You can almost make many hard sounds (*k*, *d*, *t*) with your teeth clenched. Round attack consonants such as *b* and *p*, which make a percussive sound when you open and close your lips, also have a lot of punch. Vowel sounds, which require you to open your mouth and move air (try saying "ay" or "oh"), are almost inherently warm. Similarly, many soft consonants (*s*, *f*, *j*) and digraphs (*sh*, *ch*) are also warm. To many English-speaking ears, spoken French has a certain *je ne sais quoi* because of its heavy concentration of soft sounds. There's a reason it is called the language of love.

What's in a Name?

As with any other words, our names convey strength and warmth. Novelists, playwrights, and screenwriters have often used this to great effect, as we see with memorable character names from Holly Golightly to Dirk Diggler. Unless you are in showbiz you are unlikely to do much about your name, but it is worth being aware of how others might perceive it.

A big part of a name's likability is based on how easy it is to pronounce. Recall our earlier discussion of halo effects—in this case, fluency creates a halo effect. This is not such good news for those of us with names that are not clearly phonetic in English. Similarly, research suggests that certain characteristics of our first names, such as popularity and number of syllables, enable people to make reasonably accurate predictions about how wealthy and well educated we are, which speaks to perceptions of strength.

As you might expect, researchers have found that this bumps up against cultural stereotypes, particularly regarding names that "sound black." Names are deeply intertwined with race, geography, and class, all of which can trigger positive or negative associations. Many Americans could hazard a reasonable guess about which part of the country somebody named Billy Ray comes from, and that guess will likely come wrapped in some cultural information, accurate or otherwise.

Researchers have also determined that the strength and warmth cues from a name can even shape judgments about whether a person is a good match for a particular professional position. In the absence of other information, people with warm-sounding names like Amanda and Ryan are judged as warmer, more sincere, and less powerful than people with cold names like Nicole and Derek, making them seem more suitable for warm jobs (daycare worker) than for those requiring high competence (administration). Names can also augment judgments about physical appearance. A person with a mature face and a warm name is perceived as more suited for a warm job than a person who looks the same with a cold name, but the person with the warm name also is deemed less capable of leadership. There are also gender effects: A woman with a mature face and warm-sounding name is viewed as more sincere than a similar-looking woman with a cold name.

There are limits to how much we can read into names—Barack

Obama was elected president despite having a name that sounded utterly foreign to most Americans—but they remain a prominent piece of information we use to make social judgments about each other.

I Am from Mars, We Are from Venus

The use of pronouns such as "I" and "we" tells a lot about strength and warmth, as well as offering clues about gender, education, and status. Some of these clues are obvious, while others are less so. Most of us have learned somewhere along the way, for instance, that the overuse of "I" suggests self-centeredness or egocentrism, which asserts strength but undercuts warmth. This behavior may also suggest this person has some major insecurities they are trying to mask. In either reading of the strength signals, overdoing the "I" is not warm. Conversely, the use of "we" generally demonstrates an awareness of other people and offers a way to show that you recognize or even understand their thoughts and feelings. At a fundamental level, this projects warmth by conveying a sense of shared concerns and interests. When "we" is used this way, we think of it as "circle language"; as we said earlier, it gets you in the circle with your audience by drawing it around both you and them.

At the same time, psychologist James Pennebaker has found that people who use "I" frequently are more likely to be telling the truth than people who use less forthright language that deflects attention from them. And using "I" to talk about one's own feelings and experience is integral to the warm, feelings-focused communication style used by many women.

Men, on the other hand, tend to think like the hero of Nick Hornby's *High Fidelity*, who obsessively ordered and reordered his music collections. This tendency to systematize and classify speaks to demonstrations of analytical competence. Men typically use more abstract and complex language with less emotion. Leaders of organizations use "we" a lot, but they use it to speak on behalf of the whole organization, which often creates emotional distance rather than bridging it. When a superior tells a subordinate, "We need to get this done," with the clear implication of an order, there is nothing warm or empathetic about it.

There are all sorts of ways men and women use language differently that echo the divide between strength and warmth. Psychologist Simon Baron-Cohen (yes, the comedian's brother) has developed a theory about the extent to which a person leans more toward empathizing, a focus on relationships among people, or systematizing, a focus on things and the rules that describe how they work. It will come as no surprise that women typically do more empathizing and men more systemizing.

On a related note, boys tend to raise their hands and get called on more than girls in school, and men tend to talk more than women in professional meetings where status is at stake. Outside work, where talking means connecting, women talk more than men. Linguist Deborah Tannen, whose work has been hugely influential in illuminating the differences between men's and women's conversational styles, explains that men typically focus on independence, while women focus on intimacy— another instance of the strength-warmth divide.

Stories

There are two rhetorical forms that naturally project strength and warmth together: stories and humor.

It is no secret that a story is a powerful way to convey a thought, feeling, or idea. Storytellers from Aesop to Jesus knew that using tales and parables made it easy for broad audiences to understand, recall, and even spread a kernel of wisdom. So where do strength and warmth fit in? There is a significant body of research demonstrating that our brains are wired for stories. We can tell our friends what happened in our favorite movies far more easily than we can reel off the five points of a strategic management plan, because the devices that make stories work—heroes and villains, plots and subplots—stick with us. That makes them the very best way to get in the circle: Everyone likes stories. We have all been listening to them since childhood, and doing it relaxes our critical faculties and lowers our guard. In that respect, sharing a story with others is an inherently warm experience.

Stories work best when they feature people doing and feeling things, and when they create visual images in the minds of the audience. Research by Harvard psychologists Joshua Greene and Elinor Amit has found that when people are confronted with a scenario that poses a moral dilemma, stories that create mental pictures are more likely to trigger emotional responses than stories without them, which tend to trigger rational responses like cost-benefit thinking. Good guys and bad guys are essential as well: They draw the line for the audience between right and wrong.

Seth likes to say that a good story acts as a Trojan horse for our point of view. The act of telling it is almost like giving a gift to an audience, and they do not even realize that you have packed it full of messages and values until they are already hooked and hanging on your every pause, waiting to hear what happens. As a result, the ability to tell a good story is a display of competence. People who master it have the most potent rhetorical tool at their disposal, one that is shared by prophets and con men alike. Stories can persuade us to follow leaders, invest our savings, vote for a candidate, or support a good cause. That is strength.

Telling stories also offers a great opportunity to demonstrate how you project nonverbal strength and warmth signals. If there is conflict in the story, strength nonverbals may add to the emotional impact, and if it ends well (or maybe just starts well), you can dial up your warmth as the storyteller. If you are lucky enough not to experience too much conflict on a day-to-day basis, or if you are in an environment where warmth expressions are viewed with suspicion, telling a story is a way to show your audience that you have both in you.

Humor

Nothing is less funny than analyzing humor, so we will keep this point brief. Humor can project strength and warmth at once, because it displays verbal dexterity at the same time it creates a shared experience of laughter. We respect people with the ability to make us laugh, particularly those quick enough to use it as a weapon—ask any comedy club heckler who has been cut down to size—and we like them, because they are fun to be around as long as we are not the butt of their jokes. The best humor in a professional context is usually self-deprecating, because it shows that you do not take yourself too seriously, and it does not risk hurting the feelings of others. A well-timed joke or humorous aside can puncture a tense atmosphere in a meeting like nothing else.

Humor can also bond people, drawing a circle around those who get it and excluding those who do not. These are inside jokes, and as often as not the joke is that there is no joke at all, that it is just some random dumb thing someone once said and someone else repeated. Once the inside joke is established, though, everyone in the know is amused by how perplexing the rest of the world finds it. This kind of exclusion also happens when someone is the butt of a mean joke. That person is now relegated to the outside of the circle.

Our one word of caution about humor is to ignore the age-old advice of starting presentations or speeches with a joke, unless you are the kind of person who was voted "funniest" in your high school class yearbook. There are few places in the world that you would less rather be than in that room facing that audience after your opening joke bombs.

Apologies

One of our friends made an error at work that went undetected until his organization put something out publicly with the error in it. When a reporter zeroed in on it, it ended up making national headlines for a day. With the credibility of his organization on the line, he stepped up and issued an apology to clarify that the responsibility was his alone.

The first rule of apologizing is to mean it. That means feeling and expressing genuine empathy for the people you have done wrong. You have to do the uncomfortable work of imagining what they feel in order to find the right words to express your sorrow for hurting them. As we learn when we are kids, saying "sorry" is not enough. If you do not check the warmth box, your apology does not count.

If warmth is step one, strength is step two. The other essential is a statement of your determination never to repeat this mistake. To make it convincing, cite the specific steps you are taking (or have already taken) to ensure it will never happen again. If you forget this and stop at "sorry," your apology, however heartfelt, will convince no one.

Wordsmithing

Not long ago, a friend of ours was at a delicate stage in a long-distance relationship, and it was not clear if the relationship would survive the stresses of separation. She knew well enough to avoid getting into emotional phone calls with her boyfriend, yet she wanted open and honest communication. She began drafting a letter in which she spelled out clearly what she wanted and expected from the relationship, but she was worried about getting the tone right: Straight talk would make it seem like she could handle honesty, but it risked pushing him away. Warm language might coax him into sharing his feelings, but that ran the risk of making her look weak. She reread the letter and asked herself sentence by sentence whether she was projecting a balance of strength and warmth. In places where she seemed too vulnerable, she would add tough, funny, or matter-of-fact language to bolster her strength. When she realized that something might sound accusatory, she would rephrase the point solely in terms of how she felt, and acknowledge that he was in a difficult position. Looking at her writing through a strength and warmth lens gave her a way to find the right balance between showing affection and demanding respect. This is a useful exercise for any written context, from love letters to website copy.

Making It Happen

"I want to be the person my dog thinks I am."

—Seen embroidered on a pillow

We have explored a variety of ways you can dial strength and warmth up and down using language and nonverbal signals. The next question is how to put all that to good use in your own life.

Changing the habits of thought and behavior that define us to the rest of the world is within our control. But that does not mean it is easy, which is why there are so many different approaches to personal change—finishing schools; character-building activities; joining the army; psychoanalysis, behavior therapy, and most every other kind of psychotherapy; and even psychotropic drugs. Some of these are more helpful than others, and no one approach works best for everyone. But each in its own way is trying to do the same thing: to rewire the residue of our accumulated experience—the positive and negative associations we have with the people and things in the world around us—so we respond differently to life's challenges than we have in the past.

This all starts by figuring out what you are doing now.

The Funhouse Mirror

There is a small town on the Minnesota prairie where all the women are strong, all the men are good-looking, and all the children are above average. Garrison Keillor's tongue-in-cheek tag line for his fictional world says so much about the way we tend to see ourselves that social psychologists call this distorted sense of self-perception the Lake Wobegon effect: Most of us think we are better than average in a variety of ways. Very few people describe themselves as below average in driving skill or intelligence, but by definition half are above and half are below. If you tackle a task with a group of people, you are likely to think your own contributions are more valuable than your fellow group members or disinterested observers do. Just about everybody has a hard time with this, regardless of age, education, or intelligence.

Where warmth is concerned, we presume that our own intentions are good—most of us see ourselves as basically decent people. When we do questionable things, we usually have seemingly reasonable rationales to reconcile our actions with this conception of ourselves as good people. We also sometimes overlook the reality that other people do not automatically assume we have good intentions.

In assessing our own strength, we also have a variety of blinders. We like to see ourselves as strong. Unlike with fuzzy subjective warmth, though, there are plenty of objective ways to evaluate our strength, to see how our skills measure up. Instinctively, the mentally healthy among us tend to grade our own strength on a curve: We attribute bad outcomes more to luck and good outcomes more to our sterling strength. People who are harder on themselves tend to be less happy, and often less warm. So most of us generally trust in our own competence. And it is easy to expect our competence to speak for itself, and to overlook the importance of physical bearing, assertiveness, and all the other signals that show strength.

The reality is we generally have very little sense of the nonverbal cues we give off as we walk through life anyway. These include basic things like the default expressions we wear on our faces, the tilt of our heads, or the gestures and vocal cues that our friends would say define us.

Taking Stock 1: Experiences

So how can you find out how you come across to the world? One approach is just to think about your place in the world and consider a few questions. How much do you shape your social world? Do you ask or do you command? Do you veto others' suggestions? When do you feel most powerful—are there particular activities that bring out your strength? Who sees you in those moments? And is that a feeling you could somehow tap into at other times to feel more confident?

Similarly, how connected do you feel to others? How much time do you spend with them? How often do you laugh? When do you feel most happy in your own skin and connected? Are there particular activities that bring out your warmth? Whom do you share those with? And could you bring some of that attitude into other settings to share with people?

You may already be aware on a deeper level of patterns in your relationships that suggest imbalances in strength or warmth. If you have had a string of bad relationships that have ended the same way, you may want to look closely at the common dynamics. Were respect and liking present in more or less equal measures? The same can be true with bosses or coworkers. If you feel like you never get the attention you deserve at work, for instance, it may be because you expect your competent performance to speak for itself, when you may need to make a greater effort to make your presence known. Depending on the circumstance, these patterns can shape our character profoundly, and change can be a long-term prospect.

Taking Stock 2: The Person in the Pictures

Look at pictures and video clips of yourself. This is not the same thing as looking in a mirror; when we look in a mirror, we automatically adjust our posture and facial expression and sometimes our hair to look our best. If you are good at posing for pictures, posed pictures may be similar (or if you are bad at posing for pictures, they may be worse). Try to find candid pictures and videos that catch you looking the way others see you.

Ask yourself how you would react to meeting someone who looks the way you do in these images. Pay attention to what you notice first. What about you projects strength or weakness? What about you projects warmth or coldness? There is always something on either side of the ledger. Many of us will never be able to see ourselves clearly because we get hung up on some particular aspect of our appearance—looks or body type or dress. Still, it is worth checking your own intuitive reaction first anyway. Then you can go through the elaborate taxonomy of strength and warmth cues in this book as a checklist to help you make sense of what you are seeing.

Because we instinctively pose for the mirror, the person revealed in candid shots and videos can be a little disappointing. But take heart. First of all, there is a lot more to your strength and warmth projection than what the pictures capture: Nonverbal behavior is captured only partially, and vocal and verbal habits not at all. More broadly, whatever you see in those images is good enough to have gotten you the reactions you have been getting from people to this point. Once you understand your overall strength and warmth projection more clearly, you will be able to do even better.

Taking Stock 3: A Little Help from Our Friends

Those closest to us can see us much more clearly than we can see ourselves. Research has found that for most of us, a survey of our friends yields a more accurate picture of our personalities than our own self-assessments.

Getting honest feedback from people you can trust is invaluable, but it is not easy. Parents, spouses, and siblings are sometimes too close to be objective. And even good friends will be reluctant to tell you things they fear will hurt your feelings ("You're great—really").

If you want to try to talk to someone you trust about this, it calls for a careful approach. Realize that you are putting your friend in a potentially awkward position, and resolve to be grateful and sympathetic no matter what you hear. Do not ask for feedback like you are fishing for compliments or being neurotic and in need of reassurance. It is important to explain why you are asking, and to show that you have already come to terms with the idea that you might have some shortcomings: "I feel like I have not been connecting with people lately, and I'm trying to figure out what that is about. I wonder if I might be saying things that seem off to people, or if my intensity level sometimes creates a disconnect. I can't really put my finger on a specific example of anything; it is just a general sense." If you start the conversation by proposing possibilities, then your friend does not have to be the first one to bring them up. And if you have brought up the wrong ones, your friend can put your mind at ease about those by pointing you to the real story.

After you ask, you will want to listen carefully. Just do not start reading dark meanings into every note in your friend's voice; there is a reason psychologically healthy people are not too self-critical. And even a good friend's opinion is still just one opinion. If you think you have heard an important piece of feedback, explain to your friend what you think you heard and ask if you have the right idea. If you do end up with a big pile of constructive criticism, do not despair; things are no worse than they were before you had this new perspective. You do not have to tackle everything all at once. But now you can see the way forward.

Coaching Yourself

When people try to improve their skills, whether in soccer, surgery, or social relations, it is handy to have someone to work with: a friend, a therapist, a coach. Since such people are not in your head, they are not working with all of the information you are, but they also have a much clearer perspective on the qualities you are projecting to others, because they have had the experience of being in your presence. They can tell you when you are hitting the mark and when you are not. But unless you are a top CEO with a big training budget, they usually cannot be around all the time, or even when you need them the most.

Fortunately, you can also learn to be your own coach. Your perspective will always have limits, but you can improve your ability to identify and monitor important signals and recognize how to adjust in response, just like a coach would advise you. In fact, the shared secret of most exceptionally compelling people is that they were not born that way—they worked hard at it, and continue to. Ronald Reagan had decades of professional acting experience before he brought his grandfatherly cowboy persona to the national stage. Even after years as a successful politician, Bill Clinton still sought out every expert he could find to learn how to connect with people better. The best communicators are the ones who realize how much room they still have for improvement.

When we play the coaching role for people, whether we are working together for one session or continuously, one of our principal objectives is to help people learn to coach themselves. Reading this book cannot replicate the experience of getting coaching. But as you think about how all of this relates to you, it is useful to consider how this kind of personal change happens. When we help people evaluate the way they move through the world, we begin with a few overarching issues:

Skill: Does this look right?

Most of us send all kinds of signals we are not aware of, mostly rooted in emotions we may not even consciously realize we are feeling. After decades of this, our muscles may have forgotten how to make fluid, confident gestures, and many of us say "aah" between words more often, and louder than the words themselves. Almost all of us could stand to shake some bad behavioral habits and develop a few better ones, so our nonverbal and verbal signals paint a picture of us as confident and personable.

Remember, in keeping with the hydraulic effect, almost every signal we send adds strength or warmth and reduces the other, just not in equal measure. The challenge is putting together the right combination of signals to get you into the upper-right quadrant. But since our bad habits are often rooted in unhelpful emotional reactions, the best way to get rid of them is to rewire those reactions. Likewise, the better behavioral habits we are trying to develop are going to be more effective and more lasting if they are rooted in an authentic (and positive) emotional experience. So while we spend time with people focused on learning and unlearning various behaviors, we also focus on letting go of feelings of weakness and dialing up feelings of strength, getting past cold, detached attitudes and engaging genuine feelings of warmth. Developing a positive attitude makes the dance steps come easier too.

Confidence: Can I pull this off?

Most of us have some level of inhibiting anxieties around how we conduct ourselves around others, not only in front of large audiences but also in more intimate but still high-stakes settings, such as job interviews or pitch meetings. You do not have to get rid of that anxiety to make a good impression, but you do want to learn to manage it—to get the butterflies in your belly to fly in formation, as the saying goes.

Emotional Alignment: Does this feel right?

When you are at your best, your actions are expressions of your strength and warmth. If you want to be at your best, you want to do more than just turn down your anxiety and go through the motions: you want to turn up feelings of strength, and warmth too. If you can affirmatively develop a clear sense of your own strength and your own warmth, you can tap into that in high-stakes moments so you feel confident and happy to be there. Then all your good new habits are not just motions you go through—they flow directly from your feelings and character.

We often think about our coaching as working in two different ways, "outside in" and "inside out." Outside in is basic instruction in how to perform particular actions, in the same way teachers, trainers, and athletic coaches everywhere show us how to do things. Some of that definitely has a place in our work. We show our clients the magic ball, and they practice using it until it feels as natural as it looks. But we also do a lot of inside-out coaching, focusing first on rethinking attitudes and mental frameworks and feelings. This naturally shapes all the small but critical behaviors that we otherwise have a lot of difficulty changing consciously. At the end of the day, the best way to project strength is to feel strong, and the only way to project warmth is to feel warmth.

Inside-out coaching can be done using imagination exercises or games to shift the associations that guide their natural reactions. Imagination games are nothing new: Maybe as a kid you made a game out of an otherwise unpleasant household chore, or made a tough decision by imagining a reckless friend of yours whispering to you from one shoulder and a more responsible friend warning of the risks from the other. The imagination games we use work by setting up emotional associations that kick in when you face a challenging situation to put yourself in a more effective frame of mind. You are preparing your mind ahead of time, a little like Ulysses lashing himself to the mast, only usually not so excruciating. These games are useful along the way to help you develop good habits and get by in the meantime. Once you have had success, and get used to the feeling of expressing your strength and warmth naturally through your actions, the imagination games may feel less like a tool and more like a crutch you no longer need. We have mentioned a couple of our favorites already—getting in the phone booth, getting in the circle—

and will describe others in upcoming chapters, particularly in the section on how to manage anxiety in public speaking.

Dialing Up Strength

Your strength is firmly grounded in your confidence. Do you believe you will be able to get the job done? Are you tough enough to hold your own with other strong-willed people whose interests are not the same as yours? This is an internal test of your mettle, and it is not a matter of competence. It is a matter of will.

Summoning that strength often takes effort. Sometimes we are tired, sometimes we are nervous, sometimes we are just not feeling it when the important moment comes. While we cannot rewire our natural responses completely, we can still create change when we need it through brute force of will. Just focus on why the task is important and how it connects to your values and your sense of who you want to be in the world. Then resolve to do it, no matter how it feels. Finally, make yourself do what needs to be done, even if that is not at all what comes naturally to you in the situation.

Psychologist Brian Little describes his own struggles as an introvert forcing himself to lecture to large audiences at Harvard and around the world. He simply made himself walk up to the podium and speak the words. It was painful and exhausting, but necessary to achieve what his principles and passion called on him to achieve. For most of us, if we force ourselves to do something enough, we will adapt to it somewhat and it will become less onerous and more natural. But even if it never gets any easier, it can still be done. And that then boosts our sense of our own strength, which is its own reward.

We project strength through the nonverbal cues we discussed earlier: upright posture, controlled gestures, a level brow, a focused gaze, a low vocal pitch, minimal filler, and no uptalk. These are all things we can practice and get better at. As uncomplicated as it sounds, simply stand-ing tall is often half the battle. If your moves are a little off, keep practic-ing and you will get better, just as with any other physical skill. And if your courage is still faltering, you can do most of this consciously, al-though if you have a belly full of butterflies your results will be uneven.

Many people do not project much strength because they have an uneasy relationship to it. We are keenly aware of its misuse, and never want to be party to that, so most people prefer to lead with warmth so they are perceived first as nice. If you work at it, you can get pretty far in life this way. But without the complementary strength, there are lim-its. For warmth-focused people, it is important to think about all the worthy things that strength accomplishes—and to imagine all the wor-thy things that will be left unaccomplished without it, including helping others. For some people, it is critical just to realize that they deserve respect, and they can claim it only by asserting themselves, by showing strength.

For the more introverted, it is worth remembering that just trying on an extroverted persona can be a fun trick. You do not always have to be the life of the party, but extroverted behavior enables you to project strength and warmth at the same time. And the research suggests that it can run your happiness and confidence circuits in reverse, giving you a boost of good feeling.

Dialing Up Warmth

One of the political candidates we have worked with initially said that he was not particularly a "people person." He did not really like meeting people or engaging in the give-and-take of "retail politics." He saw it as a necessary duty, not an enjoyable part of the job. You may ask why he chose that line of work. The truth was that he was driven by a passion for serving the public good and thought the best way he could do that was to represent his neighbors in Congress. With some coaching, he was able to translate those intentions into warmth that people could feel.

The simple truth is that if you want to be admired, you have to be liked. And if you want to be liked, you have to like people. It is a basic reciprocity effect: If you like other people, they are inclined to like you, and vice versa. Granted, there are plenty of excuses not to like people, but you can find fault with anyone. If your goal is to be admired by others, you have to find reasons to like them—especially if you want to persuade them to see things your way later.

When you sense the need to make a deeper connection with people, there are a couple of questions worth asking yourself: Why do I like these people—or if I don't, why might I come to like them? What are our shared concerns and interests? How can I make it clear that we want the same things or are on the same team? Look for ways that mirroring might send nonverbal cues that you feel the same way as the person you are trying to reach. In choosing your words, your first move is to find a way into the circle. What feelings can you validate that will demonstrate that you "get it"—that you see the world similarly? This calls for a lot of listening and a genuine interest in finding common ground.

But it is not just an intellectual exercise. To effectively project warmth to people, you have to *feel* warmth for people. It is possible to physically trigger feelings of happiness, running your warmth circuits in reverse, just as we saw with power poses and strength. You can move the muscles around your mouth and eyes into the position of a genuine smile and hold that position until it starts to make you feel happy. It is far better, though, to use the inside-out approach and find a reason to be happy where you are. In challenging situations, this may even require laughing ruefully at life. That is often good enough to put a genuine smile on your face. But if you can focus on the people you are with, and why you are happy to be there, the rest generally falls into place.

The Warm-up Routine

Making all of this happen when it really counts is not easy, not least because that is when we are naturally at our most anxious. For most of us, the quality of our communications tends to follow a bell curve distribution. Sometimes they are exceptionally good, sometimes they are pretty bad, and most of the time they fall somewhere in between. Much of the frustration stems from the feeling that there is little rhyme or reason to the lack of consistency. This is one of the principal goals of coaching, to communicate not only compellingly, but consistently—to lop off the left end of the bell curve and shift the whole thing up to the right. For people whose professional success is directly tied to their personal communication, even just a few missteps avoided or a 10 percent shift to the right can pay huge dividends.

The best way to make sure you are reliably at your best is to develop a warm-up routine that puts you in the right physical state and frame of mind to project the right energy for the occasion. This need only take a minute, or even a few seconds, but this time makes everything that happens next go better.

Recall the advantages to making yourself big for just a minute or two, increasing your testosterone and decreasing your cortisol, so you are more confident and less anxious. Some people also like to limber up with a few favorite stretches. Find something you like and stick with it—the familiarity helps you feel comfortable and grounded.

Then while you are making yourself big, you want to get your attitude straight. Recall the phone booth exercise we mentioned earlier; remember what it feels like when you are happy and in command. Whatever works for you is what you should do. For example, one of our clients often faced hostile questioning in his public appearances. For him, in this moment in his warm-up routine, he would think about the word "generous," because that was how he wanted to present himself to his audience, even—or perhaps especially—when they were not feeling generous toward him.

Reading Others Redux

But it's not all about you. No matter how strong and warm you feel, no matter how well prepared you are to share your good ideas, you can fall flat if you fail to tune in to your audience's signals. To be effective in the moment, you need to pay attention to your audience.

Whenever you encounter someone, you make your initial judgment: Do I like this person, and do I respect this person? To understand more, though, think about how that judgment happened. What emotional reaction hit you first? Were there notes of fear, or pity, or contempt? Then ask yourself what led you to that impression. Just notice what about this person jumped out at you first. If you were describing the person to a friend, what would you say? You would likely start with the basics—gender, ethnicity, height, age, build, hair color, and dress—each of which might or might not have much to do with your character judgment. Beyond that, there are usually several other distinctive things you might recall next: posture, facial expression, vocal tone, gestures, maybe even specific words or phrases. Focus on those defining signals—they are most likely the key ingredients in your strength and warmth judgments. Each one projects a unique kind of strength or weakness, warmth or coldness that shapes your overall impression.

Then you can take a closer look at those key signals to see if they really mean what they first seem to. It is important to distinguish between what people are doing deliberately and what they are doing unconsciously, because their intentions are how you judge warmth. Some nonverbal behavior is the equivalent of walking around with your pants unzipped: Everyone knows about it but you, and it is not flattering. Imagine, for instance, a man seated at his desk having a casual conversation with his female boss, who popped in and is standing in the doorway of his office. If he absentmindedly picks at his cuticles while they're talking, that may or may not reflect chronic low-level tension. If he seems unaware of it, chances are it does not say anything about his intentions. On the other hand, if he is conspicuously checking his fingernails, that likely reflects a conscious choice to be informal in her presence, which could signal a lack of respect.

Of course, there is no way to get a reliable impression of someone with just a glance, or even after a few minutes. But you do learn something important even in those first few seconds: Your first impression is likely very similar to the impression this person has made on many others over the years. Knowing this impression, you can imagine how other people have treated this person over time, and that can give you an idea about the response you might expect.

You will often find people taking steps to blunt the negative impact of things they cannot easily change, like gender, ethnicity, looks, or body type. The former linebacker flashes a big smile to put people at ease. The pretty girl wears a scowl to ward off unwanted attention. The young black man dresses impeccably to avoid racial profiling. The overweight girl is funny and gregarious to keep from being ignored.

Though your first impression is useful, keep watching. A young woman seems friendly and gregarious, but perhaps she is actually very suspicious and that is her way of testing people. Her hip is cocked at a funny angle— is that attitude, or does she have a bad knee? Sometimes with just a little more observation you can distinguish the signals from the noise.

One of the things you are trying to find out is this person's attitude toward different kinds of strength and warmth projection. Do they value jovial humor to project warmth and confidence, or dismiss that as bluster and favor a more understated demeanor? Often their own signals are your best guide to how they would like to be approached.

Remember, when you encounter new people, you are on a two-way street—judgment is being passed on you too. If you decode their signals quickly, you can figure out how to put your best foot forward.

Strength and Warmth
in the World

Into the Wild

True story: Our friend's dad did not want a dog, but one day Mom and the kids brought one home anyway. What was worse, they picked a tiny, yappy dog, and they called him Peanut. He was mostly well behaved, but Dad just had no patience for him. Peanut would slink up to Dad and wag his tail and try to lick him, and Dad would yell for someone to get "this dog" away from him.

Then one day, a big black bear comes ambling through their backyard. Everyone runs to the back window to see, and everyone is laughing and taking pictures, until somebody says, "Where's Peanut?" Suddenly, Peanut comes streaking across the backyard at the bear, barking like a maniac. The bear sees this crazed dog hopping around in front of him, little fangs bared, and wants none of it; he turns away, retreating at a trot, Peanut barking furiously all the while.

Now Dad has a whole new attitude. Not only does he not mind the dog; he takes him for walks every day. And when he gets the leash, he says, "You wanna go find a bear? Let's go find a bear."

Why didn't Dad like Peanut before? In part, Peanut may have been a symbol of Dad's weakness in his own household, but that was not the real issue. The problem was that Peanut was a sissy dog, weak, unworthy of respect. But when Peanut proved tougher than a bear, that was good enough for Dad.

So far we have looked at all sorts of different ways we humans project and perceive warmth and strength. Now it is time to see how all these projections and perceptions play out in a range of everyday settings: the office, the stage, the bar, the living room. Looking through the strength and warmth lens at how people judge each other helps explain how things unfold in each of these situations. And wherever you find yourself, at the executive or entry level, campaigning for office or campaigning for a second date, it also lets you see how dialing up your own strength or warmth might be just the thing to get you where you want to be.

At Work

A friend of ours once had meetings with senior executives at two Fortune 500 companies—a bank and a media conglomerate—in the same week. For her bank meeting, she presented herself very conservatively: dark suit, hair up, plenty of poise in her demeanor and grace in her movements. Not surprisingly, this fit their culture and expectations, and her meeting went well. Later that week she went to the media company, and she showed up dressed and carrying herself the same way. It took her a few minutes to realize something was not right. Initially she thought it was great how friendly everyone was to her. But it slowly dawned on her that they were also very skeptical of her steely demeanor. She found herself tap-dancing quickly to convince the people at the media company that she was a good fit with their culture, which placed a premium on openness, creative expression, and collaboration.

Looking at our friend's experience through the lens of strength and warmth, we see a few different dynamics in play. While both companies place a premium on strong market performance, the bank's culture is colder and the media company's culture is warmer. Our friend showed up at both places looking and acting all business, which projected strength. At the bank, that helped earn their respect, and it also helped show that she shared their sensibilities.

At the media company, her appearance and demeanor suggested that she was out of sync with their culture. Her hosts likely saw her as strong but not warm. They may also have seen her as neither warm nor strong: Since she misjudged their company, they may not have respected her.

As any Ayn Rand acolyte can tell you, a modern capitalist economy is all about getting things done—all strength. On the other hand, an organization where people are aligned around their collective mission is a team that shares a bond of warmth. And even when the shared interest is not so clear, getting things done in organizations means dealing with people effectively, which usually requires warmth. There are some organizations that see themselves as all business, with no time for warmth. But many organizations see some form of warmth as key to their effectiveness, whether it is good client service, appealing marketing and branding, or attracting top talent by keeping employees happy.

Strength judgments at work are based on more than personal presence and job performance. The workplace is full of status symbols that confer strength. The most obvious of these is someone's place in the organizational hierarchy, but status signals like access to decision makers, compensation, and even distance from the proverbial corner office also count. A senior position carries prestige and often direct authority to make decisions that affect coworkers' lives. Job status is won and lost based on a variety of factors ranging from hard-won experience to nepotism. But it is exactly because life is complicated that we use social status signals like job titles as shorthand.

These three strength elements—presence, performance, and position—exist in a balance at work. Over time, the shorthand of position does not always match the reality, and when someone in authority neither projects a strong presence nor gets the job done, position alone will not be enough to maintain coworkers' respect, and they will start to question whether that person is a good fit for the job. If you look the part, you may end up getting and keeping the job even if the results are not what they should be, to some extent because acting the part will help divert people's suspicions that you might be the problem. On the other hand, if you are achieving outstanding results at work, you may buy yourself latitude in the way you present yourself. This recalls the old saying that the difference between a crazy person and an eccentric is that an eccentric has lots of money; success creates a buffer of respect.

The Interview

One of the most important moments of self-presentation is the job interview, especially if the candidate has no prior connections at the company. As always, the candidate's basic goal is to project strength and warmth, but the stylized ritual of the interview has its own particular challenges.

From the interviewer's perspective, there are three basic questions to answer:

1. Can the candidate do the job? This is the competence aspect of strength.

2. Does the candidate want to do the job? This speaks to the candidate's determination, also a dimension of strength.

3. Do our people want to work with this candidate? This is warmth.

Projecting strength is an applicant's primary goal, and the hiring process reflects that. If you know people at the company or have been recommended by an intermediary, you may have made a first impression before the formal process even starts.

The typical first impression is made on paper through a resume, an important though increasingly dated means of projecting strength. What institutions have you been associated with, and for how long? How expansively can you describe what you did there without calling your honesty into question? And not least, how flawlessly can you present all of this information? People who buck tradition and try to stand out by adding displays of warmth to their resumes might luck out once in a while, but for the most part they are missing the point. The resume is about documenting evidence of strength. The cover letter offers slightly more latitude to humanize oneself. You can express emotions here, but the expectation is still that your primary emotion is joy at the prospect of helping your potential employer get the job done. Lots of people now also use professional networking sites to post professional profiles that can be enhanced with photos and videos. Anything that goes beyond the information on a paper resume should add to the overall portrait of you as a capable professional, not distract from it.

Once your resume has gotten you in the door, the interview brings all of your other strength and warmth signals into play. Like our friend who forgot to recalibrate her approach when moving between the worlds of high finance and media, in person you will be judged on your appearance and attire. But your demeanor will generally speak loudest. Do your posture and stride project confidence? Does your facial expression show you are happy to be there? Are you fidgeting or twitching in ways that suggest more than the usual amount of nerves? In an instant, the preliminary judgment has been made, and all other incoming information starts to be filtered through the lens of that initial impression, which hardens by the second.

But the applicant is not the only one being judged. As the applicant, you are also judging the interviewer, and it is critical to get that judgment right. The interviewer's strength and warmth is your best clue. People generally project what they value. Watch your interviewer and figure out which signals get dialed up and which get dialed down. The winning strategy is to meet strength with strength and warmth with warmth.

This can be hard, as the high stakes of an interview can make any candidate nervous. And since you want the job, you also want people to like you, which will tend to make you behave in a more ingratiating manner. The best way forward is to follow your interviewer's lead—not to be manipulative or condescending, but to be respectful of this person and their values.

As always, projecting effective nonverbal signals is all in the attitude, because our external behavior reflects our emotional state. Since in interviews we are meeting strangers for the first time and want them to see us as good people, we are often polite and modest when describing ourselves and our accomplishments. This is a mistake. Your interviewer generally wants to like you too, but you are not just any old stranger; you are a potential team member whose strengths are likely to directly benefit them. Interviewers may or may not have read your resume, but either way they want to be reassured that you know what you are doing, and you can do that by showing confidence, not modesty. Research finds that narcissistic personality types do very well in interviews. For the rest of us, finding the right balance can be a challenge. You do not want to hide your accomplishments, but if you brag too enthusiastically, you risk appearing conceited. A good happy medium is to frame your accomplishments in terms of how you have helped others, such as how you enabled your team or organization to meet its goals. Thinking this through during your warm-up routine before the interview can be invaluable.

If you advance to the final round of interviews and end up in a head-to-head matchup, a contrast effect is likely to develop between you and the other candidate. Your interviewers will likely see one of you as the slightly stronger candidate and the other as the slightly warmer one. If you have gotten this far, chances are you have cleared some basic threshold on strength and warmth already, but now is the time to shore up your case. Again, follow the lead of your interviewers and try to emphasize whichever quality seems most important to them, but do not overlook the importance of making sure your prospective employer sees both qualities in you.

In the Office

Congratulations; you're hired! Now what? Now you get to meet all of the coworkers who were hidden from you during the interview process.

At work, we are judging and being judged by colleagues on multiple levels at once. We get to know our coworkers as people, but they are there first and foremost in the role of professionals getting paid to do a job. Strength is often judged first in the professional role—nurses, bond traders, and airline mechanics all need their coworkers to be highly competent, even if they emphasize different qualities in their personal lives.

The kind of reception you get from colleagues depends not only on what qualities you project, but on what kind of culture you are entering. While most private-sector workplaces prioritize the bottom line, there are different conceptions about how best to maximize it. Some companies stress cooperation, while others encourage competition. Susan Fiske, of Princeton University, has studied the influence of cultural factors on individual interactions. In a more cooperative setting, coworkers regard one another as potential assets and value both how personable and how competent someone is. In a more competitive environment, coworkers are regarded as potential threats and competence is king.

The reality is that most workplaces have elements of both: some necessary cooperation on tasks, and some unavoidable competition for status. These crosscurrents can make life in the modern workplace emotionally fraught for even the most well-adjusted, competent, and cheerful among us. Since we judge other people both by how capable they are and by whose team they are on, tensions between cooperation and competition make these judgments doubly difficult.

Beyond the competitive-cooperative dynamic, some workplaces have "hard" cultures driven by hierarchy and top-down decision making, while others have "soft" cultures that emphasize collaboration and getting buy-in for decisions. These cultural dynamics are usually a direct reflection of the organization's priorities. A company that explicitly focuses on customer service and customer experience as core values will likely place more of a premium on warmth from its employees than one that seeks to project lots of strength as a means of maintaining investor confidence.

It is possible to build a high-functioning organization around a culture of strength. Some people thrive in a hard-charging atmosphere, and for them, that appeal is all the warmth they need, at least until they burn out. Organizations that hire for this quality can perform at a very high level. In these environments, internal decision making still requires both strength and warmth to persuade people to adopt new ideas, but bottom-line performance is all that matters. The downside to this approach tends to be lower employee quality of life and higher attrition. Many organizations find not only that an environment with more warmth improves quality of life for everyone, reducing employee turnover costs, but that happy employees are productive ones as well.

Communicating Up, Across, and Out

Nearly all of us have a complicated set of relationships to navigate at the office. The first is communicating up, or managing direct and indirect bosses and senior influencers.

There are obvious limits to how much strength you can bring to this task, and every boss is different. An insecure boss may interpret a show of strength as a threat. At the other extreme, a friend in middle management at a global technology company has been told repeatedly by his very aggressive boss that he is not forceful enough when making his case in their conversations. Not all bosses are like that; the trick is reading and matching, as we said earlier about interviewer styles.

One of the tried-and-true techniques for projecting warmth with just about any personality type is appealing to concerns that will help your boss either look good or stay out of trouble. If, for instance, you are able to pass along useful intelligence because you have an ally in an office higher up the food chain, your boss can prepare for incoming fire before it reaches her desk through formal channels. The "no surprises" rule is another golden oldie; most bosses appreciate advance notice about developments that may wind up on their desks. This projects warmth by demonstrating your loyalty to the team.

If your boss gives you a fair amount of free rein, proactive engagement can be a good way of shaping your own agenda and demonstrating your competence as a self-starter. With micromanagers, many respond well to a steady flow of information about your activities. Micromanagers are typically high in two aspects of strength: assertiveness and competence. Regular reminders that you also value competence can be a good way to set your micromanager's mind at ease. Whether your organization talks in terms of shareholder value, key performance indicators, project milestones, or team goals and objectives, the micromanager will appreciate hearing that you care about hitting those same targets.

When communicating with people at lower levels in the organization, keep in mind that they see you differently than you see yourself. If you are an unknown quantity, it can be important to establish a basis for respect. This can be achieved through a combination of the words you choose and nonverbal cues, including posture and dress. In other cases, your position may confer status that gives you a halo, or it may make you the source of envy or even resentment. This is common in organizations where there is a clear line between "the suits," or management, and "the field." One potential way to inoculate against this is to acknowledge it in a lighthearted way at the outset: "So you're probably looking at me and thinking, 'Here's the suit from headquarters who has no idea how the work really gets done around here.'" By demonstrating that you know how they feel about you, you can disarm skeptics and help establish warmth that can serve as a basis for a solid working relationship.

Communication with peers is often shaped by the competition-cooperation dynamic mentioned earlier. A shorthand frequently develops among people working at the same level in an organization, and speaking that language is a way of projecting warmth. These relationships can include a lot of good-natured insider kidding, which can build camaraderie, though it can also look completely savage to someone not in the club.

When you head out into the world on behalf of a company, you are its proxy. In that first moment when you walk in the door and introduce yourself, everything that your hosts know or sense about your organization—brand, reputation, and credibility all rolled into one—gets projected onto you. Understanding how your organization is perceived before you show up is the first step in figuring out what you need to dial up or down as its representative on the ground, whether you're meeting a customer, client, vendor, or other stakeholder.

The same way your organization's reputation attaches itself to you, the impression you make is a reflection on the company. Your behaviors and mannerisms—whether friendly or formal, organized or disorganized, high energy or low key—will either conform to your hosts' expectations of your organization or deviate from them. It is possible to play against type to your advantage here. If your firm has a reputation for being very buttoned-down, you might pleasantly surprise someone by showing more warmth. The same dynamic can work in reverse. Imagine that you work for a nonprofit organization and you are meeting a prospective corporate partner for the first time. If there are questions hanging in the air about the managerial competence of nonprofits in general (or your organization in particular), you can help address them by dialing up strength, in both what you say and how you present yourself.

Strength vs. Warmth, Part 1: The Manager's Dilemma

Managing others is something most of us aspire to, because it means control and status. But it also comes with responsibility, not least learning to balance strength and warmth in interactions with the people you manage. In many ways this is similar to other leadership roles we have seen modeled all our lives, like parent or teacher—it requires being both cheerleader and disciplinarian. Playing the role well requires some range.

This can be particularly hard for certain types of people. A friend of ours tells the tale of a peer of hers becoming a supervisor. Insecure in his new position, he felt it necessary to establish his authority as a leader by issuing an e-mail memo about curbing leisurely coffee breaks. Soon morale was down and the break room conversations that often yielded useful information and ideas were a thing of the past. On the other hand, the sidekick type of boss, who wants above all else to be loved— see the inimitable Michael Scott character from TV's *The Office*—may unwittingly invite subordinates to game the system and not do their best work. This can easily lead to various crises requiring forceful interventions the boss is ill-equipped to perform. Out-of-balance bosses create problems either way. Control freaks and screamers command respect but no loyalty, while hesitant and conflict-averse managers may lack the backbone to make tough calls.

Suppose you work with a guy named Henry, who sometimes has trouble getting things done on time. A few months after he joined the company, he was supposed to have part of a proposal finished, but he missed the deadline. This was not the first time—he had been a little late once before. And maybe that was the problem: When it happened before, everyone recognized that his work was sharp, so while he knew his lateness annoyed his colleagues, he still felt he had permission to take his time. But now his lateness seriously hurt their proposal's chances.

If you were supervising Henry, you would have lots of options for how to handle the situation. You might administer concrete punishment for the missed deadline. You might chew him out in private, or in front of the team. You might take his part of the work away from him at the deadline, denying him the satisfaction of producing good work, and get the proposal out the door as best you can without his best efforts. You might sit down and talk with him alone and ask what you can do to help him get it done on time. Every manager has a unique style, and every situation and employee presents a slightly different challenge. While it is hard to know in advance what approach will work best when subordinates screw up, an all-strength approach often creates as many problems as it solves, a point made memorably by the apocryphal management edict "The beatings will continue until morale improves." Everyone interprets supervisory actions differently, but most people respond well to knowing that there are both personal costs of failure and real rewards—recognition, satisfaction, raises—for contributing to the larger group effort.

Unless the organizational culture demands otherwise, there is a good argument for trying warmth before strength when managing employees: It builds trust first, and sends a message that everyone is presumed competent and motivated. This kind of trust reduces friction and promotes sharing important information. A culture of fear, in which employees' overriding concern is avoiding trouble, can keep important ideas and information underground if people are too concerned about survival to speak up.

Strength vs. Warmth, Part 2: The Marketer's Dilemma

In the marketplace, potential customers pass judgment on companies and their wares, and once again strength and warmth considerations are at the fore. Suppose you are marketing bed linens. For you to make the sale, consumers need to see your sheets as promising a set of features that they are interested in—for instance, the color is appealing and the package says they are soft. Consumers also need to see the sheets as being able to deliver on that promise—for example, your brand is one they know and trust, and the package offers a money-back guarantee if the color fades. Matching the consumer's needs and reliably meeting them is both warm and strong.

But while any product has to meet some basic strength and warmth criteria, successful products can emphasize strength and warmth differently in appealing to consumers. Suppose your sheets are up against snazzier sheets that sell at a slightly higher price point and brag about their higher thread count and exotic foreign fibers. You could cede the strength appeal to the competition and counter with a warmth appeal: Your sheets are not exotic and new; they are just like the sheets you grew up with—basic, homey, with simple, friendly colors. Alternatively, you could focus on your sheets' lower price point as a strength, directly challenging the competition on strength by portraying their features as overhyped silliness and your sheets as the sensible choice—all the sheet you want at the price you want to pay. Depending on how efficiently you communicate and how much time your customers have to think about sheets, you could also pitch both points.

Susan Fiske and her colleagues examined popular corporate brands and found that consumers look for the same qualities—capability and intention—when thinking about consumer brands as they do when judging people.

These influence both purchasing decisions and brand loyalty. Take, for instance, Campbell's soup. Consumers have good feelings about it, and the company is seen as capable of delivering the goods. This combination of high warmth and high strength makes it an admirable brand. On the flip side, perceptions of BP in the aftermath of the Deepwater Horizon disaster are that its officers were neither competent nor concerned about anything beyond their own narrow self-interest. This leads to feelings of contempt or disgust.

Organizations earn reputations as either capable or incapable of delivering what they promise, and as easy or difficult to work with—usually a reflection of how much they account for the shared interests of their partners. In a competitive marketplace, many factors contribute to judging performance. Customers may prefer a warmer working relationship with a "good enough" partner to an annoying experience with one that is better by certain objective measures.

Strength vs. Warmth, Part 3: The Salesperson's Dilemma

Sales can be a rough line of work, particularly in the Willy Loman or *Glengarry Glen Ross* model of pitching your wares to one customer at a time. Salespeople have to show customers enough warmth to build trust while staying strong enough on the inside to cope with rejection. Core to the sales profession's traditions is the strategic choice between leading with strength and leading with warmth, also known as the hard sell versus the soft sell.

In the soft-sell scenario, the salesperson uses the full complement of warmth signals to show concern for the customer's well-being, so the customer feels like the salesperson has the customer's best interests at heart. This can include everything from long discussions about the customer's needs to free trial periods to free tickets to the big game.

In the hard sell, the salesperson creates a very different dynamic, and it is heavy on strength. When the hard-sell salesperson initially introduces the product to the customer, the salesperson is confident and up-beat, with both strength and warmth. But the salesperson soon switches gears and becomes almost aloof. Unlike the attentive and needy soft-sell salesperson, the hard-sell salesperson's demeanor is one of supreme confidence. The product is definitely going to sell—there might even be a bidding war pushing the price up before long. The message is clear: The salesperson does not need the customer. Take it or leave it; it does not matter to the salesperson. In fact, the customer is lucky to have the opportunity to buy this spectacular product at this price. After all, plenty of people will recognize a great deal being offered, so there is no need to waste time with a customer who does not. The salesperson is trying to create a dynamic where the seemingly great strength of the product makes the customer want to get in on that action. It is a classic case of using strength to draw people in—to create warmth, in other words.

If the customer does not come around, the salesperson has one last move to try: expressing disbelief and contempt that the customer would be so stupid as to pass up this deal, and actively threatening to punish this stupidity by withdrawing the offer—in which case the would-be customer will clearly regret having missed this chance. Here the salesperson is using straight strength to create urgency and compel the customer to respond.

If there is any question about which way to go, salespeople can and do hedge their bets by leading with warmth, and only turn to strength if it is necessary to close the deal. The time spent building rapport up front still helps when the heat is on. If instead a salesperson starts with the hard sell and fails, there is probably not much hope. Remember the tomato rule: Cold impressions last, which means you are going to have a hard time reestablishing trust after being a jerk.

The Big Pitch

In high-stakes situations like a big pitch, whether for a venture capital investment, a hefty contract from a client, or a partnership, you are being evaluated on a number of dimensions that correspond to strength and warmth. Your would-be partner wants to know you have something of significant value to offer, that you have a strong sense of the relevant business dynamics, and that you can deliver—all strength factors. They also want to know your interests are aligned, and that there is a good personal fit for a long-term relationship.

To close the sale, your story will have to include both a compelling way of establishing a shared interest as well as the business case for the proposal. The rest—a character judgment—will depend on earning the confidence of the other party and demonstrating that you are their kind of person. Depending on what kind of people they are, this may not call for high-wattage gregariousness—it may be about making clear your commitment to providing return on investment to shareholders, or some other serious concern that determines personal fit from their perspective. The warmth challenge in a big pitch is first and foremost about getting in the circle.

The most common mistake we see in presentations large and small is an overreliance on a PowerPoint deck to tell the story. A slide deck is a standard part of many big pitches, but too often it is used as a crutch—or worse, it tells the whole story, rendering you redundant. A self-explanatory slide deck you might e-mail someone to read on their own does not belong in a projection behind you, because that makes you irrelevant, or worse.

A friend of ours had a brother in the military, and he was given the critical assignment—and huge opportunity—of briefing a general on a mission-critical issue, with two weeks to prepare his presentation. He worked his butt off and got every slide just perfect. When the moment came, he walked the general through the first slide and then the second. As he turned to the third, the general spoke: "Is everything you need to say on those slides?" "Yes sir," he replied. "Fine," said the general. "I will tell you when to flip." After weeks of preparation, the rest of his big meeting with the general he spent in silence, flipping slides "like Vanna White," as he told it.

Most audiences will not be so candid with you. More likely, they will read each new slide you show them, and then go back to looking at their smartphone until you finish talking and turn to the next slide.

Ultimately your audience needs to believe in both you and your idea. Your deck may sell your idea, but it will not sell you. That means you should be the center of attention, not your slides. Know what you want to say first, and then use slides to illustrate key points along the way— but not every point, so you stay relevant and keep your audience's attention.

Having a strong narrative is key. The story should be developed first, before the slides or other supporting materials; as we said earlier, it is the number one way into the circle. Even jaded skeptics will expect and respond positively to a good story, regardless of whether they proceed to challenge your business case and all the assumptions behind it.

We once worked with a health care company that called us in a week before a big pitch to help them rehearse. In the first run-through, the team members each spoke to several slides of a PowerPoint deck. They moved through it relatively smoothly, but the larger issue was that the presentation was about as memorable as a preflight safety briefing. There was no story that gave meaning or context to the problem the team was proposing to solve. After an hour or so of talking through this, one of the team members casually recounted an anecdote about a doctor involved in the project who had worked in a poor country that needed this breakthrough. A perfect story had been sitting in plain sight. After retooling the presentation around it, the team realized that the doctor protagonist would actually be the best messenger to bring the emotional element to life. A few phone calls later, the doctor agreed to tell his story on video as part of the pitch. We helped simplify the slides to support the overall narrative. The team called us the next week, excited that they had won the account. It was not magic; it was just good storytelling.

A good business case projects more than just competence. The assumptions and projections within it make a concrete statement about how you think the world works. Getting your audience to see the world as you do is a challenge of creating shared understanding—again, it comes back to the circle.

Fake It Till It's Real

Many, many people play a destructive imagination game with themselves known as the "impostor syndrome." Having attained some success, they have been elevated into positions of leadership and are not quite sure of themselves. This then becomes their dark secret: They suspect they are the only ones who are not quite sure what they are doing, and that they must have been given this responsibility by mistake. As a result they feel vulnerable, because they are sure they will be exposed and shamed and drummed out of their positions. This feeling is serious, debilitating, and very common. Now, it is true, as the Peter Principle suggests, that some people get promoted and promoted until they finally land in a job that is beyond their ability to do well, and there they stay. But most people suffering from impostor syndrome are right where they should be.

Their problem is they have allowed themselves to be fooled by the confidence of those around them.

When we are kids, we first think adults know everything, and then we start to suspect maybe they do not, and as we become adults ourselves we confirm that. Similarly, in most professional settings, many people at the top of their fields are flying largely by instinct. A lot of them will see their luck turn or have new developments overtake them at some point.

Until that happens, though, many of them will not admit any self-doubt, because it makes it harder to summon and project the confidence it takes to do the job. But they are not necessarily as infallible as they seem.

People who start to get the feeling they are in over their head can usually partially talk themselves out of it, both by considering that the supreme confidence of most people around them may be folly and by remembering the accomplishments that got them to where they are. But in the moment, faced with a daunting professional situation and having a mild panic attack, there is also a little game you can play to buck yourself up.

Frank Abagnale was a professional impostor. He passed himself off as a pilot and a doctor, among other professions, and he faked his way through most of it just fine. How? By now you know the answer: He was confident, comfortable in his own skin (and someone else's uniform), and compelling. Eventually he did get caught, but even then the people who caught him liked him so much they hired him. Frank wrote a book, *Catch Me If You Can*, and Leonardo DiCaprio played him in the movie version. So if you are feeling like an impostor in your job, imagine how a good impostor like Frank would handle himself in your situation: He would smile, stride around confidently and relaxed, make good eye contact, and listen intently to colleagues. You can do all of that too. And not only that, unlike Frank, you have the tremendous advantage of actually knowing something about what you are supposed to be doing.

Words at Work

One of the hardest things with writing is to imagine how the person on the receiving end of your communication will interpret what you have labored so hard to express. E-mail has only exacerbated the opportuni-

ties for miscommunication, since we all now write to each other expo-
nentially more than we did a couple of decades ago.

What Not to Do

Memos to your team that overreach on strength run the risk of undermining morale. The Internet is filled with e-mails from bad bosses; we
will take just one particularly egregious example. On Good Friday
(which falls during Passover), a managing director of an investment
bank, seeing many empty desks, wrote an e-mail that started: "Unless
you are an orthodox something, please get into the office." He closed by
disparaging the work ethic of those who were out, writing, "Join Wells
Fargo and become a teller if you want to take bank holidays."

This is almost comically bad, and there are any number of ways to
handle it better. Even a robotic HR e-mail ("I am writing to remind you
that Good Friday is not a company holiday. If you would like to take it
off, you must use a personal or vacation day") would be an improvement
over this jerk's tone. A more winning approach that would cost nothing
in terms of authority might be:

> One of the things I enjoy most about our firm is that we are a diverse
> group with lots of different beliefs and traditions under the same
> roof. The one downside of that is that we cannot build everyone's
> holiday traditions into our company-wide vacation schedule. For
> those of us for whom today is a religious holiday, the time is yours to
> take, just please record it either as a vacation or a personal day.
> Thanks for your understanding, and enjoy the holiday.

This acknowledgment that people have different customs around religious holidays does not take any great effort or undermine company
policy; it simply makes people feel like you value them as individuals.

Getting It Right

The first decision to make is whether or not to commit something to writing rather than saying it in person. If you're a leader trying to communicate something to hundreds of employees in multiple locations, e-mail may be the most efficient way to do that. But before you hit "send," consider the following questions: Will your message evoke strong emotions that can be tempered if people see your expressions, hear your tone of voice, and sense the authenticity of your intent? Is there an alternative means for communicating with everyone, such as an all-hands meeting or teleconference? Do you want to foster a real-time dialogue or an ongoing exchange, or is this a one-way flow? Do you want to establish a correspondence that people can refer to in the future? Every situation is different, but these considerations can help you choose the right course.

Once you've identified your audience and determined that it is best to put your message in writing, the next step to figure out is what you want people to do once they read it. In sales and marketing, this is called the "ask"—the change in behavior you want to see.

When Things Go Wrong

Tony Hsieh, CEO of Zappos, used a very different style in communicating with his employees after a hacking incident breached one of the company's customer databases in January 2012. His first line underscored the importance of what he was about to say: "Please set aside 20 minutes to carefully read this entire email."

After describing the basic facts of what had happened, including the involvement of law enforcement, he explained the tone of his message: "Because of the nature of the investigation, the information in this email is being sent a bit more formally." He emphasized in all caps that no customer credit card information had been compromised, and stated his top priority with unmistakable clarity: "The most important focus for us is the safety and security of our customers' information."

He then shared the e-mail that customers would be receiving, which included specific steps to solve the problem before reiterating his commitment to the customers with language that made clear his personal anguish about what had happened: "We've spent over 12 years building our reputation, brand, and trust with customers. It's painful to see us take so many steps back due to a single incident." He briefly described a training process that all employees would undergo immediately to help customers through this, and closed with a simple but powerful appeal: "We need all hands on to help get through this."

Crisis communication is something everyone would rather avoid having to practice, but even the best, most reputable firms in the world have found themselves wrong-footed at one time or another. The Zappos communication covered the fundamental bases that can help to project both strength and warmth in any crisis:

Project Warmth:

- Validate how people feel—scared, anxious, frustrated, or otherwise.
- Express appropriate remorse.
- Release timely, accurate information to show you are not hiding anything

Project Strength:

- Express your determination to fix things.
- Express a clear and thorough understanding of the problem.
- Explain the concrete actions you are taking to fix things.

The ultimate goal is restoring credibility and trust. Crisis communication is considerably more complex in practice than in the abstract, but projecting strength and warmth is always paramount. The people affected need to know that the responsible organization is doing everything possible to protect them, and that it is working in good faith toward a shared goal of getting things back on track.

Social Media at Work

If you are using social media for business, the great advantage of platforms like Twitter is that you can engage with customers, readers, activists, enthusiasts, and fans around the world in a way that was impossible a decade ago. Social media works best as a two-way conversation, not as a one-way "push" of information. Warmth is the general dynamic involved; you have to demonstrate that you truly care about listening as well as talking. If your goal is to grow an online community, the principles we discussed for projecting verbal warmth (the circle) definitely apply.

Oftentimes a social media post is used to encourage people to check out a blog, article, or website. Since these have to be brief (e.g., 140 characters for a tweet), there are some tricks for writing catchy updates that will attract people to click on hyperlinks. These are many of the same skills that good headline writers use to draw attention to stories. A few tried-and-true techniques include:

- Intrigue (One thing you didn't know about . . .)
- Self-deprecating humor (The most embarrassing thing I will never do again . . .)
- Lists (Fifty ways to . . .)
- Questions (Should you . . . ?)
- Advice, how-to (Don't leave home without . . .)

Verbal agility like this demonstrates strength by showing command of language. These are good skills to have and use on occasion, but if your goal is to truly engage an online community, it is far more effective to write in your own clearly identifiable voice (which displays warmth) than to rely on rhetorical devices. For instance, a friend who is an entrepreneur in Silicon Valley once tweeted, "Start-ups are better than sex . . . when they work." There was no mistaking the authenticity of his tone; he was not playing a role or using the tools of the PR trade.

Leadership

When we consider how organizations select leaders, there is often an imbalance between strength and warmth. Not only are the people involved in the selection process typically most concerned about choosing someone who can get things done, they are likely to have seen only the sunniest side of the subordinates they are considering promoting. In a hierarchy, everyone is taught to kiss up to those above them, but not everyone is so nice to those below. So warmth often gets shortchanged or is undervalued.

Yet when we look at the skills good leaders need, it is clear that warmth and strength both count. Think back to our original chart on strength and warmth, and the rare air of the upper-right quadrant, where we find high strength and high warmth. These are the people we admire as leaders. As you may have guessed, there is more to say about the connection between strength and warmth and leadership.

There are any number of competing models of leadership, including transactional, transformational, adaptive, and charismatic, to name just a few. One way to get a grip on all of these was developed by Matt's old boss, Harvard political scientist Joseph Nye. He surveyed the leadership studies landscape and then used an existing study of presidential leadership to create a taxonomy of six principal leadership skills: emotional intelligence, communications, vision, organizational skills, Machiavellian political skills, and contextual intelligence.

Emotional intelligence enables leaders to understand themselves and others in a way that allows them to move people to action. Nye notes that emotional intelligence has two components: mastery of oneself and outreach to others. Self-mastery projects strength. Recall our discussion of strong nonverbal cues and the importance of poise, which shows control of your body in space. The same is true when you demonstrate control in your use of language. Outreach to others, on the other hand, is about warmth. The ability to get in the circle, for instance, requires the emotional intelligence to read your audience before making an appeal to shared concerns or interests. Also remember the biological tension between strength and warmth. Testosterone inhibits oxytocin, making it difficult for strong leaders to feel and project empathy. At the same time, not being too warm may make strong leaders better judges of character; unusually warm people can tend to suffer from the "rose-colored glasses" syndrome, in which their sympathies override warning signals about people who do not share their best interests.

Communications, as we have discussed throughout, can project both strength and warmth. The skill of being an effective communicator is an aspect of a leader's strength, while the ability to connect with stakeholders is an exercise in warmth. Nye points out that leaders have to communicate with a variety of internal and external audiences in a variety of settings—large audiences, small groups, one-on-one, and via words alone—all of which require slightly different skills.

Vision is a leader's way of describing the present and articulating an idea for how to arrive at a (presumably better) future state. Noel Tichy, who headed GE's famous leadership institute in Crotonville, N.Y., once wrote that it is a leader's responsibility to define reality. Developing a vision is the act of defining the present and future reality. The ability to create a compelling vision is a powerful way to establish a sense of shared interests that we equate with warmth. While conveying a vision is a way of projecting warmth, great visionaries are not always warm people. Henry Ford and Steve Jobs both had tremendous visions for the future of their respective industries, but neither would have been called cuddly.

Organizational skills allow leaders to understand, design, and implement systems that direct the resources needed to keep an organization running effectively. The other half of Tichy's definition of leadership is the ability to mobilize resources. Some of these fall under traditional definitions of management—taking charge of personnel, schedules, and budgets to meet defined goals or objectives—while others speak to adaptive skills, such as moving an organization through a period of change. Achieving these ends may require varying degrees of warmth when the resources being mobilized are people, but the net effect of having superb organizational skills is one of strength.

Machiavellian political skills are perhaps the most easily identifiable manifestation of strength. This is the side of strength that makes the all-warmth crowd queasy. It is the ability to size up others for wheeling and dealing in what Nye calls "hard power" situations that require either incentives or coercion, carrots or sticks. Knowing how much support you have before the votes are counted and how much arm-twisting you can engage in without causing future problems is a skill that projects strength. Accordingly, we view people who prioritize this skill at the expense of others as cold and bloodless.

Contextual intelligence is the ability to read a situation and determine an appropriate approach to the leadership challenge that it poses. As Nye points out, this requires aptitude in dealing with organizational culture (warmth), power politics (strength), the needs of people within an organization (warmth), and information flows (strength). Nobody is capable of doing this well in all circumstances. History is replete with examples of leaders who thrived in one setting and failed to adapt when the context shifted.

All these skills are essential for tackling significant leadership challenges, though their relative weight and importance depends on the setting. Leading people ultimately demands satisfying two primary needs for the group: projecting enough strength to protect it from threats and keep it on track, and projecting enough warmth to recruit and retain others who will help realize the group's vision. Leadership resides in the ongoing balancing act between strength and warmth, and leaders need to project both actively in the presence of people who work for them. The dynamics that come with maintaining that balance—the halo effect and the hydraulics—apply to leaders as much as anyone, though positional authority confers status that can help mitigate some of the penalties associated with being the boss. The most admired leaders are the ones who project consistently high levels of strength and warmth and have the contextual intelligence to know how to use it. We remember them long after they exit the stage.

In Public Speaking

If your phone rang right now and you were told that very shortly you would be asked to speak to a large crowd of people, how would that make you feel? Would it make a difference if they were all people you knew or strangers?

Of all the moments of judgment we face in our lives, few feel as momentous as standing in front of a large group of your fellow human beings, seeing all their faces, and speaking to them. Whether it is a logistical announcement, a wedding toast, or a persuasive speech, most of us are not accustomed to facing the glare of that much attention all at once. Even if you are just communicating rote information, you know that at some level the way you express yourself leads everyone in that audience to make some sort of character judgment about you. On top of that, when a lot of people are asked to pay attention, usually the topic is important, and occasionally big outcomes ride on whether you do a good job or not.

After long experience coaching people to deal with public speaking situations, we divide the challenge of speaking well into two buckets: first, managing your nerves, and second, everything else. Surveys consistently show that we fear public speaking more than almost anything else; many people, it seems, would prefer to be eaten by a shark. The old joke is that most people at a funeral would rather be in the coffin than giving the eulogy.

This can easily create a self-defeating cycle. When you are at the front of the room, whatever emotions you project into that room strongly influence how everyone in your audience feels. If you are uncomfortable being at the front of the room, your audience will be uncomfortable watching you. Whether they like you or not, if they are sitting there, they want you to own the room, so they know that their experience will at least be a comfortable one. The heart of projecting strength is projecting confidence—and nowhere is this more true than at the front of the room.

A Sensible Fear

The anxiety attached to public speaking is in fact more reasonable than is usually understood. Consider for a minute that if you are having a conversation with one person, you expect that while you are talking, you will get a steady stream of nonverbal feedback: nods, uh-huhs, grunts, and facial expressions, all of which communicate understanding of what you are saying. If you are not getting any feedback, just a blank, silent stare, you will quickly get a strong feeling in your gut that something is wrong: This person hates you, or is maybe deaf, or does not speak the language. Without the nonverbal feedback, it feels like your communication is hitting a brick wall.

But when you speak in public, you are completely in charge of the room, and unless you are a teacher who cold-calls students, the audience understands that it is off the hook. They are not expected to do anything but watch: to them, you are television, or perhaps a play. So instead of the nonverbal feedback that tells you that you are being heard and understood, you get nothing. And if looking at one blank face in a one-on-one conversation gives you the feeling that something is off, looking out at a sea of blank faces staring silently back at you sets off all kinds of alarms, including cortisol, the unpleasant feeling in the pit of your stomach, and adrenaline, which gets your pulse pounding.

When you are unsure of your own performance, it is easy to imagine that every other witness to it shares your doubts and worse. Now, just because you are being paranoid does not mean they are not actually judging you harshly, and in some environments people will be. But most of the time, people want you to succeed. There is nothing more uncomfortable for an audience than to witness a meltdown, so a good performance is a win-win for both you and them. Just realizing how much of the judgment you feel is in your own head and how little is in other people's can make projecting both strength and warmth come much more easily.

Most significant things in life require work, study, and most important, practice. We take baby steps—riding the bike with training wheels, wearing water wings in the shallow end of the pool, steering the car around an empty parking lot—to build up to the key situation in which skill makes all the difference. With public speaking, as often as not, we skip all of that. Professionals who take years refining their craft are rewarded for their efforts by being asked to speak in front of ballrooms full of their peers with little preparation at all.

In part this represents a logistical difficulty: It is pretty impractical to assemble large practice audiences just for people to get used to standing in front of them. Moreover, public speaking is often treated as something easy—all you have to do is stand up and speak your mother tongue, after all—or as something you just have to deal with: You will feel awful; just keep talking and you'll get through it. While practice is in fact an invaluable resource for improving one's public speaking ability, these attitudes usually do much more harm than good. When it comes to reforming habits, there is no substitute for video. Seeing yourself from the perspective of others tends to be both very humbling and very useful. As you watch, you imagine how your audience would interpret what you see, or how you would react to someone like you if you had just been introduced. When you see yourself doing things you wish you had not, and imagine what your audience must have thought of you, it registers on a gut level that makes it much less likely you will do that again in the future. You can also notice what went right, and monitor your progress as you improve.

Speaking in public—even if you are seated—is a performance. It is not exactly athletic, but it takes energy. You are "on" the whole time you are at the front of the room, projecting energy into the room. Professional speakers have a saying: Your audience is never going to be more enthusiastic about your topic than you are. Maybe your talk is not a pep rally and you do not want people spontaneously jumping out of their seats, but to keep them interested enough to pay attention, you have to show some interest and enthusiasm nonverbally.

Since your energy largely dictates the energy in the room, it is a good idea to set aside a few minutes to go through your warm-up routine to put yourself in the right physical state and frame of mind to project the energy you want to your audience. Physically, there are both moving and still warm-ups. You want to physically relax by stretching out tight muscles, shaking out your limbs and bouncing on your toes. Then recall the advantages of making yourself big for several minutes, increasing the testosterone and decreasing the cortisol, a.k.a. butterflies. There is an old saw in public speaking, which we have already touched on briefly, that everyone gets butterflies; the trick is to teach them to fly in formation. That is the point of the warm-up routine.

Mentally, use the time while you are stretching out and bouncing around to take stock of how you are feeling: Is anything bothering you—maybe an argument from this morning or a deadline tomorrow? Identify anything that is affecting your mood, and reassure yourself that for the next few minutes while you are talking that situation will not change. Give yourself permission to set it aside and not worry about it for the duration—you can pick it up again later. Then while you are making yourself big, you want to get yourself mentally in the mood. Remind yourself why you are talking to this audience, who they are, and the emotional energy you want to project their way. For example, people who tend to race through their material will sometimes use this time to breathe deeply and repeat a mantra like "slow and smile" to ease themselves into a physical state that leads them naturally to proceed at a more deliberate pace.

There are no rules to this. Whatever works for you is right. The important thing is to recognize that when you stand up in front of a crowd, or look into a broadcast camera lens, you are in a resource-constrained situation. You are being watched, you have a lot of things you need to do right nonverbally and verbally, and it is hard to consciously keep track of where your hands are when you are also trying to assemble the right words for your next sentence. And that is a best-case scenario. If you are nervous, your mental bandwidth is constricted even further as your forebrain surrenders control to your lizard brain. These constraints mean you want to do anything you can to make the nonverbal parts of your presentation automatic, unconscious, and second nature. Anything you can do to get yourself into a state where that takes care of itself frees your brain to do more with both your content and your delivery.

When it comes to reducing anxiety, there is no substitute for repetition. Just going through a situation over and over makes it progressively more familiar, which drains away the fear of the unknown until it seems commonplace. Of course, most high-stakes situations come around only once in a while, so you do not get too many live dress rehearsals. Luckily, you can still do repetitions alone in the theater of your imagination. Walking through visualization exercises is extremely useful, because they allow you to create the effect on your brain of practicing without the logistical hassles of assembling an actual audience. Olympic athletes close their eyes and visualize themselves going through every turn on the ski run even when they are nowhere near the mountain. Legend has it that Hall of Fame quarterback Joe Montana used to sit at his locker before every game and run through every offensive play from scrimmage in his head. In the same way, even if you cannot practice in front of a live audience, you can give your brain a very similar experience just by picturing and walking through the experience in real time. Matt has done this same exercise with musical gigs that required learning lots of new material. It is not a substitute for the real thing, but it has the advantage that you can control the outcome much more easily, picturing yourself delivering your talk perfectly, with all the nuances and precision you like. If you can get yourself to the venue ahead of time, you can make it even more realistic, because you can picture the room just as it will be (minus the people). If the room is empty, you can even picture the seats full and walk through your paces.

Late in his career, Lawrence Olivier, the world's most celebrated stage actor, inexplicably began to develop a crippling case of stage fright. He felt like every time he set foot on stage, his enormous reputation, everything he had worked for, was on the line, that one slipup could expose him as a fraud. He eventually found his way to a solution: Before every show, he would peek out at the audience from backstage for several minutes and curse them as contemptible scum. That way, when he strode out on stage, he had so demeaned them in his own mind that he didn't care at all what they thought of him. This is not a good way to forge bonds of warmth with your audience, any more than picturing them in their underwear is. But if your nerves are really getting the better of you, imagining your audience in a way that dampens your awareness of or concern for their opinions can be very helpful. Famed Hollywood therapists Barry Michels and Phil Stutz work with a lot of people facing career-defining and nerve-racking pitch meetings, and they recommend imagining everyone sitting in judgment covered in a thick blanket of dust, like they had spent a century in an attic, to dim the spotlight of their attention. When taking the edge off your anxiety can make all the difference, this is a great game to play.

Speaking of mentally demeaning your audience, there can be times when you need a quick shot of extra strength to handle a particularly tough situation. While we hope these are rare, they do come up. As snarling punk rock legend John Lydon says, "Anger is an energy." If you need to project aggression toward someone, imagining that they insulted you or kicked your dog can get the right emotions flowing. Michels and Stutz advise their clients to imagine themselves uttering a long scream at the top of their lungs, akin to what Walt Whitman called his "barbaric yawp," to vent their frustration and summon their energies. This is just a quiet version of what martial artists do when they strike someone, or what many football players do in the locker room just before they take the field.

Once you have gone through your warm-up routine and entered the room where you will be speaking, another way to get comfortable in your surroundings is to chat casually with people before kicking off your talk. This helps establish your warmth in the room as a friendly person, and it can also help burn off nervous energy and set you further at ease in those sometimes unsettling moments as people are trickling in before things get started.

Not Your Father's Podium

Investing time learning and practicing the skill of public speaking used to be common, not rare. As recently as the past century, *rhetoric* was not a derogatory term—it was an academic subject studied and practiced by the most educated citizens. In ancient times, public speaking was not just a chore to be endured from time to time; it was central to the culture. Before histories were written down, history was an epic poem like *The Iliad* and shared with the masses in public performances. Even after the written word, literacy was far from universal, so for news to be widely shared, it needed to be read aloud in the public square. And before movies, most entertainment took the form of plays and stage shows—more people speaking in public.

The evolution of technology has not only made public speaking less common, it has changed our expectations about what it should look like. Orators in ancient times had to project their voices long distances to be heard in the back of big crowds, so they would tip their heads back to send the sound over the heads of the front row and gesture broadly so the folks in the back could see. We can still see remnants of this oratorical style in formal speech making today. With the advent of movies and television, though, we have become accustomed to seeing even famous and powerful people up close and personal in interviews and casual settings. That means audiences have come to expect not the stilted delivery of prewritten lines, but a natural conversational expression of a speaker's feelings in the moment. Orations are out—conversations are in. If you watch the most popular TED talks, for instance, most of the speakers talk to the audience like it's a large crowd of friends rather than an assembled mass of strangers. They neither read from a prepared text nor use notes. The tone is intimate, not didactic.

While some may pine for old-school formality, the new, more emotionally expressive style makes very good sense. Studies have shown that a recitation of information from a live speaker is a very inefficient way to transmit information from another. Especially in this age, with so many communications options, pulling a large group of busy people together in one place is a major investment of resources when an e-mail attachment or Web chat might do. The reason we still get everyone together in one place is because it allows us to communicate emotionally, with all of our nonverbals readily evident, to really impress upon an audience what is important about a topic. That kind of interaction is still hard to replicate through technology-enabled remote communication. When we gather in person, emotion is the point.

The old, more formal style dies hard, though. Despite the shifting norms of emotional intimacy facilitated by video technology, the professional workplace still seems to many like a place where the way to project competence includes suppressing other emotions. Old-school formality projects strength, the thinking goes. Authority and competence are strong and appropriate for the workplace, but as we know, they are not the whole story. The other reason for the lingering popularity of the more formal oratorical style is that people think it seems easier to pull off when they are anxious. They devolve into a bundle of nerves when they are about to speak, so they do their best to hide those feelings behind a formal facade. It is not a crazy strategy, but it gets in the way of emotionally connecting with the audience.

The emergence of the more conversational style has created a common conundrum for public speakers: How much of what you intend to say should you write word-for-word ahead of time? When the oratorical style reigned, preparing the text ahead of time was the preferred approach—it could be read aloud and also passed along to scribes to keep a record and distribute in faraway places. While preparation is undoubtedly invaluable, this approach does create an emotional fissure between the speaker and the audience. Speaking extemporaneously expresses thoughts and feelings in the moment. Reciting a speech is a totally different activity, more akin to reciting lines in an acting performance. We understand that the speaker endorses the words, but we cannot even be sure he or she wrote them. Even if the speaker does manage to put emotion into the delivery, that emotion is mediated through the prewritten speech. It is very difficult to project as much warmth or strength reading a speech as you can speaking from the heart.

Needless to say, speaking without notes or memorized remarks presents its own difficulties, especially on sensitive topics, in which a few ill-considered words could be taken the wrong way. The ideal approach, if you have the time to prepare and deliver it correctly, is to think through all your points and stories and potential problems ahead of time, and then have minimal notes at the ready to remind yourself of the points you want to cover and the stories you want to tell. To pull this off, you have to know your material enough to be able to talk about it fluently. This approach lets you show off your mastery of the material with full emotional transparency, so you project your full measure of strength and warmth.

If you are stuck with a script, make sure you look up and out at your audience frequently to maintain an emotional connection and not dilute the strength and warmth you are projecting. This is especially important at the ends of sentences, because the pause between one sentence and the next, even if it is brief, is a moment of nonverbal connection. In a one-on-one conversation, that is the moment the speaker reads the listener's reaction and decides how to proceed. On a lighted stage, the speaker may not even be able to see the audience, but from the audience's point of view, it is important to see the speaker looking out toward them in that moment, to feel they are being taken into account. You do not need to make eye contact with everyone—just move your eye contact around the room so no one subtracts warmth points for ignoring their section. This is not about sweeping across the audience like a ship's radar, either: You are giving different audience members each a turn being the person you are connecting with at the end of each sentence, so you look at one person, pause, and then move on.

Assuming you can see them, one type of audience member will likely stand out: the friendlies. These are the people who, instead of turning off their faces like they are watching TV, light up with big smiles and exaggerated encouragement like a parent at a preschool play. In some situations these may be friends or colleagues of yours, while other times they may be complete strangers who just happen to be unusually empathetic. This condition makes them terrified that you are going to get nervous or mess up, because if you did, they would be even more mortified than you would. It can be useful to focus on their smiling, nodding faces through the beginning of your presentation until you get more comfortable, at which point it is good to take in the rest of the folks in the audience.

Even better than looking around the room is moving around the room. By physically closing the distance between yourself and audience members in different parts of the room, you create more warmth, and by being brave enough to come out from behind the podium or table and move confidently through the space, you project serious strength. Moving also has the advantage of helping you burn off excess adrenaline-fueled energy. And the same way kids stop passing notes in class when their grade-school teacher patrols the aisles, when you spread your warmth around the room, you are much less likely to lose your audience's attention to their phones and laptops.

There is a difference between moving comfortably through the space and pacing like a lion in a cage. Ideally, you spread your physical presence walking around the room similarly to how you spread your eye contact around the room (only slower): You go to one area, then move to another, and so forth. Depending on what the room looks like, you may not be able to easily leave the front, so you might just move from side to side, and you probably do not want to spend a lot of time behind your audience if they all have to turn in their chairs to see you. The key distinction is that just like with eye contact, you want your movements to be deliberate: You are moving to a spot to be able to connect better with a part of your audience there. You go to that spot, then you stop, and talk from there for a bit, connecting most with the people nearest to you, and only then do you move on.

The most common way people undercut their strength at the front of the room is with extraneous movement. Whether it is fidgeting with a ring, aimless shifting weight back and forth from leg to leg, or one hand repeatedly squeezing the other, that excess energy often finds its way out in conspicuous and distracting ways. Rather than simply telling yourself not to do that, it is much more helpful to find an affirmative behavior to replace the offending habit. If you are tempted to shift your weight, walk to a new spot and talk from there. If you feel energy in your hands, gesture—if you are talking, it would probably help for you to be gesturing anyway. If all else fails, find a less conspicuous way to burn off that energy; for instance, some people tighten all the muscles in a foot or a leg.

Voice

The old oratorical style favored vocal strength over vocal warmth. Over the years a standard technique developed that is sometimes called "clap-trap," not because it is hokum but because it induces large audiences to show their approval by clapping. There is nothing more uncomfortable for an audience than sitting silently while a speaker gets his timing wrong and leaves a gaping pause, expecting a burst of applause for a line that doesn't earn it. Those same speakers also often get the big response when they least expect it, and as a result they talk over the crowd rather than letting the noise settle naturally.

We discussed earlier how the easiest way to project a lot of strength with your voice is to end a sentence with successively lower pitches while maintaining your volume, and then pause afterward. That kind of delivery may earn you applause if your audience strongly approves of whatever you just said. If maximum applause is your goal, the more reliable cadence is the one we all know from fawning introductions of game show hosts to the set and sports stars to the arena: The pitch and volume rise together in a great crescendo. While we all notice the high note, what makes it work comes just afterward: There is a slight but audible decline in pitch at the very end—like a pole vaulter who dramatically pushes over the bar, and then begins to drift down toward earth. This slight lowering of pitch relieves the tension created by the high note and signals the audience that the crescendo is over and it is time to clap. Without that last note to take the edge off, you would create a sense of alarm that would stand the audience's hair on end.

The more conversational, intimate style also projects strength, and it adds considerable warmth as well. It sounds like chatting with an old friend, with lots of variety in pitch and volume and rate. Using these speech patterns sends a powerful signal of intimacy that can be used to create a sense between people who just met that they are old friends. Radio, TV, and movies have established the expectation of emotional intimacy and honesty, and this also works when speaking live to a large audience. Some speakers are warm and casual most of the time, with occasional moments of determined, assertive strength. Others tend to be more strong, more old-school oratorical, but have learned to punctuate that formality with moments of revealing warmth. Either way, if you demonstrate moments of each, your audience is likely to come away admiring you.

In Politics

"Governor, if Kitty Dukakis were raped and murdered, would you favor an irrevocable death penalty for the killer?"

The sheer audacity of the question is still breathtaking nearly a quarter century later. When moderator Bernard Shaw posed this hypothetical to Massachusetts governor Michael Dukakis about his wife to kick off the second presidential debate with Vice President George H. W. Bush in the fall of 1988, it was a naked challenge that went directly to the issue of character: "Show us what you are made of."

Rather than assert himself by flashing a sense of righteous indignation at the horrific hypothetical scenario, Dukakis answered it like any other policy question. "No, I don't, Bernard, and I think you know that I've opposed the death penalty during all of my life. I don't see any evidence that it's a deterrent and I think there are better and more effective ways to deal with violent crime," he said. It was precisely the manner one would expect from a bloodless technocrat.

Dukakis's response was not warm, because he was the only person listening not aghast, and he did not connect to that emotion at all. But it was also not strong: It was all competence, but no guts, no willfulness. Dukakis had set the stage for this question earlier in the campaign. "This election isn't about ideology. It's about competence," he had said, choosing to emphasize the performance of the Massachusetts economy during his tenure as governor. The debate misstep was not the only problem Dukakis had projecting strength throughout the race, but it spoke directly to the limits of relying on competence alone.

The business of politics is more about character judgments, and nonverbals specifically, than most of us would care to admit. Alex Todorov, at Princeton University, and his colleagues found that people can predict who will win elections seven times out of ten by judging their relative competence from just brief glimpses at official campaign photos. Around the same time, the two of us worked with Jesse Shapiro and Dan Benjamin, economists then at Harvard, on an experiment that showed subjects ten-second silent video clips of two gubernatorial candidates and then asked them who they thought won the race. The judgments based on these quick impressions proved to be a more accurate predictor of the winner than campaign spending.

With well-known politicians, we all form images of them based on our repeated exposures to their natural features and nonverbal cues. If you close your eyes, you can probably conjure up a still image of any recent president in a matter of seconds. Is he smiling? Now do the same thing with the candidate who opposed him. Politicians who overlook the importance of creating a lasting image that projects both strength and warmth do so at their peril.

As with elements of personal identity such as gender and ethnicity, political identity is also tied to our attitudes about strength and warmth. One study found that physically strong men are more likely than physically weaker men to hold political views that promote their economic self-interest, whether they are richer or poorer. Physically strong one-percenter men support policies that leave money with whoever prevails in the market, while physically stronger working-class men favor policies that level the economic playing field. Weaker men are less likely overall to advocate for their economic self-interest politically.

Since the Vietnam War, the two fundamental stereotypes that have helped shape American politics are that conservatives are presumed strong but not warm, while liberals are presumed warm but not strong. This manifests itself in any number of ways, from the issues associated most closely with each side to presumptions about the traits of leaders. Republicans, for example, are thought to be more aggressive on matters of national security, while Democrats are linked more closely to domestic issues such as health, education, and civil rights.

Using the metaphor of family, linguist George Lakoff has suggested that conservatives and liberals can be understood in terms of "strict father" and "nurturant parent" archetypes. The two opposing world-views that Lakoff attributes to these types are somewhat reminiscent of our earlier discussion of Ayn Rand and the Beatles. The strict father model stems from the view that "life is difficult, and that the world is fundamentally dangerous." The nurturant parent model, on the other hand, "is one of being cared for and cared about, having one's desires for loving interactions met, living as happily as possible, and deriving meaning from mutual interaction and care." Accordingly, the strict father embraces a philosophy of tough love toward his children, while the nurturant parent strives to build a secure bond with them. In the political sphere, these models shape ideological beliefs about discipline, order, and hierarchy (strict father/strength), as well as empathy, compassion, and fairness (nurturant parent/warmth).

In the press, this sometimes gets boiled down to generalizations about the "Daddy Party" and the "Mommy Party." These stereotypes help set the terms of political debate: Is the liberal tough enough to fight the bad guys? Does the conservative care enough about people who have lost their jobs to extend unemployment benefits? Candidates inevitably face the challenge of having to project whichever quality they are presumed to lack, depending on whether there is a (D) or (R) after their name on the ballot.

If it fell to Lakoff to help liberals make sense of this, Karl Rove, the political strategist behind George W. Bush's victorious presidential campaigns, did the same for conservatives in a way that reflected his more tactical background and outlook. Having spent his whole career as a political operative working campaigns and reading countless polls, Rove surmised that voters subconsciously ask themselves three questions when choosing between candidates: First, which candidate is the stronger leader? Second, which one do I trust more? And third, which one cares more about people like me?

The first and third questions align pretty clearly with strength and warmth, respectively. The trust question emphasizes the importance of nonverbal communication: We trust people when all of their communication signals—facial expressions, posture, gestures, vocal tone, and the actual words they say—line up to tell a consistent story. By contrast, when different signals are telling different stories at the same time, we suspect that person is trying to hide something, and we lose trust.

Some politicians understand the appeal of strength and warmth and make conscious efforts to portray themselves as striking a balance. George W. Bush ran in 2000 as a compassionate (warm) conservative (strong). The terms used to describe Sarah Palin did much the same thing: hockey mom, pit bull with lipstick, mama grizzly. Others are intensely aware of the need to transcend stereotypes, as we saw with Hillary Clinton and Barack Obama.

The emphasis on projecting strength and warmth through language appears to be part of a larger trend among American politicians. An analysis of inaugural addresses found that presidents since Franklin Delano Roosevelt have relied more on intimidation (a show of strength) and ingratiation (efforts to increase likability) in their speeches than earlier presidents. Similarly, a study of governors over the past forty-five years found that those who used language conveying enthusiasm (warmth), activity, and realism (both strength) were more successful at pushing their legislative agendas than other governors.

With all this in mind, timing is everything in politics. The importance of a candidate's strength and warmth balance is determined in large part by the external factors shaping the election. In years when voter sentiment runs toward "Throw the bums out!" being lucky sometimes trumps being good.

Online

Back in 1993, when the World Wide Web was still in its infancy, a cartoon in *The New Yorker* by Peter Steiner defined the essential paradox of online life: "On the Internet, nobody knows you're a dog."

This means that others, including people you may never meet in person, now form perceptions and judgments of you based on how you come across on a two-dimensional screen, whether through photos, videos, chat boxes, or just static text. With people who already know you, your digital presence just augments their existing sense of who you are. Where strangers are concerned—and these can range from potential employers to potential mates—there is more at stake, because what they see on-screen will serve as their first impression of you. To use an old-school analogy, think of this as your baseball card. Granted, many of us have had the experience of meeting people face-to-face after seeing only online photos, and there is often a striking difference between the digital and the real that melts on contact. But when we do not have the opportunity to close that gap, our online presence is all the more critical because it is the only way we have to represent ourselves. For the most part, the same fundamental principles that we have outlined so far about strength and warmth apply in the online realm, but there are some unique wrinkles worth noting.

Posts

Anything we post as comments, links, quotations, book recommendations, or other likes and dislikes becomes part of our online strength and warmth portrait. Again, audience awareness is the first step in deciding what to post where. If you use Facebook for staying connected to people, you probably focus mostly on warmth without even thinking about it: You share things your friends will like. Some people use Twitter or blogs to comment on an area of expertise, which speaks more to strength.

The broader question to ask before posting something is what you hope to achieve by putting it out for the world to see. What does it say about strength or warmth? Even the volume of online sharing makes a statement. It is definitely possible to "overshare," and not just in the sense of providing too much information about your personal life.

Oversharing hurts strength—and maybe even warmth too, if it drives others away.

Photos

The popularity of online photo sharing has only enhanced the importance of understanding nonverbal communication through visuals. Remember the experiment in which people were able to successfully pick out the winners of elections based solely on campaign photos? You may not be campaigning for office, but you could be campaigning for a job or a date, and online images will provide the same kind of fuel for social judgments about strength and warmth.

In addition to looking at your profile and photos, people checking you out also make judgments about the attractiveness of your friends. Researchers in the Netherlands found that an individual is considered more likable and a better potential friend if surrounded by good-looking friends. On a certain level, this is reminiscent of where we started off on the playground: We have always made social judgments by association. The difference is that your profile is always on the digital playground, even when you have logged off.

There are two kinds of photos of us online: the ones we put there, and the ones our friends post of us. Some sites offer some control of your image, but for the most part it is best to assume that people can find any photo of you that is floating around online. Given that cameras are now as ubiquitous as mobile phones, a certain degree of photo savvy is a helpful skill. Most of us have been posing for pictures since we were kids, and when someone points a camera at us, we have one face that we make, which may or may not resemble saying "cheese." Check your pictures and see how that face you make is working for you. All of our faces are built differently, and even beautiful faces can do funny things you might rather not memorialize in pictures, like flaring nostrils or baring gums or bottom teeth. But remember, nothing says "fake" like a forced smile in a photo. If you look happy, you look good, and for the most part simply being happy to be with the people in the group should be enough to make you smile naturally. If not, avoid the temptation to mechanically plaster on a phony smile. Think about something else that makes you happy instead.

Videoconferences

Live video meetings and webinars are becoming increasingly common, and this trend is likely to continue as technology and bandwidth improve. A webcam setting is typically the same as the setup on a TV news program in which the guest is not in the studio with the anchorperson: All the viewer sees is a head shot. This means that all the strength and warmth projection happens from the neck up and through your words.

In addition to the strategies we have covered already, there are some relatively easy things you can do to improve your presence during videoconferences, particularly if you are a featured presenter.

Practice using your webcam before you need it, and review the video to make sure the backdrop looks good, your gaze is focused in the right place, the lighting is adequate, and any background noise is minimized.

Avatars

Interacting with an avatar is a decidedly new experience for most of us, but there is already evidence that avatars can appeal to us with the same kinds of cues that project warmth in the physical world. Specifically, Jeremy Bailenson, of Stanford's Virtual Human Interaction Lab (VHIL), found that when avatars mimic the gestures and posture of the people they are speaking with, they are judged to be more persuasive, credible, trustworthy, and intelligent than avatars that do not engage in mimicking behaviors. This verges on the creepy—we can all imagine a not-too-distant future in which finely tuned avatars will seem so *familiar* to us that we treat them like long-lost friends. In the meantime, it is helpful to understand these effects and realize that they validate just how powerful similarity expressed through nonverbal cues can be.

The use of an avatar can alter perceptions of our own strength. Researchers at VHIL found that people who were given 3-D avatars that were ten centimeters taller than their actual physical height negotiated more confidently in a simulation than people given an avatar ten centimeters shorter than their physical height. The effect did not only occur online; it also carried over afterward into the physical realm, even when people were negotiating with others who were the same height. Similar to the research on power poses, this suggests that your brain gives itself a boost after assuming a temporary state that feels more powerful.

A Constantly Changing Dynamic

If we had written this when we first started thinking about strength and warmth, we would have missed the importance of social media—Facebook and Twitter were in their infancies at the time. Even as platforms and websites come and go (Friendster, anybody?), the importance of online presence will continue to grow as kids who have never known

a world without the Internet become adults. The digital tools for projecting strength and warmth will likely change too, as our discussion of
avatars suggests, but the goal should remain the same: congruence between your digital and physical presence.

In Love

*"Most women desire someone who makes them laugh
and also feel safe. So basically a clown ninja."*

—Internet meme

Someone once said we should have as many different words for "love" as
Eskimos supposedly have for "snow." The ancient Greeks had at least six
different words for different types of love, and we have some related
terms as well: affection, lust, crush, etc. Still, we rely on the word "love"
to mean many different things, each of which is plenty complicated on
its own without mixing it up with the others.

Pioneering love researcher Helen Fisher points to at least three distinct biological phenomena that we commonly call "love." First is romantic love or infatuation, that intoxicating, aching desire that gets and
keeps us focused on one (hopefully) suitable partner. This near-delirious
state is governed by a complex mix of hormones including dopamine,
the chemical of ecstatic pleasure, and norepinephrine, a source of energy and focus (and partly responsible for all the great art created by the
lovelorn). Second is lust, which obviously promotes reproductive activity, acting largely through the hormone testosterone in both genders.

Lastly there is the deep, affectionate attachment we feel for family
and close friends. This kind of love keeps us bonded with our group, so
parents raise their children and we take care of each other more generally. This love is closely associated with the hormone oxytocin (and its

partner, vasopressin). The action of these hormones is complicated, but as we said earlier, oxytocin is as close as there is to a warmth hormone. Paul Zak, a leading oxytocin researcher and author of *The Moral Molecule*, ran an amazing test in which he drew blood from everyone at a wedding before and just after the ceremony, and found that everyone's oxytocin levels surged during the ceremony, with the family and close friends of the happy couple experiencing especially pronounced bumps. Zak refers to oxytocin as the "trust molecule," for its propensity to create that connected feeling of sharing interests that we call warmth.

As the saying goes, the heart has a mind of its own, and how we spot and meet and court and love each other is not just about judgments of character, or we would all fuss a lot less over looks. But with both looks and character, the strength and warmth signals shape our experience every step of the way. Let's examine how this plays out.

What Women (and Men) Want: Part 1

When a guy (let's call him Jack) first walks into the proverbial bar, before he figures out where to sit himself down, he is going to look around the place and see if anyone is looking back at him. Straight guys love the sight of an attractive woman smiling at them. It floods them with pleasant hormones, dopamine chief among them. It just feels nice. It also signals to Jack that the woman in question (let's say Jill) is open to talking to him, which makes her extra appealing, since approaching a woman socially and getting shot down is not much fun.

When Jill sees Jack with a happy smile on his face, it creates a totally different effect. Assuming they are at about the same level of attractiveness and status, a big warm smile is a fine overture of friendship, but it is likely to squash any sense of possible romance between them. In guys, warmth with no strength is not sexy. Again, not all smiles are created equal. If Jack is wearing a flinty-eyed expression with his smile, that is a potent romantic combination. And if he radiates strength some other way—say, Jack is actually a movie star, to take an extreme example—then a big smile by itself will not necessarily quash Jill's interest. But most people seek out people who are of similar social standing and attractiveness level as themselves, and in that scenario, Jack would have to show some seriousness of intent to spark Jill's attraction. A happy Labrador retriever puppy smile lands him in the lower-right quadrant, the "nice guys finish last" pile.

This emasculating smile effect has a similarly ardor-dampening counterpart for women, as documented by Professor Jessica Tracy and her colleagues. While a big goofy grin proved to be quite attractive on women (and anything but on men), pride displays—like a raised chin or slightly smug smile—did the opposite: Proud men seemed very attractive to straight women, whereas prideful women were judged not attractive. This makes some sense: If Jack is already wary of Jill rejecting his advances, any extra pride on her part might as well be a big sign saying, "Danger: Keep Away." But what, then, explains the attractiveness of prideful guys?

This is the bad-boy effect, where women find it attractive when guys act like jerks, projecting lots of strength and little warmth. Jill may feel an occasional attraction to tough, high-testosterone guys for short-term romantic fun, and that is common, normal, and arguably healthy (though acting on those impulses can obviously carry risks). Some research suggests women even find facial scars sexy on guys they are considering as short-term prospects, at least if the scars come with a good story.

It is worth noting that bad-boy arrogance comes in slightly different flavors, and Professor Tracy has documented differences between dominance signals and prestige signals. Dominance is just strength without warmth, our upper-left quadrant, while prestige is strength with enough warmth to be seen as admirable, edging toward our upper-right quadrant. Prestige is usually conveyed by some signal that the community admires this person for exemplifying a shared value. For instance, a jerk wearing a Yale class ring will still be regarded as arrogant, but the association with Yale, esteemed temple of higher learning, implies a justification for his arrogance: He's cocky because he's good. Given the choice between dominance and prestige in a potential partner—between the Yale jerk and the just plain jerk—women prefer the prestige version. Even with the bad-boy phenomenon, a little warmth still helps.

What Women (and Men) Want, Part 2: Online

If Jack and Jill are the kind of people who would rather not meet by chance at the proverbial bar, they may well meet online first. There are dozens of online dating sites that offer varying levels of service and exclusivity, but the differences among them do not matter so much for our purposes. If you are establishing a profile in order to meet someone online, you want to attract the kind of person you want to date. As noted earlier, men find happiness to be the most desirable trait in a woman, while women look for confidence as the most desirable trait in a man.

This leads to an interesting surprise in the way women assess men in an online dating context. Rebecca Brand, of Villanova University, found that when women saw photos separate from their written profiles and were then asked to judge men on a variety of parameters (confidence, sense of humor, masculinity, and overall attractiveness), they could tell which men were attractive just based on confidence expressed in their written profiles—they did not even need to see the photos to sense the projected strength. Attractive men are likely to come across as confident, Brand concluded, because they already have a sense of their appeal as a mate.

In an era of online "hot or not hot" ratings contests, it will come as no surprise that men rely heavily on profile photos to determine happiness and overall attractiveness. While photos are important, words also matter; the language should be congruent with the emotion in the photos. One cautionary note: A written profile that signals cynicism about the dating scene will read as unhappiness or an indication that you have "issues" with relationships.

On the Prowl

However promising a prospective partner looks from across the room, the process of forging a romantic relationship has only just begun. The first hurdle is beginning a conversation. If Jack and Jill have not already been introduced to each other, someone has to get things moving. This challenge is a good indication of how much our social expectations around gender roles have and have not evolved. Traditionally, Jill's role in this first step was limited to maybe projecting a little warmth in Jack's direction with a smile or a furtive look to suggest she was interested in talking and would like him to come over. Today, it is perfectly socially acceptable for Jill to walk up to Jack and introduce herself. But the expectation is still that that is Jack's job. This is not because approaching Jill demonstrates warmth, though it does do that. No, the approach is Jack's responsibility because it requires strength. It takes courage to walk over and say hi, because it is an admission that he finds Jill interesting, which gives her power over him to reject his advances and bruise his ego. In taking that risk, Jack demonstrates his strength.

If Jack is having trouble summoning his courage, one trick he might try is firmly and confidently declaring aloud to himself that he is going to walk over to Jill and do this crazy thing. This can help with getting used to the idea of being the kind of person who does such things confidently. Not only does it build strength; it refutes and silences any voices of self-doubt. It may take a few repetitions to move from anxious and hesitant to strong and confident, but that is okay. (Note: This technique can work just as well for Jill.)

This is the traditional dynamic of courtship: The guy pushes his luck, and the woman sits in judgment of his efforts until she is won over and throws caution to the wind. She may be disappointed with the quality of the guys who present themselves for her consideration, but once the courtship begins, as long as they obey the law, she is in charge. In this model, all she has to do is to project warmth proportional to how much further she wants her suitor to pursue her. These roles have broken down and blurred as Western societies have gradually grown more egalitarian and less sexist, and men and women now look for all kinds of qualities in a potential long-term partner, who is expected to serve as lover, co-parent, business partner, and best friend.

But the ancient dynamics still exert a pull, and conversation still often proceeds with Jack trying to impress Jill more than she tries to impress him. This is reflected in the recent phenomenon of so-called pick-up artists, young men who share strategies online for how to talk women into bed. Their favored methods include a variety of ways for men to better project strength in the courtship conversation: "peacocking" around in mildly outlandish clothes or hairstyles to attract attention and show that they are not afraid of the judgments of others; "demonstrations of higher value," like doing a quick card trick or palm reading, or flashing prestige signals like an American Express black card or a car key with Ferrari's yellow shield and prancing horse. Their most infamous strength-projection trick is known as "negging," which means directing some mild criticism toward the woman in question—basically teasing without the humor. This is meant to bruise her ego slightly so she is less likely to judge herself too good for her suitor, and motivate her to prove herself to him. It is also really annoying, which is why young women have caught on to this gambit and warn their female friends to avoid these characters.

Traditional teasing is also meant to get someone's attention, maybe rattle their confidence a bit, and motivate them to engage in more conversation. But teasing is done with a smile. It can be mean, in which case the teaser's smile is laughing at the victim, but it can also be playful, in which case the smile is a genuinely warm one. This combination of strength and warmth makes playful teasing alluring and lots of fun, one of the most potent forms of flirting.

Unspoken Signals

Sexuality is among the most uncomfortable and embarrassing conversation topics in almost any culture. Like religious beliefs or income, it is an important aspect of our lives that is nevertheless not perceptible in everyday interactions. But sex is particularly scary because sexual arousal so dramatically alters our nonverbal behavior that it seems to turn us into different people, if not actually into animals. The movements, noises, and facial expressions that sex conjures out of us more closely resemble demonic possession than social interaction. We like to think we do not discuss sex because it is such a profound and intimate act, and there is truth to that. But it is also true that we are embarrassed at the idea of revealing that side of ourselves because those behaviors emphatically do not fit with the way we present ourselves socially.

Courtship and flirting behavior involves less dramatic but still distinctive nonverbal signals. For the most part, we perform all these courtship displays involuntarily around people we find attractive, often without even noticing ourselves (which is why your friends may notice whom you find attractive even before you do). For guys, the classic courtship nonverbal signals are stereotypically strong. When Jack notices a particularly attractive woman, you will often see him instinctively adjust himself to puff out his chest the way male birds and monkeys do during mating season. Guys have a range of strength posing they can adopt, from sitting or standing up straight to sprawling out their limbs in a self-consciously casual way. Guys often choose the slouchy, hips-first gait perfected by Elvis ("the Pelvis"), sometimes hooking a thumb in a belt loop for good measure.

At this point, you might expect to hear that just as guys traditionally use strength signals for courtship, women must use lots of warmth signals. Women do use warmth signals in courtship, as we saw with the allure of a warm smile. But sex is different. Sex is not about character judgments. Sexual attraction has its own inscrutable logic, and that goes for lust and infatuation too. (It gets difficult to disentangle these things when the hormones really start flowing.) And for sex, the female complement to men's signaling strength is not signaling warmth—it is signaling weakness.

Just as Jack puffs himself up for attractive women, Jill will often react to the appearance of a handsome suitor by curling up slightly into a submissive, almost bashful posture, shoulders hunched, toes turned in, head down. The signature move here is the duck-and-peek: Jill looks at the object of her affection with her head turned slightly away so she's glancing at Jack from one side, and then she pitches her forehead slightly downward so she's also peeking at him out from under her upper eyelashes. She projects both shyness and interest. Executed without a smile, this move is striking. Add a warm smile as well, and it is inviting. Either way, Jack is going to do a double-take.

And if Jill uses a flinty smile, she can turn this move into a playful jest, restoring its strength. Even if traditionally, or even instinctively, female courtship signals project weakness, we are much more complex creatures than the beasts from which we evolved, and there is plenty of room for female strength displays, playful or otherwise.

Some courtship displays simulate surrender into the intoxicated bliss of sex itself. The classic here is the look universally known as "bedroom eyes," a heavy-lidded gaze practiced by several generations of pin-up models and perfected by Marilyn Monroe. (Science has even stepped in to confirm that looks with lowered eyelids are more consistent with "short-term mating strategies" than open-eyed looks.) In addition to slow-motion blinks, other slow, fluid movements of limbs and shoulders can carry a similar connotation, which is one of the reasons dancing can look so alluring. Where the curling up signaled Jill's weakness by moving to protect herself, these displays leave Jill looking defenseless, the height of weakness. Often her head leans to one side, a move that does double-duty: By leaning away from Jack, she displays demure reticence, and in exposing her neck to him, she suggests surrender.

These sexy surrender signals are not just for women; guys can use them too. Jack might look silly batting his eyelashes at Jill, but a little tilt of the head, slightly droopy eyelids, or a more languid gait can all amp up Jack's sex appeal too.

In fact, despite the basic instinct for guys to puff up and women to curl up, many other sexual signals work both ways. Among the most potent interest signals is steady eye contact, often lingering a little longer than one might expect in normal interaction. As mentioned earlier, depending on the facial expression it is paired with, extended eye contact can project strength or warmth or both. Similarly, if either Jack or Jill touches the other in socially sanctioned places more often than social norms suggest for casual conversation, it is a sure sign of warmth. Some people make unusually frequent touching their social trademark, part of a conspicuously warm persona. But especially in environments where touch is rare, the mild shock of contact creates a feeling of excitement and connection that can presage more intimate contact to come.

Long-Term Goals

If their first meeting was intriguing enough, then comes the next challenge: the Mexican standoff around who contacts whom first to arrange the next meeting. Nowhere in life is the trade-off between seeming warm but weak or strong but cold quite as stark as with the so-called three-day rule—or was it four, or two? By long-standing tradition, young men of previous generations were supposed to wait several days after their last in-person contact with a love interest before contacting her again. Reach out too soon, the theory goes, and Jack looks desperate and weak. Wait too long, and he seems uninterested and cold. Times have changed somewhat, and one of the beauties of evolving gender roles is that now Jill is empowered to contact Jack too, so now she too can wonder whether to reach out and if it will make her look desperate.

Assuming our protagonists manage to make a date, it is not uncommon for either or both to come down with a case of nerves. If you are on a date and want to avoid getting nervous, pretend your date is off-limits romantically and just someone to have a nice time with. (This parallels a common experience: many people find that once they are coupled and off the market, they become much more relaxed and charming around potential love interests.) Your more casual sense of intimacy invites reciprocity, and allows you to project both strength and warmth as you naturally would. As for the date itself, an adventurous expedition or even just a good, tense movie affords opportunities for Jack to show off both his strength, by remaining unfazed, and his warmth, by displaying sympathy with Jill's reactions and maybe some humor. If Jack instead shows a lack of strength or warmth, that is useful for Jill to know too.

In this getting-to-know-you phase, there can also be a strong temptation to embellish the personal resume. Research shows people tend to lie more to potential partners they find more attractive to shore up their own value relative to these highly marketable prospects. These fibs can burnish either strength or warmth, but there will be a significant warmth penalty to be paid if and when these lies are eventually found out.

Assuming our heroes can sort out each other's stories, they may face the question of what each should be looking for in a good longer-term partner. Being generally strong and warm for one another is a good start. But there are other issues of compatibility too. Some of that is based on culture and background, sharing experiences and expectations. But compatibility is more than just demographics—it is also based on temperament, on how we're wired.

Based on her research into both hormonal influences on behavior and online dating interactions, Helen Fisher has developed a four-part typology of temperaments that shape our dating and mating behavior, which she terms "explorers," "builders," "directors," and "negotiators." We all have all four temperamental tendencies to greater and lesser degrees, Fisher has found, but usually one is dominant.

Explorer and builder tendencies are largely complementary. Explorers, as the name suggests, seek out new experiences and pleasures. In the Big Five personality scheme we discussed earlier, they are high on openness and extroversion, and in biological terms, they have an active dopamine system that drives them to seek pleasurable stimulation. In social life, explorers are adventurous and also often gregarious, unafraid and friendly—strong and warm.

Builders do not yearn for all things new. Instead they pay more attention to what is already in their world, nurturing stronger, closer friendships, though fewer of them. In Big Five terms, they are more conscientious, and in hormonal terms they have active serotonin systems. In many ways they are the opposite of the strong and warm explorers, but they have a strength and warmth of their own. Their conscientiousness gives them control over their environs, a powerful form of strength, and their loving embrace of the familiar is very warm.

While explorers and builders each have a balance of strength and warmth, directors and negotiators each have a clear favorite. Directors are driven to understand and control their worlds. They are all about analyzing things, getting the right answer, and taking the right action; feelings matter only insofar as they facilitate or get in the way of getting things worked out. Directors tend to be very confident that they understand the right way to go about things, and socially they like to be dominant. In Big Five terms, they tend to be lower than average on agreeableness, and biologically they have a surplus of testosterone. Directors are all about strength, not so much about warmth.

Negotiators, by contrast, just want everyone to get along. They are all about feelings and empathy. Socially they are facilitators, and they make excellent listeners—though their aversion to conflict often makes negotiators more likely to lie to avoid hard truths than other temperament types. In Big Five terms they are highly agreeable, and biologically they show lots of estrogen activity. In our terms, their priority is warmth, and strength is secondary.

What does this typology suggest for long-term compatibility? For many years, two competing clichés have echoed through our culture: Opposites attract, and birds of a feather flock together. Fisher's research suggests both are true, because what she has found is that on one hand explorers flock with other explorers and builders flock with other builders. But directors and negotiators do not flock with their own kind. Instead, these opposites find themselves attracted to each other. Maybe it is just because bossy directors like pliable negotiators, who in turn appreciate the direction that directors provide. But on some level, each type seems to recognize that the other offers something they lack. The combination of strength and warmth not only completes a person; it completes a partnership.

On the Rocks

Unsurprisingly, partnerships that are in trouble do not exhibit much strength and warmth. In fact, research on couples headed for the rocks points clearly to specific strength and warmth deficits as the prime culprits. As memorialized in Malcolm Gladwell's *Blink*, University of Washington professor John Gottman has devised an elaborate set of tests and measures to ascertain whether a couple is likely to last. Specifically, he can predict with 95 percent accuracy whether or not a couple will be married fifteen years after they submit to testing at his lab. After years up to his ears in this research, though, Gottman can tell a couple's fate almost as accurately without instruments. The deadly signs of relationship decline he calls the "four horsemen": criticism, defensiveness, stonewalling, and last and worst, contempt.

In practice, this sounds all too familiar to most people. Jill might say: "You're so insensitive. You never listen when I tell you things." Translation: I am not getting any warmth from you, Buster. Or perhaps it is a more specific complaint: "How many more times am I going to have to ask before you call the doctor's office already?" In other words, are you so lacking in strength that I have to do everything for you?

Once the argument is on, the criticism often leads to Gottman's other horsemen. Jack may respond with defensiveness, a plea for understanding: "Honey, I told you, I'm waiting for Susan to get back to me before I call because I think it would be better to know how she dealt with it." You just don't understand, in other words. You lack warmth.

Stonewalling is even more dramatic. Now, sometimes when people get upset, it can be very helpful for them to take time out and compose themselves before they try to talk with their beloved. But if the purpose of the pause is not clearly and respectfully communicated, not responding to a partner in distress is a deeply hostile gesture. It is disrespect: I am not even going to bother talking with you, because you are not worth it. While this gesture is not phrased as a complaint, it clearly conveys that the stonewaller is not perceiving any strength in the criticizer. (Stonewalling is not warm either, but the stonewaller may still be feeling some warmth from the criticizer.)

Most fearsome of all the horsemen, though, is contempt, our instinctive reaction to people we no longer respect or like. When one partner regards the other as lacking both strength and warmth and expresses that directly, watch out. The signs are not hard to spot: rolling eyes, sarcasm, a snorted "hmph," saying something "stinks"—which connotes disgust, a close cousin to contempt. These signals often come disguised as playful, and sometimes they genuinely are, in which case they are usually followed by some affirmative signal of warmth or shared humor. But without a genuine "just kidding" signal afterward, these signals are corrosive, alienating, and destructive. Gottman even found that a lot of contempt signals predict catching a cold, presumably because living in emotional misery is bad for the immune system. Living with contempt actually saps our strength.

If things really have fallen apart, and the time comes to part ways, even the partner who calls things off can often feel intense regret. One common explanation for this sadness goes something like "The grass is always greener" or "You don't know what you've got until it's gone," and there is some truth to that. Yet sometimes there is more to it. Sometimes the split happens in part because one partner seems weak to the other, who loses interest. But if that supposedly weak partner then confidently moves on, or even initiates the final split, the now-former partner suddenly sees them as strong again, which increases the sense of having lost someone desirable. Whether that strength was missing in the relationship or was there but no longer noticed, some kind of change was probably for the best.

Happily Ever After

But plenty of relationships do survive. When we forge romantic partnerships, we take on more and more roles with each other: lover, financial partner, chore sharer, sometimes even caretaker. Each of these new roles comes with its own goals, which means our assessments of strength and warmth—do you share my goals, and can you help us achieve them?—shift accordingly. And when people also take on the role of parents, the tension between strength and warmth once again takes center stage.

Joan was the first in her family to go to college, and she embodied the American Dream her parents had worked hard to give her. By the time she became a first-time parent at age thirty, she earned more than twice what her father had as a carpenter. Yet she wanted a very different childhood for her kids than the one she'd had. Her parents had grown up in the Depression, and bequeathed her their constant anxiety that everything could go wrong overnight. They demanded excellence in her schoolwork, and by age ten, she was also fixing lunch and dinner for the whole family so her mother could work extra hours as a seamstress—and she helped with her mother's sewing too. So Joan had a great work ethic, as did her eventual husband, Robert, but they wanted their kids to have what they had not: freedom from the discipline of constant work, a childhood unburdened by the responsibilities of adulthood.

Their son, Jason, was speaking in full sentences by his first birthday. They found a good preschool so they could both keep working, and in the brief hours between Joan picking him up from daycare and his bedtime they marveled at how quickly he absorbed new concepts. Joan was so immersed in her son's world during those precious evenings that she scarcely noticed as Jason's interests turned into demands. She never said no, and Robert didn't either. When Jason began to lash out, even pounding his tiny fists on them, they dismissed his behavior as normal childhood tantrums. They were profoundly shocked when Jason's preschool teacher called them in to discuss their son's selfish and disruptive classroom behavior. The teacher had seen all of this before, and she put it to them plainly: "He doesn't respect you."

Parents deal with the balancing act between liking and respect every day. Joan and Robert chose to shower affection on their son and set no limits. They were both comfortable projecting strength in their professional environments, but they wanted to be free of that at home, based in large part on their mixed feelings about their own childhoods. Both interpreted the strict discipline they had grown up with as a lack of warmth, even though as adults they maintained positive, loving relationships with their parents. They did not blame their parents for unhappy childhoods—they just wanted something less regimented for Jason. The mistake of thinking of strength and warmth as opposites rather than complements led to a hydraulic effect: they gave away strength, to the point where they lost their son's respect.

Nancy Rambusch, who founded the American Montessori Society in the early 1960s, called this the permissive model of child-rearing, and it represents the all-warmth reaction to the all-strength industrial model that Joan and Robert had lived through. Just as attitudes toward kids shifted in the home, there was a parallel shift in the classroom. The origins of the American public education system in the mid-nineteenth century mirrored the culture of the Industrial Age. Desks were bolted to the floor in rows like a factory floor. Teachers enforced strict discipline, and students did as they were told. In terms of behavioral expectations, this authoritarian model of education paralleled what happened at home. Children spoke only when spoken to, and corporal punishment was the norm, not the exception. This model held in most of American culture for roughly a hundred years, until the end of World War II.

As the baby boom generation first reached school age, a more child-centric culture emerged. Advances in psychological research focused more attention on children's emotional development. From Jean Piaget to the medically based advice of Dr. Benjamin Spock, this new way of thinking about schooling and parenting called for adults to understand and empower children as individuals. As this generation became parents and fell in love with their children, strict discipline gave way to teachable moments and an emphasis on building self-esteem. This is the model Joan and Robert embraced.

In the early 1990s, Rambusch advocated for a hybrid between authoritarian and permissive child-rearing approaches, which she called "authoritative." If the role of the adult in the authoritarian model was someone who "means business," and the adult in the permissive model was "a nice guy or gal," she suggested that the authoritative parent or teacher was "a nice guy or gal who means business." In short, strength and warmth had to work in concert. The basic strategy of this approach is to maintain a consistent warmth message that the parent is on the child's side, even when that means making sure bad behavior is dealt with appropriately. Note how this fits with the tomato rule dynamic we discussed earlier, that even one cold, uncaring moment can color a relationship forever. Punishment clearly projects strength and does not feel warm, so the authoritative approach to punishment requires explaining how the child's behavior is not acceptable, and so the parent needs to be strong about not rewarding it.

To pull this off, parents need to manage their emotions first: to respond, not react, when their kid does something outrageous. Children read their parents' nonverbal signals very well, and they know the difference between parents who are disappointed and exasperated but are making the effort to teach a kid a lesson, and parents who are just reacting based on emotions, getting back at the kid for making their life hard. While the authoritative approach takes patience, it also teaches patience by example. Research shows that authoritative parenting leads kids to perform better on the famous marshmallow test—demonstrating the willpower to resist eating the first marshmallow and earn the second one—which bodes well for all kinds of successes later in life.

This same strength-plus-warmth approach proves especially effective for classroom teaching as well. Doug Lemov, a managing director of Uncommon Schools, a network of charter schools, spent years studying the specific practices of good teachers, which he compiled in *Teach Like a Champion*. One of Lemov's many practices that involve projecting strength and warmth is called "warm/strict," in which the teacher lays down the law while showering the student in warmth cues to make it clear that a student's bad behavior has consequences exactly because the teacher is rooting for the student to succeed. Lemov states flatly, "The fact is that the degree to which you are warm has no bearing on the degree to which you are strict, and vice versa." While the story is more complicated than that, his point is clear: By projecting with energy, you can, and should, project both strength and warmth at once.

In addition to balancing their own strength and warmth, parents face the challenge of helping their children navigate this balance in relations with siblings and peers. This brings us to lessons from the playground (and backseat): Some children intuitively understand the need to stand up to a bully, and others are challenged to learn it. The process of growing up is largely one of gaining strength physically and cognitively, whereas socially and emotionally both strength and warmth need to be learned. These skills come more easily when parents and other caring adults offer praise for appropriate displays of strength or warmth and corrections for inevitable missteps. And they come even more easily when those adults model considerate and assertive verbal and nonverbal behavior consistently themselves. It may sound old-fashioned, but steady and patient guidance to nurture the qualities of character is perhaps a parent's greatest gift to the next generation.

Epilogue

When you feel and project strength and warmth at once, several things happen. You feel strong, and you command respect. You feel warm, and you draw out empathy in others. But when these feelings are paired, they are more than the sum of their parts.

For one thing, when you feel both appreciative of humanity and unthreatened, you feel happy and contented. Even when you are by yourself, this lets you feel secure about your place in the world and open to new experiences.

Your effect on people is also different. Since people see you as warm and feel connected to you, when they also see you as strong, they feel reassured, confident that you and your strength are there for them if they need it. They may also feel validated: They respect your strength, so when you show warmth and treat them like a worthy colleague they feel strong too. When you project both qualities at once, your presence is a gift to people. It makes them feel better, more relaxed and happy, and reassures them that things are going to be all right.

In the end, strength and warmth are not just character traits in tension. They are energies, basic life forces, and they work together too. Strength gives us a sense of mastery, and warmth gives us a sense of belonging. Mastery and belonging are how we hold back our primal anxieties, and when we are lucky, feel the thrill of living. Strength enables warmth, creating room for it. Strong people stand up for themselves, and stronger people stand up for others. Warmth enables strength too, healing our wounds and giving us something to be strong for. This effect is as pedestrian as it is profound: Researchers have even found that watching videos of puppies and kittens or reruns of a favorite show—a.k.a. spending time with familiar fictional friends—recharges depleted willpower. Both strength and warmth have their individual benefits, but it is when they happen together that life gets good.

This is the last step, where everything comes together. It is more than not being afraid of your own shadow, more than learning the moves. It is actually emotionally engaging in the moment, understanding and feeling your own actions as expressions of your strength and your warmth. In those moments, you feel powerful and deeply connected to people. That makes you compelling to others, because it makes you compelling to yourself.

Admiration

If admiration is your goal, a good question to ask is, "Why *should* someone admire you?" While on some level it is natural to want others to admire us, knowing your own motivations and intentions is an important part of reading yourself. Remember, admiration is reserved for those who are both respected and liked—who matter in the world and put their strength to use in service of shared concerns and interests.

If you are doing both of those things, you are already in relatively rare company, but that does not mean you are outwardly projecting these qualities. You may think that should not matter. But ultimately people value you for your presence and your example as well as your deeds. If your words and nonverbal communication suggest that you feel hesitant and unsure of yourself, or are not concerned with other people's feelings, that matters. And if you have done great and selfless things and still seem ill at ease in life, you remind the rest of us that even success may not bring happiness.

There are some people who manage to project strength and warmth when we first encounter them but whose deeds tell a different story. Our admiration for them is usually short-lived. The rest of us figure out soon enough that they are all hat, no cattle.

The Morality of Strength and Warmth

We are born into this world with little more than the ability to project warmth. Think of an infant's first smile and the effect it has on a new mother, right down to the oxytocin boost she gets from looking into that cherubic face. We figure out how to assert ourselves by crying, but otherwise lack any means of projecting strength; we are utterly dependent on those who care for us. From that starting point, we begin the process of acquiring strength. By the time we are on the playground, we are already sizing up physical strength and willfulness relative to peers. This growth continues through puberty and adolescence, which many cultures mark with a rite of passage to adulthood that demands a display of strength—physical, intellectual, or otherwise. In late adolescence and early adulthood we approach our physical peak, though other elements of strength such as professional competence and social skills are often only beginning to bloom.

We learn more about warmth along the way as well. As any parent knows, young children go through a process of losing their egocentrism—they discover that other people have different perspectives and feelings. As we grow up, we figure out how to make and keep friends, empathize with others (both cognitively and emotionally), and develop intimate relationships. As our social circles expand, we join groups and affiliate ourselves with like-minded people who are on our team in life. Most of us go on to raise families, which become our innermost circle of shared concerns and interests. We are not equating familial ties with happiness, but there is a reason for the cliché about blood being thicker than water.

Strength and warmth are part of our nature. They have a biological basis in the hormones that drive everything from physical size to behavior. We can choose to favor one quality over the other, but both are present in just about every facet of our lives. The tension between them is innate and ubiquitous.

What about the dark side of that nature? Despite what people at the extremes may think, strength and warmth are not inherently good or bad. The morality surrounding their uses depends wholly on the intentions of the person who projects them. As far as faking it to achieve truly malicious ends, false warmth is usually easy to spot if you know what to look for. (We have tried to highlight some of those signs.) Yes, there are con artists, and yes, some people are more gullible than others, which is why due diligence goes beyond strength and warmth judgments. But the utterly charming psychopath who can lie convincingly without contradicting or betraying himself is far more common on TV than in reality.

As far as the morality of strength and warmth, the Golden Rule embodies the concept of reciprocity, but it does not follow that all moral decisions are based solely on warmth. Strength is essential for protection and survival if someone seeks to do harm to you or those who share your interests or concerns. To paraphrase Ecclesiastes 3:8, there is a time for strength and a time for warmth. Strength should be met with strength, and warmth with warmth.

The question of how to use strength and warmth in your own life begins with your intentions. Who do you want to be? What are you trying to achieve? Does the strength and warmth expressed through your deeds align with what you project in your everyday social interactions? Do you use your strength in the service of others? Do you use your warmth to minimize painful conflicts when you can? Only you can answer for yourself, and there is nothing simple or straightforward about it. It takes courage (strength) to be rigorously honest about your intentions (warmth).

Reflecting on questions like these will bring a richer understanding of the foundational role strength and warmth play in our interactions with the people who surround us. We live most fully when we cultivate both in our lives, when we balance a high degree of individual capability with an unflagging regard for the needs and interests of others. Only then are we worthy of genuine admiration.

Acknowledgments

This book has been several years in the making at this point, and you would not be reading it without the efforts of many enthusiastic and talented people.

First among these is our agent, Mel Flashman, who had the foresight to realize the potential of these ideas and the patience to stick with us for the long haul. Megan Hustad has also been a co-conspirator since the proposal phase, gracing us with her insights and impeccable taste. Our editor, Caroline Sutton, at Hudson Street Press, has both believed in this project and helped focus it in ways that have made this a stronger book. And Kym Surridge's judicious copyediting sharpened the text significantly.

The core ideas here were developed by reflecting on our work with our clients. We have learned so much from them, and are humbled by the trust they have placed in us over the years. Our business partner and friend Seth Pendleton, the "P" in KNP Communications, is the invisible presence throughout these pages. The concepts in the book grew out of our work together and our shared quest to develop a new approach to helping people deal with one another.

Two very special people, Ilyse Hogue and Betsy Kohut, supported us throughout, balancing strength and warmth as sharp readers and infinitely patient partners. We would not have made it without them. You are both owed many evenings, weekends, and vacations.

Amy Cuddy, of Harvard Business School, has been an invaluable friend and colleague. Having worked with her as thought partners and in the classroom for several years now, we are deeply grateful to her and proud to call her a collaborator and kindred spirit. Special thanks also to Todd Rogers, now at the Harvard Kennedy School, for instantly recognizing the connection between our work on strength and warmth and the research on warmth and competence, as well as for introducing us to Amy. Many experts have freely given their time to discuss their work with us. Tori Brescoll, Dana Carney, Tanzeem Choudhury, Susan Fiske, and Jessica Tracy all provided key insights about their research. And Jordan Pringle has helped to school us on style.

Many friends and colleagues weighed in with important insights, intellectual contributions, and encouragement, including Rich Benjamin, David Brock, Matt Butler, Carol Hedlund, Charlie Honig, Will Jenkins, Sally Kohn, Jean Lenihan, Cathey Park, Andrew Ranson, Sarah Rigdon, Rinku Sen, Gong Szeto, Barry Winer, Henry Winkler, and Christine Zinno.

John is deeply grateful to his parents. Their wisdom is reflected throughout. This book would not be possible without the many lessons his parents taught, not to mention the serene confidence they showed in their only son as he walked away from the worlds of law and consulting to go his own way. John would also like to thank Sara Watts, nee O'Connell, for helping him recognize and seize the opportunity in front of him.

Matt would like to thank Liz Coleman and the Center for the Advancement of Public Action at Bennington College, Donna Connell, Max Crandall, Samantha Dodge, and Haley Stephenson. And dating back long before this project, Andrew Kohut and Marybeth Kelman have provided endless encouragement and love.

Notes

Global

We have changed the names of everyone in the text except for authors, researchers, and famous folks.

After much discussion, we have used third-person plural pronouns (they/their) throughout when referring to a person of indeterminate gender, rather than slowing down the text with "he or she," "s/he," or other clunky compromises. There are lively debates among grammarians about the need for written English to catch up with the spoken language here, and we take comfort in the fact that George Bernard Shaw adopted this same usage at least once. May our English teachers forgive us.

The Big Idea

The Gandhi quote appeared in *Young India* (1:52 [1919]), the weekly journal he published for several years.

The concept we call strength is closely related to a number of other terms and concepts. We chose to call it strength because that denotes a personal quality, as in Gandhi's quote. The closest synonyms are "agency" and "capacity." We did not go with either of those because they have extra syllables, and sound a little too clinical and Latinate for our liking. "Power" is also closely related, but power suggests an external force that can be gained and lost, granted and taken away, rather than a quality of character. (For instance, recall the saying "power abhors a vacuum.") The disadvantage of "strength" in a research setting is that its common association with physical strength means that any broader meaning requires an explanation. "Competence" denotes just skill, to the exclusion of will, and our political experience teaches that being seen as a smart technocrat is no substitute for being seen as tough. (Compare the picture of Dukakis in the tank with George W. Bush's photo-op on the aircraft carrier, and consider who got elected president twice.) But in most cases, *competence* is a good proxy for *strength*, and because it is a more precise term, it is easier for research subjects to assess. This points to a larger research question of finding ways to study this broader concept of strength, or looking at willfulness and determination in isolation from competence and even physical attributes.

The classic marshmallow study is by Walter Mischel. See Walter Mischel, Ebbe B. Ebbesen, and Antonette Raskoff Zeiss, "Cognitive and Attentional Mechanisms in Delay of Gratification," *Journal of Personality and Social Psychology* 21, no. 2 (1972): 204–18.

Two recent books offer a good overview of the science behind willpower: Roy F. Baumeister and John Tierney, *Willpower: Rediscovering the Greatest Human Strength* (New York: The Penguin Press, 2011); and Kelly McGonigal, *The Willpower Instinct: How Self-Control Works, Why It Matters, and What You Can Do to Get More of It* (New York: Penguin Group, 2011). A different way to think about willpower is through the lens of the Harvard Law School Program on Negotiation (PON) model, founded by Roger Fisher and William Ury, which accounts for interests, emotions, and identity. In the case of our friend who started jogging, her interest was in achieving physical fitness, the emotional payoff was feeling good about herself after exercise, and her identity was tied to seeing herself as the kind of person who does not quit.

For some of the science on testosterone, see A. Booth, G. Shelley, A. Mazur, G. Tharp, and R. Kittok, "Testosterone, and Winning and Losing in Human Competition," *Hormones and Behavior* 23, no. 4 (1989): 556–71; and A. Mazur and A. Booth, "Testosterone and Social Dominance in Men," *Behavioral and Brain Sciences* 21 (1998): 353–97.

J. K. Burgoon and N. E. Dunbar, "An Interactionist Perspective on Dominance-Submission: Interpersonal Dominance as a Dynamic, Situationally Contingent Social Skill," *Communication Monographs* 67, no. 1 (2000): 96–121.

Clifford Nass, of Stanford University, has done a series of really interesting experiments about negative responses to strength displays, which are recounted in Clifford Nass and Corina Yen, *The Man Who Lied to His Laptop: What Machines Teach Us About Human Relationships* (New York: Penguin, 2010). One recent study also suggests that confidence may weigh more heavily than competence, validating the Peter Principle and the strength-detractor cynics. See Cameron Anderson, Sebastien Brion, Don A. Moore, and Jessica A. Kennedy, "A Status-Enhancement Account of Overconfidence," *Journal of Personality and Social Psychology* (2012, in press). For a summary, see University of California–Berkeley Haas School of Business, "Why Are People Overconfident So Often? It's

All About Social Status," *ScienceDaily*, August 13, 2012, http://www.sciencedaily .com/releases/2012/08/120813130712.htm.

Our friend and colleague Joseph Grady, of Topos Partnership, talked about primary metaphors in his 1997 Ph.D. dissertation, "Primary Metaphors and Primary Scenes." George Lakoff and Mark Johnson identified "affection is warmth" as a conceptual metaphor in *Metaphors We Live By* (1980), and discussed primary metaphor theory in the afterword of their 2003 edition.

Lawrence E. Williams and John A. Bargh, "Experiencing Physical Warmth Promotes Interpersonal Warmth," *Science* 322, no. 5901 (2008): 606–7.

Chen-Bo Zhong and Geoffrey J. Leonardelli, "Cold and Lonely: Does Social Exclusion Literally Feel Cold?" *Psychological Science* 19, no. 9 (2008): 838–42.

The Bill Murray quote appeared in the February 21, 1999, issue of *Parade*.

Primatologist Frans de Waal has written and spoken extensively about empathy. See *The Age of Empathy: Nature's Lessons for a Kinder Society* (New York: The Crown Publishing Group, 2009). His TED talk on moral behavior in animals is also worth watching: http://www.ted.com/talks/frans_de_waal_do_animals _have_morals.html.

Barbara Ehrenreich, *Nickel and Dimed: On (Not) Getting By in America* (New York: Metropolitan Books, 2001).

A lot has been written about similarity-attraction effect. Nass's *The Man Who Lied to His Laptop* is a good place to start.

Franz R. Epting, Carol Zempel, and Charles Rubio, "Construct Similarity and Maternal Warmth," *Social Behavior and Personality* 7, no. 1 (1979): 97–105.

See Helen Fisher, *Why Him? Why Her? Finding Real Love by Understanding Your Personality Type* (New York: Henry Holt, 2009). Also check out Fisher's TED talk: http://www.ted.com/speakers/helen_fisher.html.

Dr. Paul J. Zak has written a book on oxytocin called *The Moral Molecule: The Source of Love and Prosperity* (New York: Dutton Adult, 2012). Also check out his TED talk: http://www.ted.com/talks/paul_zak_trust_morality_and_oxytocin.html. This is an exciting, emerging, and controversial area, and researchers continue to explore oxytocin's implications for how we interact with one another. One interesting avenue of exploration beyond oxytocin's role in creating affinity between members of a group is its role in reacting to outsiders in a relatively more hostile way. See, for instance, C. K. W. De Dreu, L. L. Greer, G. A. Van Kleef, S. Shalvi, and M. J. J. Handgraaf, "Oxytocin Promotes Human Ethnocentrism," *Proceedings of the Na-*

tional Academy of Sciences USA 108, no. 4 (2011): 1262–66; and Professor Carsten De Dreu's website: http://dedreu.socialpsychology.org. Evidence thus far tends to suggest oxytocin acts by enhancing affection for friends, rather than by enhancing animosity toward foes. This can certainly still contribute to differential treatment, though.

Niccolò Machievelli, *The Prince*, chapter 17, "Concerning Cruelty and Clemency, and Whether It Is Better to be Loved Than Feared." Note that Machievelli warns not only against not being feared, but also against becoming hated: "Upon this a question arises: whether it be better to be loved than feared or feared than loved? It may be answered that one should wish to be both, but, because it is difficult to unite them in one person, is much safer to be feared than loved, when, of the two, either must be dispensed with. Because this is to be asserted in general of men, that they are ungrateful, fickle, false, cowardly, covetous, and as long as you succeed they are yours entirely; they will offer you their blood, property, life and children, as is said above, when the need is far distant; but when it approaches they turn against you. And that prince who, relying entirely on their promises, has neglected other precautions, is ruined; because friendships that are obtained by payments, and not by greatness or nobility of mind, may indeed be earned, but they are not secured, and in time of need cannot be relied upon; and men have less scruple in offending one who is beloved than one who is feared, for love is preserved by the link of obligation which, owing to the baseness of men, is broken at every opportunity for their advantage; but fear preserves you by a dread of punishment which never fails. Nevertheless a prince ought to inspire fear in such a way that, if he does not win love, he avoids hatred. . . ." *The Prince* can be found online from Project Gutenberg: http://www.gutenberg.org/ebooks/1232. For an account of Machiavelli's decision to write *The Prince* in order to curry favor with the Medicis, see Pasquale Villari, *The Life and Times of Niccolò Machiavelli*, Vol. 2 (London: T. Fisher Unwin, 1892), 166. (Available free as a Google e-book.)

In addition to the dueling hormones in our blood, there is also new evidence that the neurons required for empathy and analytical thought suppress one another.

See Anthony I. Jack, Abigail Dawson, Katelyn Begany, Regina L. Leckie, Kevin Barry, Angela Ciccia, and Abraham Snyder, "fMRI Reveals Reciprocal Inhibition Between Social and Physical Cognitive Domains," *NeuroImage*, October 27, 2012. See a summary: "Empathy Represses Analytic Thought, and Vice Versa: Brain Physiology Limits Simultaneous Use of Both Networks," *Science Daily*, October 30, 2012, http://www.sciencedaily.com/releases/2012/10/121030161416.htm?

Bogdan Wojciszke and Andrea E. Abele, "The Primacy of Communion Over Agency and Its Reversals in Evaluations," *European Journal of Social Psychology* 38, no. 7 (2008): 1139–47.

Janine Willis and Alexander Todorov, "First Impressions: Making Up Your Mind After a 100-Ms Exposure to a Face," *Psychological Science* 17, no. 7 (2006): 592–98.

For a good summary of the research on overcoming a single instance of cold-ness, see Amy Cuddy, Peter Glick, and Anna Beninger, "The Dynamics of Warmth and Competence Judgments, and Their Outcomes in Organizations," *Research in Organizational Behavior* 31 (2011): 73–98. This is perhaps the single most useful resource if you are looking for a recent overview of the breadth of academic re-search on warmth and competence judgments. Also see it for references to halo and hydraulic effects, and the studies of who gets sued for medical malpractice. It is available online at: http://www.people.hbs.edu/acuddy/in%20press,%20cuddy ,%20glick,%20&%20beninger,%20ROB.pdf.

There is an interesting echo of the choice between strength and warmth in the classic prisoner's dilemma scenario, in which the prisoner can choose either to maximize return for himself at the expense of his confederate in the adjoining interrogation room, or keep faith with his confederate so they collectively end up better off. Ayn Rand's choice is clear, as is the warm one. This is also the choice structure behind the tragedy of the commons.

To be clear, plenty of normal, well-adjusted people have read and enjoyed Ayn Rand's books at some point in their lives. We personally know someone who in a moment of despair was so inspired by the vision of strength in her works that he credited them with keeping him from suicide, and for that we are grateful. Rand herself was a bit of a ghoulish character, however, even lavishly praising William Hickman for kidnapping, raping, and murdering a twelve-year-old girl. Rand said it showed great "strength" to so thoroughly disregard social mores and put his own desires first. Enough said.

"The strong do what they can," from Thucydides, is almost shorthand for the realist theory of international relations. *The Peloponnesian War* is available online from Project Gutenberg: http://www.gutenberg.org/files/7142/7142-h/7142-h .htm.

Fritz Heider was the godfather of the contrast effect. See *The Psychology of Interpersonal Relations* (Hillsdale, NJ: Lawrence Erlbaum Associates, 1958).

Great warmth can lead to generally acknowledged strength, whereas great strength without some other warm aspect will not appeal to all audiences. By it-self, great strength will only create warmth with some folks. In our practice, we refer to these two dynamics as "strength as warmth" and "warmth as strength."

These connections also help explain a linguistic paradox: why we warm to people we call "cool." The modern term is affectionate, and affection is deeply connected to the idea of warmth—the literal opposite of coolness. The word "cool" was originally used to compliment a person's ability to stay calm and composed under pressure. It came to be used more broadly to describe people who resist pressure from the outside world and confidently do their own thing. That kind of strength is attractive, something we aspire to have ourselves and want in people on our team, and we are drawn to it, which introduces an element of warmth. It is this combination of strength and warmth elements that has turned "cool" into an enduring compliment for almost anything we approve of.

Read the full text of Dr. Martin Luther King's "power and love" speech here: http://www.thekingcenter.org/archive/document/mlk-address-tenth-anniversary-convention-sclc#.

Susan T. Fiske, Amy J. C. Cuddy, and Peter Glick, "Universal Dimensions of Social Cognition: Warmth and Competence," *Trends in Cognitive Sciences* 11, no. 2 (2007): 77–83. Their work focuses more narrowly on the concept of competence, rather than on the broader concept of strength, which includes both competence and willfulness. But in most cases, competence is a good proxy for overall strength. This paper also includes a great overview of the history of psychologists' versions of this duality, dating back to the middle of the twentieth century.

Our emotional reactions to people who project lots of strength and low warmth depend on the social context and our priorities. If we are feeling strength-averse, we are more likely to react with fear than envy. If we admire strength, we are more likely to react with some envy. And the more we admire strength, the more likely we are also to be drawn to this strength; this is the strength-as-warmth dynamic mentioned earlier. It is not uncommon for people to have some feelings of envy toward others they consider genuine friends.

Neither of us has ever seen Gene Simmons with a vacant look in his eyes, but we imagine it must have happened once or twice.

For a relatively accessible overview of the Big Five, see Oliver P. John and Sanjay Srivastava, "The Big-Five Trait Taxonomy: History, Measurement, and Theoretical Perspectives," in L. A. Pervin and O. P. John, eds., *Handbook of Personality: Theory and Research*, 2nd ed. (New York: Guilford, 2001), 102–38. The paper is also available online at http://pages.uoregon.edu/sanjay/pubs/bigfive.pdf. The popular Myers-Briggs test is based on the Big Five, minus the neuroticism dimension, possibly in part because it is harder than the other factors to paint as value-neutral.

By some (necessarily imprecise) measures, strength and warmth account for more than 80 percent of our value judgments of others, while other kinds of personality differences account for the rest. See Bogdan Wojciszke, Roza Bazinska, Marcin Jaworski, "On the Dominance of Moral Categories in Impression Formation," *Personality and Social Psychology Bulletin* 24, no. 12 (1998): 1245–57.

Christopher Peterson and Martin E. P. Seligman, *Character Strengths and Virtues: A Handbook and Classification* (New York: Oxford University Press, 2004).

Pretty much anything we pass a value judgment on can be analyzed through the lens of strength and warmth, respect and liking. And that is not limited to things we anthropomorphize; it includes pretty much anything we think of as a thing: a company. A product. A logo. A brochure. A letter. A number. A work of architecture. A work of literature. A piece of music. A food dish. A vacation. Generally speaking, if we admire something enough to approve of it, we see aspects of both strength and warmth in it.

The Hand You Are Dealt

The hand you are dealt can be surgically altered these days, through cosmetic surgery or even gender reassignment surgery. We do work with people for whom these can be reasonable options. Except in very limited circumstances, we usually counsel against plastic surgery. Pretty much the last thing we would want people to do is to limit the natural expressive range of their faces.

Daniel Kahneman, *Thinking, Fast and Slow* (New York: Farrar, Straus, and Giroux, 2011). This book is a treasure trove.

For the comprehensive model of how stereotypes map to warmth and competence judgments, see Amy J. C. Cuddy, Susan T. Fiske, and Peter Glick, "Warmth and Competence as Universal Dimensions of Social Perception: The Stereotype Content Model and the BIAS Map," in M. P. Zanna, ed., *Advances in Experimental Social Psychology, Vol. 40* (New York: Academic Press, 2008), 61–149.

Larissa Z. Tiedens, "Anger and Advancement Versus Sadness and Subjugation: The Effect of Negative Emotion Expressions on Social Status Conferral," *Journal of Personality and Social Psychology* 80, no. 1 (2001): 86–94.

Amy J. C. Cuddy, Susan Crotty, Jihye Chong, and Michael I. Norton, "Men as Cultural Ideals: How Culture Shapes Gender Stereotypes," Working Paper 10-097, *Harvard Business School* (2010).

Peter Glick and Susan T. Fiske, "The Ambivalent Sexism Inventory: Differentiating Hostile and Benevolent Sexism," *Journal of Personality and Social Psychology* 70, no. 3 (1996): 491–512.

See Frank Flynn's description of his findings about the Heidi/Howard experiment: http://www.gsb.stanford.edu/news/headlines/wim_martin07.shtml.

Victoria L. Brescoll, Erica Dawson, and Eric Luis Uhlmann, "Hard Won and Easily Lost: The Fragile Status of Leaders in Gender-Stereotype-Incongruent Occupations," *Psychological Science* 21, no. 11 (2010): 1640–42.

All of those penalties kick in just for projecting strength by being competent. If a woman is also, heaven forbid, socially assertive, there are extra penalties. Research shows that managers look less favorably on women who exhibit dominant body language than on those with submissive body language. Once again, the opposite tends to be true for men.

L. Babcock and S. Laschever, *Women Don't Ask: Negotiation and the Gender Divide* (Princeton, NJ: Princeton University Press, 2003).

Amy J. C. Cuddy, Susan T. Fiske, and Peter Glick, "When Professionals Become Mothers, Warmth Doesn't Cut the Ice," *Journal of Social Issues* 60, no. 4 (2004): 701–18.

M. C. Bolino and W. H. Turnley, "Counternormative Impression Management, Likeability, and Performance Ratings: The Use of Intimidation in an Organizational Setting," *Journal of Organizational Behavior* 24, no. 2 (2003): 237–50.

Victoria L. Brescoll, Eric L. Uhlmann, Corinne Moss-Racusin, and Lonnie Sarnell, "Masculinity, Status, and Subordination: Working for a Gender Atypical Supervisor Causes Men to Lose Status," *Journal of Experimental Social Psychology* 48, no. 1 (2012): 354–57.

Jack Zenger and Joseph Folkman, "Are Women Better Leaders than Men?" *Harvard Business Review, HBR Blog Network*, March 15, 2012, http://blogs.hbr.org/cs/2012/03/a_study_in_leadership_women_do.html#.T2jQJnyK4-Q.facebook.

Victoria Brescoll has done some of the most insightful work on the topic of women and anger in the workplace. See Victoria L. Brescoll and Eric L. Uhlmann, "Can an Angry Woman Get Ahead? Status Conferral, Gender, and Expression of Emotion in the Workplace," *Psychological Science* 19, no. 3 (2008): 268–75. We are grateful for the many insights she shared when we besieged her with follow-up questions.

Cuddy et al., "The Dynamics of Warmth and Competence Judgments." See also Susan T. Fiske, Jun Xu, and Amy J. C. Cuddy, "(Dis)respecting Versus (Dis)liking: Status and Interdependence Predict Ambivalent Stereotypes of Competence and Warmth," *Journal of Social Issues* 55, no. 3 (1999): 473–89.

In some cases, the rules for women are that you fit in by getting the work done to exacting specifications. If you are at NASA mission control directing a manned flight, that environment calls for commanding respect through a combination of technical competence and confidence. Warmth in that setting is about showing how committed you are to the team and its mission, and not letting anything get in the way of performing to the highest possible standard of professionalism so your astronauts return home safely.

Cuddy et al., "Warmth and Competence as Universal Dimensions of Social Perception." Also summarized succinctly in Cuddy et al., "The Dynamics of Warmth and Competence Judgments." See also Eric L. Kohatsu, Rodolfo Victoria, Andrew Lau, Michelle Flores, and Andrea Salazar, "Analyzing Anti-Asian Prejudice from a Racial Identity and Color-Blind Perspective," *Journal of Counseling and Development* 89, no. 1 (2011): 63–72.

We have partially redacted the *n*-word here. This was not done lightly. When we considered this, we got great but conflicting advice from several wise black friends. Ultimately we went with partial censorship because we did not feel comfortable writing out a word that we would not use in conversation.

Alfiee M. Breland, "A Model for Differential Perceptions of Competence Based on Skin Tone Among African Americans," *Journal of Multicultural Counseling and Development* 26, no. 4 (1998): 294–311.

The "hot-blooded" Latino stereotype can also be lampooned as silly and not deserving of respect, as illustrated by Sofía Vergara's character Gloria on the sitcom *Modern Family*. It is easy to make the case that the Gloria character perpetuates disrespectful stereotypes about Latinos. In the show's defense, however, she is not just a minor comic relief character; she is a major character whom viewers get to know as a person, and she is portrayed very sympathetically by Ms. Vergara.

Terri D. Conley, Joshua L. Rabinowitz, and Jerome Rabow, "Gordon Gekkos, Frat Boys, and Nice Guys: The Content, Dimensions, and Structural Determinants of Multiple Ethnic Minority Groups' Stereotypes About White Men," *Analyses of Social Issues and Public Policy* 10, no. 1 (2010): 69–96.

Nicolas Kervyn, Vincent Y. Yzerbyt, Stephanie Demoulin, and Charles M. Judd, "Competence and Warmth in Context: The Compensatory Nature of Stereotypic Views of National Groups," *European Journal of Social Psychology* 38, no. 7 (2008): 1175–83.

Robert W. Livingston and Nicholas A. Pearce, "The Teddy-Bear Effect: Does Having a Baby Face Benefit Black Chief Executive Officers?" *Psychological Science* 20, no. 10 (2009): 1229–36.

See "Do Black Women Have More or Less Freedom as Leaders? Understanding the Roles of Race and Gender," which is based on the research of Robert W. Livingston of the Kellogg School of Management, Ashleigh Shelby Rosette of Duke University, and Ella F. Washington, also affiliated with Kellogg. Available online at: http://insight.kellogg.northwestern.edu/index.php/Kellogg/article/do_black_women_have_more_or_less_freedom_as_leaders.

Hilary B. Bergsieker, J. Nicole Shelton, and Jennifer A. Richeson, "To Be Liked Versus Respected: Divergent Goals in Interracial Interactions," *Journal of Personality and Social Psychology* 99, no. 2 (2010): 248–64.

John Blake, "Why Obama Doesn't Dare Become the 'Angry Black Man,'" CNN, June 8, 2010, http://articles.cnn.com/2010-06-08/politics/rage.obama_1_president-obama-barack-obama-race-relations?_s=PM:POLITICS.

Amy J. C. Cuddy, Mindi S. Rock, and Michael I. Norton, "No Right to Be Mad: Denying Outgroups Anger and Denying Help to Angry Outgroups" (February 2008). In Amy J. C. Cuddy & D. Small (chairs), Effects of Emotion on Judgments and Decisions About Humanitarian Aid. Symposium conducted at the 9th Annual Meeting of the Society for Personality and Social Psychology, Albuquerque, NM. Many thanks to Amy for walking through this with us.

Wizdom Powell Hammond, "Taking It Like a Man: Masculine Role Norms as Moderators of the Racial Discrimination–Depressive Symptoms Association Among African American Men," *American Journal of Public Health* 102, Suppl. 2 (2012): S232–S41, http://ajph.aphapublications.org/doi/abs/10.2105/ajph.2011.300485.

Amy J. C. Cuddy, Michael I. Norton, and Susan T. Fiske, "This Old Stereotype: The Pervasiveness and Persistence of the Elderly Stereotype," *Journal of Social Issues* 61, no. 2 (2005): 265–83.

David Perrett's book *In Your Face: The New Science of Human Attraction* (New York: Palgrave Macmillan, 2010) covers a lot of the research mentioned about faces: the wide cheeks of extroverts, hormonal effects in the womb, masculine features on women and feminine features on men, and pretty boys and pretty girls.

To picture the expression in which the lips are closed but the jaw hangs slightly open, think Liv Tyler.

Sheila Brownlow found that baby-faced speakers appeared honest but were seen as less expert than people with mature faces in "Seeing Is Believing: Facial Appearance, Credibility, and Attitude Change," *Journal of Nonverbal Behavior* 16, no. 2 (1992), 101–15.

Deborah L. Rhode, *The Beauty Bias: The Injustice of Appearance in Life and Law* (New York: Oxford University Press, 2010). For a summary, see http://alumni.stanford.edu/get/page/magazine/article/?article_id=28581.

It makes sense that looks are traditionally a bigger deal for women, because their roles in society have been more circumscribed. We know that strength and warmth signals are a component of attractiveness, as are traditionally good looks. Men are encouraged to show all kinds of strength signals, from big biceps to big bank accounts, and those contribute to their attractiveness (to a point anyway). Since women have historically been discouraged from and punished for showing strength beyond their limited traditional roles, looks play a larger part for them than for men in determining how attractive they are. There is a lot more research to be done to untangle how strength and warmth contribute to attractiveness, and we will have more to say about this later.

Jerry M. Burger, Shelley Soroka, Katrina Gonzago, Emily Murphy, and Emily Somervell, "The Effect of Fleeting Attraction on Compliance to Requests," *Personality and Social Psychology Bulletin* 27, no. 12 (2001): 1578–86.

T. K. Shackelford, V. A. Weekes-Shackelford, G. J. LeBlanc, A. L. Bleske, H. A. Euler, and S. Hoier, "Female Coital Orgasm and Male Attractiveness," *Human Nature* 11, no. 3 (2000): 299–306.

Bradley J. Ruffle and Ze'ev Shtudiner did a study that Ruffle summarized in "Photos of Attractive Female Job Seekers Stir Up HR Jealousy," *Harvard Business Review*, HBR Blog Network, March 22, 2012, http://blogs.hbr.org/cs/2012/03/photos_of_attractive_female_jo.html.

Nancy Etcoff, *Survival of the Prettiest: The Science of Beauty* (New York: Doubleday, 1999).

Kevin M. Kniffin and David Sloan Wilson, "The Effect of Nonphysical Traits on the Perception of Physical Attractiveness: Three Naturalistic Studies," *Evolution and Human Behavior* 25, no. 2 (2004): 88–101. Wilson notes that while we now consider his familiar rugged features handsome, during his lifetime, Abe Lincoln was considered so ugly that he once quipped, "If I were two-faced, do you think I would be wearing this one?"

Etcoff's *Survival of the Prettiest* explains the "average" beauty concept.

The flavor-of-the-month teenybopper idols in *Tiger Beat* are a good guide to the pretty-boy type (except for the baby-faced ones).

Rhode's *The Beauty Bias* explains the universal appeal of the shoulder-to-waist ratio for males and the waist-hip ratio for females.

There is an old chestnut of a concept of three body types—ectomorphs, endo-morphs, and mesomorphs—that we learned in school back in the Dark Ages. On closer inspection, those categories are based not in human physiology but in psychology, and at this point the whole concept seems a little quaint.

Jens Agerström and Dan-Olof Rooth, "The Role of Automatic Obesity Stereotypes in Real Hiring Discrimination," *Journal of Applied Psychology* 96, no. 4 (2011): 790–805.

Eric Clausell and Susan T. Fiske, "When Do Subgroup Parts Add Up to the Stereotypic Whole? Mixed Stereotype Content for Gay Male Subgroups Explains Overall Ratings," *Social Cognition* 23, no. 2 (2005): 161–81.

Jim Rendon, "Post-Traumatic Stress's Surprisingly Positive Flip Side," *New York Times Magazine*, March 25, 2012, http://www.nytimes.com/2012/03/25/magazine/post-traumatic-stresss-surprisingly-positive-flip-side.html?pagewanted=all&_r=0.

Playing the Hand

Albert Mehrabian, *Silent Messages: Implicit Communication of Emotions and Attitudes* (Belmont, CA: Wadsworth Publishing Company, 1972).

See also Mehrabian's article with Morton Wiener: "Decoding of Inconsistent Communications," *Journal of Personality and Social Psychology* 6, no. 1 (1967): 109–14.

Here is one example of the "LBJ treatment": http://www.uiowa.edu/commstud/resources/nonverbal/lbj.htm.

Dana R. Carney, Amy J. C. Cuddy, and Andy J. Yap, "Power Posing: Brief Nonverbal Displays Affect Neuroendocrine Levels and Risk Tolerance," *Psychological Science* 21, no. 10 (2010): 1363–68. See Cuddy's TED talk: http://www.ted.com/talks/amy_cuddy_your_body_language_shapes_who_you_are.html. Power posing reminds us of what Garrison Keillor says of the whole wheat in his fictional powder-milk biscuits: It gives shy people the strength to get up and do what needs to be done.

Dana R. Carney, Judith A. Hall, and Lavonia S. LeBeau, "Beliefs About the Nonverbal Expression of Social Power," *Journal of Nonverbal Behavior* 29, no. 2 (2005): 105–23.

When thinking about gestures, here's a way to make watching a basketball game (arguably) more educational. When a player steps to the line to take the free throw, watch carefully. (This works equally well for women's or men's basketball, incidentally.) Watch his demeanor as he dribbles the ball and then pulls it up to shoot. As soon as he lets it go, close your eyes and ask yourself how he seemed. Was he relaxed, comfortable, fluent in his motions? What expression showed on his face? Then make your guess: Was that shot on target, like the literally thousands of free throws he has made in the past? Or was he a little off, out of sync, and therefore probably off target?

For a good summary of the research about gestures that can signal untrustworthiness, see: Tara Parker-Pope, "Who's Trustworthy? A Robot Can Help Teach Us," *New York Times*, September 11, 2012, http://well.blogs.nytimes.com/2012/09/10/whos-trustworthy-a-robot-can-help-teach-us/.

See also Pamela Meyer, *Liespotting: Proven Techniques to Detect Deception* (New York: St. Martin's Griffin, 2010). Her TED talk is also fun: http://www.ted.com/talks/pamela_meyer_how_to_spot_a_liar.html.

Matthew J. Hertenstein, Dacher Keltner, Betsy App, Brittany A. Bulleit, and Ariane R. Jaskolka, "Touch Communicates Distinct Emotions," *Emotion* 6, no. 3 (2006): 528–33. Keltner explains this nicely here: http://www.youtube.com/watch?v=GW5p8xOVwRo&feature=player_embedded.

Greg L. Stewart, Susan L. Dustin, Murray R. Barrick, and Todd C. Darnold, "Exploring the Handshake in Employment Interviews," *Journal of Applied Psychology* 93, no. 5 (2008): 1139–46.

Paul Ekman and Wallace V. Friesen, "Constants Across Cultures in the Face and Emotion," *Journal of Personality and Social Psychology* 17, no. 2 (1971): 124–29. Ekman has written so much that it is best to visit his website, www.paulekman.com.

D. S. Messinger, A. Fogel, and K. L. Dickson, "All Smiles Are Positive, but Some Smiles Are More Positive Than Others," *Developmental Psychology* 37, no. 5 (2001): 642–53.

See also Marianne LaFrance, *Lip Service: Smiles in Life, Death, Trust, Lies, Work, Memory, Sex, and Politics* (New York: W. W. Norton & Company, 2011). LaFrance covers the waterfront where smiling is concerned. For a good summary of the academic literature on smiling as it relates to warmth and competence judgments, see Cuddy et al., "The Dynamics of Warmth and Competence Judgments."

P. B. Barger and A. A. Grandey, "Service with a Smile and Encounter Satisfaction: Emotional Contagion and Appraisal Mechanisms," *Academy of Management Journal* 49, no. 6 (2006): 1229–38.

U. Dimburg, M. Thunberg, and K. Elmehed, "Unconscious Facial Reactions to Emotional Facial Expressions," *Psychological Science* 11, no. 1 (2000): 86–89.

Kahneman, *Thinking, Fast and Slow.*

LaFrance, *Lip Service.*

Messinger et al., "All Smiles Are Positive." See also LaFrance, *Lip Service.*

LaFrance's subtitle (*Smiles in Life, Death, Trust, Lies, Work, Memory, Sex, and Politics*) makes this point about all the different reasons for smiling.

For one account of how primates raise their brows to signal submission, see Mark L. Knapp and Judith A. Hall, *Nonverbal Communication in Human Interaction,* 7th ed. (Wadsworth Cengage, 2007). (Fun photos.)

A few years ago, fashion model–turned–TV host Tyra Banks popularized the word "smizing" to denote "smiling with the eyes" but not the mouth. She is right that the flexed lower eyelid is involved with smiling: When we wear a really big smile, our lower eyelids flex and are pushed up by our rising cheeks. Tyra's full smize is slightly more involved than just a lower eyelid squint, though: It also involves flexing the scalp muscles back by the ears the way we naturally do with a big smile. Go ahead . . . you know you want to watch Tyra Banks coach Larry King on smizing: http://www.youtube.com/watch?v=LjXAnWnL9m0.

Where steely eyes are concerned, Denzel Washington is only a close second to Mr. Eastwood.

LaFrance, *Lip Service.* See also this 2005 discussion with Dacher Keltner: D. T. Max, "National Smiles," *New York Times Magazine*, December 11, 2005, http://www.nytimes.com/2005/12/11/magazine/11ideas_section3-2.html.

Megan L. Willis, Romina Palermo, and Darren Burke, "Social Judgments Are Influenced by Both Facial Expression and Direction of Eye Gaze," *Social Cognition* 29, no. 4 (2011): 415–29.

Amy Drahota, Alan Costall, and Vasudevi Reddy, "The Vocal Communication of Different Kinds of Smile," *Speech Communication* 50, no. 4 (2008): 278–87.

Alex Pentland and Tracy Heibeck, *Honest Signals: How They Shape Our World* (Cambridge, MA: Bradford Books, 2008). See also Tanzeem Choudhury and Alex Pentland, "Characterizing Social Networks Using the Sociometer," which was presented at the Proceedings of the North American Association of Computational Social and Organizational Science, Pittsburgh, June 2004; and Tanzeem

Choudhury and Sumit Basu, "Modeling Conversational Dynamics as a Mixed-Memory Markov Process," in Lawrence K. Saul, Yair Weiss, and Léon Bottou, eds., *Advances of Neural Information Processing Systems* 17 (Cambridge, MA: MIT Press, 2005). We are indebted to Tanzeem Choudhury for her insights.

William J. Mayew and Mohan Venkatachalam, "The Power of Voice: Managerial Affective States and Future Firm Performance," *Journal of Finance* 67, no. 1 (2012): 1–43.

Pentland and Heibeck, *Honest Signals.*

Hajo Adam and Adam D. Galinsky, "Enclothed Cognition," *Journal of Experimental Social Psychology* 48, no. 4 (2012): 918–25.

Walter Hamilton and Jessica Guynn, "Is Mark Zuckerberg in Over His Hoodie as Facebook CEO?" *Los Angeles Times*, August 17, 2012.

S. Craig Roberts, Roy C. Owen, and Jan Havlicek, "Distinguishing Between Perceiver and Wearer Effects in Clothing Color-Associated Attributions," *Evolutionary Psychology* 8, no. 3 (2010): 350–64.

Regarding the choices women have, makeup counts too, but we are not going into details.

Carl I. Hovland and Walter Weiss, "The Influence of Source Credibility on Communication Effectiveness," *Public Opinion Quarterly* 15, no. 4 (1951): 635–50.

The transcript of the Darrow-Bryan exchange is available online: http://law2 .umkc.edu/faculty/projects/ftrials/scopes/day7.htm.

James Geary, *I Is an Other: The Secret Life of Metaphor and How It Shapes the Way We See the World* (New York: Harper, 2011).

Our quotes from this speech are taken from the video of Robert F. Kennedy speaking rather than the official transcript, which differs slightly. Find the video here: http://www.youtube.com/watch?v=_E3-_z5YP0M.

The basic principle behind getting in the circle was articulated more than fifty years ago by psychologist Donn Byrne: "Any time another person offers us validation by indicating that his precepts and concepts are congruent with ours, it constitutes a rewarding interaction, and hence, one element in forming a positive relationship." See "Interpersonal Attraction and Attitude Similarity," *Journal of Abnormal and Social Psychology* 62, no. 3 (1961): 713–15.

Stephen F. Hayes, "Obama and the Power of Words," *Wall Street Journal*, February 26, 2008. Many people, including Obama himself, have pointed out that he generally did a better job communicating when he first ran for president than he has as president.

Kahler has written extensively about his typology. See, for instance, *The Process Therapy Model: The Six Personality Types with Adaptations* (Little Rock, AR: Taibi Kahler Associates, Inc., 2008).

Christopher Steiner, *Automate This: How Algorithms Came to Rule Our World* (New York: Portfolio Hardcover, 2012).

Drew Westen, *The Political Brain: The Role of Emotion in Deciding the Fate of the Nation* (New York: Public Affairs, 2007).

Elinor Amit and Joshua D. Greene, "You See, the Ends Don't Justify the Means: Visual Imagery and Moral Judgment," *Psychological Science* 23, no. 8 (2012): 861–68. For a summary see Shankar Vedantam, "Why Mental Pictures Can Sway Your Moral Judgment," *NPR*, September 20, 2012, http://www.npr.org/2012/09/20/161440292/why-pictures-can-sway-your-moral-judgment.

James W. Pennebaker, *The Secret Life of Pronouns: What Our Words Say About Us* (New York: Bloomsbury Press, 2011). Muhammad Ali spoke at Harvard's commencement ceremony in the spring of 1975. After his speech, a student shouted for Ali to recite a poem. On the spot, Ali summoned the primal poem of strength and warmth: "Me . . . We!"

Simon Baron-Cohen, "The Extreme Male Brain Theory of Autism," *Trends in Cognitive Sciences* 6, no. 6 (2002): 248–54.

See Deborah Tannen's classic, *You Just Don't Understand: Women and Men in Conversation* (New York: HarperCollins, 1990).

Simon M. Laham, Peter Koval, and Adam L. Alter, "The Name-Pronunciation Effect: Why People Like Mr. Smith More Than Mr. Colquhoun," *Journal of Experimental Social Psychology* 48, no. 3 (2012): 752–56.

Marianne Bertrand and Sendhil Mullainathan, "Are Emily and Greg More Employable than Lakisha and Jamal? A Field Experiment on Labor Market Discrimination," *American Economic Review* 94 (2004): 991–1013.

Jane E. Copley and Sheila Brownlow, "The Interactive Effects of Facial Maturity and Name Warmth on Perceptions of Job Candidates," *Basic and Applied Social Psychology* 16, no. 2 (1995): 251–65.

Christopher Johnson, *Microstyle: The Art of Writing Little* (New York: W. W. Norton & Company, 2011).

Oliver P. John and Richard W. Robins, "Accuracy and Bias in Self-Perception: Individual Differences in Self-Enhancement and the Role of Narcissism," *Journal of Personality and Social Psychology* 66, no. 1 (1994): 206–19.

Psychologists call this tendency to credit our virtues for good outcomes and blame the situation for bad ones the "fundamental attribution error."

Friends can help you with some things more than others. Where you really want their input is on things about you that they can perceive and you cannot. There is a concept called the Johari window—easily found online—that can be useful in thinking through what these blind spots might be.

You may have noticed these imagination games sprinkled throughout the text. All of the ones we mention in the text are collected together in one place on our website.

Brian R. Little, "Free Traits, Personal Projects, and Idio-Tapes: Three Tiers for Personality Psychology," *Psychological Inquiry* 7, no. 4 (1996): 340–44.

Strength and Warmth in the World

In medieval times, the Christian philosopher Saint Augustine declared, "It is a sin to judge any man by his post"—in effect decreeing that character should be judged independently of professional standing. But in Saint Augustine's day, there was no American Dream, no meritocracy, not even the Lotto. You did whatever job your parents did before you, and that was that. Nowadays we have at least some social mobility and some evidence that the cream rises to the top, so we tend to feel a person's "post" is fair game for judging them, both as a professional and as a person more broadly.

For a summary of the research on how narcissists perform in interviews, see University of Nebraska–Lincoln, "How Do I Love Me? Let Me Count the Ways, and Also Ace That Interview," *ScienceDaily*, April 2, 2012, http://www.science daily.com/releases/2012/04/120402144738.htm.

Ann Marie T. Russell and Susan T. Fiske, "It's All Relative: Competition and Status Drive Interpersonal Perception," *European Journal of Social Psychology* 38, no. 7 (2008): 1193–201.

There is some research suggesting that creating a "tough love" culture that mixes both hard and soft elements can lead to improved performance. Most organizational cultures already have both hard and soft elements to their cultures, but if you find yourself in an organization veering toward one extreme or the other, this suggests that there might be room for growth. See Steven Kelman and Sounman Hong, "'Hard,' 'Soft,' or 'Tough Love': What Kinds of Organizational Culture Promote Successful Performance in Cross-Organizational Collaborations?" *Harvard Kennedy School Faculty Research Working Paper Series* RWP 12-005 (February 2012).

Nicolas Kervyn, Susan T. Fiske, and Chris Malone, "Brands as Intentional Agents Framework: How Perceived Intentions and Ability Can Map Brand Perception," *Journal of Consumer Psychology* 22, no. 2 (2012): 166–76.

When thinking about leaders and character, an old piece of wisdom is that a good way to judge a person's character is by the way they treat their subordinates.

Anderson et al., "A Status-Enhancement Account of Overconfidence."

Joseph S. Nye Jr., *The Powers to Lead* (New York: Oxford University Press, 2010). See Chapter 3, "Types and Skills."

Noel M. Tichy with Eli Cohen, *The Leadership Engine: How Winning Companies Build Leaders at Every Level* (New York: HarperCollins, 1997). Thanks to Ed Hoffman for pointing this out to us.

Tony Hsieh's e-mail is on the Zappos blog: http://blogs.zappos.com/security email.

Phil Stutz and Barry Michels, *The Tools: Transform Your Problems into Courage, Confidence, and Creativity* (New York: Spiegel & Grau, 2012).

Alexander Todorov, Anesu N. Mandisodza, Amir Goren, and Crystal C. Hall. "Inference of Competence from Faces Predict Electoral Outcomes," *Science* 308, no. 5728, (2005): 1623–26.

Daniel J. Benjamin and Jesse M. Shapiro, "Thin-Slice Forecasts of Gubernatorial Elections," *Economic Statistics* 91, no. 33 (2009): 523–36. An earlier version of this paper was titled "The Rational Voter, Thinly Sliced: Personal Appeal as an Election Forecaster."

George Lakoff, *Moral Politics: How Liberals and Conservatives Think* (Chicago: University of Chicago Press, 1996).

This analysis of Karl Rove's three questions was one of the key insights that led us to the "strength + warmth" formula.

Jim Blascovich and Jeremy Bailenson, *Infinite Reality: Avatars, Eternal Life, New Worlds, and the Dawn of the Virtual Revolution* (New York: William Morrow, 2011).

Nick Yee and Jeremy Bailenson, "The Proteus Effect: The Effect of Transformed Self-Representation on Behavior," *Human Communication Research* 33, no. 3 (2007): 271–90.

Fisher, *Why Him? Why Her?*

Zak, *The Moral Molecule.*

Jessica L. Tracy and Alec T. Beall, "Happy Guys Finish Last: The Impact of Emotion Expressions on Sexual Attraction," *Emotion* 11, no. 6 (2011): 1379–87.

Rebecca J. Brand, Abigail Bonatsos, Rebecca D'Orazio, and Hilary DeShong, "What Is Beautiful Is Good, Even Online: Correlations Between Photo Attractiveness and Text Attractiveness in Men's Online Dating Profiles," *Computers in Human Behavior* 28, no. 1 (2012): 166–70.

Fisher, *Why Him? Why Her?*

Wade C. Rowatt, Michael R. Cunningham, and Perri B. Druen, "Lying to Get a Date: The Effect of Facial Physical Attractiveness on the Willingness to Deceive Prospective Dating Partners," *Journal of Social and Personal Relationships* 16, no. 2 (1999): 209–23.

Malcolm Gladwell, *Blink: The Power of Thinking Without Thinking* (New York: Little, Brown and Company, 2005).

Matt was fortunate to train with Nancy Rambusch in 1992–93 while she served as director of staff development at the Princeton Center Teacher Education.

Doug Lemov, *Teach Like a Champion: 49 Techniques That Put Students on the Path to College* (Hoboken, NJ: Jossey-Bass, 2010).

Epilogue

H. Nittono, M. Fukushima, A. Yano, and H. Moriya, "The Power of Kawaii: Viewing Cute Images Promotes a Careful Behavior and Narrows Attentional Focus," *PLoS One* 7, no. 9 (2012), doi: 10.1371/journal.pone.0046362; and Jaye L. Derrick, "Social Surrogate Resource Restoration: Familiar Fictional Worlds Replenish Resources Necessary for Self-control," *Social Psychological and Personality Science* (in press). For a summary, see http://www.buffalo.edu/news/13646. This suggests that building in breaks with fun distractions is just like managing the charge on a battery; you can do it guilt-free from now on.

Index